*Advanced Social Research Series*
*The Center for the Study of Social Research for the Enhancement of Human Well-being*
*Kwansei Gakuin University, Nishinomiya, Japan*
*Volume 3*

# A Quest for Alternative Sociology

*Advanced Social Research Series*
*The Center for the Study of Social Research for the Enhancement of Human Well-being*
*Kwansei Gakuin University, Nishinomiya, Japan*

*Series editor: Kenji Kosaka*


A Sociology of Happiness: Japanese Perspectives
*Kenji Kosaka*

Frontiers of Social Research: Japan and Beyond
*Akira Furukawa*

A Quest for Alternative Sociology
*Kenji Kosaka and Masahiro Ogino*

*Advanced Social Research Series*
*The Center for the Study of Social Research for the Enhancement of Human Well-being*
*Kwansei Gakuin University, Nishinomiya, Japan*
*Volume 3*

# A Quest for Alternative Sociology

Edited by

Kenji Kosaka

and

Masahiro Ogino

This English edition first published in 2008 by
Trans Pacific Press, PO Box 164, Balwyn North, Melbourne, Victoria 3104, Australia
Telephone: +61 3 9859 1112  Fax: +61 3 9859 4110
Email: tpp.mail@gmail.com
Web: http://www.transpacificpress.com

Copyright © Trans Pacific Press 2008

Designed and set by digital environs, Melbourne. www.digitalenvirons.com

Printed by BPA Print Group, Burwood, Victoria, Australia

**Distributors**

*Australia and New Zealand*
UNIREPS
University of New South Wales, Sydney,
NSW 2052, Australia
Tel: +61 2 9664 0999
Fax: +61 2 9664 5420
Email: info.press@unsw.edu.au
Web: http://www.unireps.com.au

*USA and Canada*
International Specialized Book Services
920 NE 58th Avenue, Suite 300
Portland, Oregon 97213-3786
USA
Tel: (800) 944-6190
Fax: (503) 280-8832
Email: orders@isbs.com
Web: http://www.isbs.com

*Asia and the Pacific*
Kinokuniya Company Ltd.
*Head office:*
Shin-Mizonokuchi Bldg. 2F
5-7, Hisamoto 3-chome
Takatsu-ku, Kawasaki 213-8506
Japan
Tel: +81 44 874 9642
Fax: +81 44 829 1025
Email: bkimp@kinokuniya.co.jp
Web: www.kinokuniya.co.jp
*Asia-Pacific office:*
Kinokuniya Book Stores of Singapore
Pte., Ltd.
391B Orchard Road #13-06/07/08
Ngee Ann City Tower B
Singapore 238874
Tel: +65 6276 5558
Fax: +65 6276 5570
Email: SSO@kinokuniya.co.jp

All rights reserved. No production of any part of this book may take place without the written permission of Trans Pacific Press.

ISBN 978-1-876843-92-2 (Hardback)
ISBN 978-1-876843-93-9 (Paperback)

Cover illustration: The term 'Sociology' written in Chinese, Indonesian, Japanese, Korean and Thai. Created by Sarah Tuke.

# Contents

| | |
|---|---|
| Figures | vi |
| Tables | vi |
| Preface  *Kenji Kosaka and Masahiro Ogino* | vii |
| **Part I: Unremedied Suffering** | **1** |
| 1  Hybrid Landscapes: Where Children are Bullied to Death  *Masahiro Ogino* | 3 |
| 2  Some Thoughts on the Wartime Removal and Incarceration of People of Japanese Ancestry  *Takeo Yamamoto, Iwao Yamamoto and Akihiro Yamakura* | 17 |
| 3  The Logic of Surveillance and the Predicament of 'the Social'  *Kiyoshi Abe* | 31 |
| **Part II: 'Taming' Suffering** | **51** |
| 4  Social Research/Action for Returned Filipino Entertainers  *Joe Takeda* | 53 |
| 5  Commercial Surrogate Mothering in India: Nine Months of Labor?  *Amrita Pande* | 71 |
| 6  Enlarging People's Choice: Reducing Ill-being by Capability Building  *Matthias Drilling* | 88 |
| **Part III: Reciting Suffering** | **103** |
| 7  Aging Japanese American Atomic-bomb Survivors in Southern California: A Case Study  *Kayoko C. Nakao and Satoshi Ikeno* | 105 |
| 8  From Victims Divided To Victims United: The Politics of War Trauma in the Netherlands, 1945–1980  *Jolande Withuis* | 122 |
| 9  Can One Still Live Happily After Chernobyl?  *Bernard Paillard* | 141 |
| **Part IV: Multidimensional Happiness** | **161** |
| 10  Village and War: Unit of Well-being in Japan under Imperial Rule  *Akira Furukawa* | 163 |
| 11  Materialism, Pragmatism and the Pursuit of Happiness in Singapore  *Chee Kiong Tong* | 183 |
| 12  The Happy Family in Contemporary Rural Vietnam  *Do Thien Kinh* | 201 |
| **Postscript** | **217** |
| 13  The Conditions Essential to Alternative Sociology  *Kenji Kosaka* | 219 |
| Notes | 241 |
| Bibliography | 249 |
| Index | 262 |

# Figures

| | | |
|---|---|---|
| 2.1 | WRA relocation centers | 19 |
| 6.1 | Spaces of capabilities | 95 |
| 9.1 | Geographical location of Belarus, Narovlia and Chernobyl | 143 |
| 9.2 | Levels of contamination, from darkest to lightest shade | 145 |
| 12.1 | Representative ideas about the concept of 'happy family' | 202 |
| 13.1 | Triadic paradigm of the enquiry | 220 |

# Tables

| | | |
|---|---|---|
| 1.1 | Numbers of *ijime* suicide cases by population of Japanese municipalities (based on data from the Japanese Basic Resident Register Population Survey) | 5 |
| 7.1 | Interview guide: Topical areas for life review | 108 |
| 7.2 | Interview guide: Topical areas for organizational history | 109 |
| 7.3 | Abbreviated chronological table: Historical events 1868–2005 | 110 |
| 7.4 | Provisional and emerging topical areas | 116 |
| 8.1 | Editorial pages about WWII in MGv | 125 |
| 12.1 | Family happiness statistics | 203 |
| 12.2 | Characteristics of individuals | 204 |
| 12.3 | Concerning material welfare | 206 |
| 12.4 | Concerning married life | 206 |
| 12.5 | Allocation of housework | 208 |
| 12.6 | Distribution of productive work and social activity | 209 |
| 12.7 | Estimation of the best fit logistic regression model for very happy families | 211 |
| 13.1 | Eight types of investigations toward the alternative | 238 |

# Preface

In 2003, the Graduate School of Sociology and Social Work of Kwansei Gakuin University was designated by the Japanese Ministry of Education, Science and Technology as one of two leading centers of excellence in the field of sociology in Japan. The overall program initiated by the Ministry for the social sciences extended for five years, and was called 'the 21$^{st}$ Century COE Program.' Our own program is the study of 'Social Research for the Enhancement of Human Well-being: Construction of a Society Which Values Cultural Diversity.' A review of the past five years of our intellectual odyssey—including some of the trial-and-error processes—is presented in the Postscript by Kosaka. As Kosaka discusses, our program aimed at a paradigmatic shift of social research from Western/American-centered perspectives to non-Western/American—that is, more universalistic—perspectives by orientating ourselves to the meeting point of three sub-goals: alternative research, alternative society, and alternative sociology. The twelve chapters of this book are each in their own way oriented toward the idea of what an alternative sociology *ought to be*, although it is difficult to demarcate our three sub-goals, since each is contingent upon the achievement of the others.

During the process of implementing a variety of projects under the umbrella program of seeking human well-being, we have become increasingly convinced that the diminution or alleviation of social suffering is more important than the increase of happiness, which has been the central focus of Western social sciences since Bentham first outlined utilitarianism. Bentham searched for some kind of algorithm that could aggregate the decrease of pain and the increase of pleasure from the individual level to the societal level. But as implied in Bentham's succinct motto of utilitarianism—pursuing 'the greatest happiness of the greatest number'—this ideal allows for the pain and suffering of some minority or minorities.

It is not unusual in the social sciences that one positive principle, even if it is fully applied theoretically, is likely to violate some other negative feature. We want to focus on suffering at the moment. Let us give two examples very briefly. First, the principle of the Pareto efficiency is meant to lead to an optimal allocation of resources given the existing structures of preferences of the members of a society; hence if all members of a society prefer social state $y$ to social state $x$, then $y$ should be seen as the desirable societal preference. No matter how fair the principle sounds, it theoretically allows a social state where a great degree of economic disparity exists. Second, the notion of 'sustainable development' has become prevalent since the report by the World Commission on Economy and Development. The principle of sustainability, ideally, attempts to avoid sacrifices to future generations. However, we are easily led to sacrifice the poorer groups who are embedded in the existing globalized socio-economic structures. As in these two examples, we always want to pay attention to social suffering even if our societies, individually or globally, make progress towards increasing human happiness or well-being.

Our COE program's sub-title refers to cultural diversity. We admit that our implicit assumption at the start of the program was the positive relation between the increase of human well-being and respect for cultural diversity in terms of language, religion, ethnicity, and so on. Different people coming from different cultural backgrounds must have different views of happiness from the very beginning. This was illustrated and confirmed through what we called the 'fieldwork of happiness'—collecting information about different views from the far corners of the globe. Yes, cultural diversity is essential to human well-being, which avoids ethnocentrism and the 'intellectual sovereignty and dominance of Europe' (Young 2001: 65) or anywhere else. However, we became convinced that valuing cultural diversity is a necessary condition for overall human well-being, since cultural diversity as such does not always alleviate individual social suffering. This is particularly so in this time of globalization, with the remarkable progress of science and technology that we face.

From this perspective, Pande discusses how surrogate mothers in India now deliver babies, under governmental policy and protection, mostly for rich Americans. This new 'industry' only became possible following developments in genetics and medical technology as well as the advanced transportation technologies that make geographical distances remarkably shorter than ever before. The underlying principle of the production of use-value for others perhaps remains as it was in Karl Marx's time, but the commodification of surrogate mothers would never have become feasible without recent developments in science and technology.

Social suffering is difficult to describe, and sometimes even to identify, since it is often kept in silence (Morris: 1997). Morris regards literature as 'the impossible project of giving "speech" to silence' by exposing 'how we simplify and betray suffering whenever we ignore its power to elude every linguistic and conceptual tool that humans can marshal to understand it' (1997: 27). We are tempted to see social research as a means of pursuing this 'impossible project', which we hope leads us to alternative sociology. Although, in the Postscript, Kosaka calls for a sociology of missed opportunities—one that attempts to examine opportunities that might have avoided suffering in the past in the hope that such suffering might never again occur—there is a tremendous amount of work required in-between: to delineate types of suffering experienced and un-remedied, types of strategies of 'taming' suffering, and reciting suffering to give speech to silence. The chapters of this book are the outcomes of this type of endeavor.

Ogino examines the situation in which Japanese adolescents suffering from their classmates' bullying continue to undergo the violence in silence, sometimes committing suicide without finding remedies. Yamamoto et al. investigate the wartime removal and incarceration of Japanese nationals and Japanese Americans in the US during World War II, highlighting the tremendous misery and hardship this initiated. The logic of the concentration camp is, as Abe argues, repeated as 'surveillance' right in the midst of contemporary Japanese society, which is reputedly more open and subject to dissent.

When suffering is experienced, life continues, no matter how painful it is. Some people contrive to 'tame' their suffering much as one might tame a wild animal. Takeda considers how returned Filipino entertainers struggle with the suffering that they experienced in Japan and continue to experience upon their return to the Philippines in the forms of social stigma, mental and physical health problems, divorce and poverty. Pande observes that working as a surrogate mother can potentially be empowering for Indian women, despite the myriad of possible ethical problems and economic difficulties at the beginning;

benefits might include the husband taking-on a role in the housework and childcare, and the possibility of improved living conditions purchased with the money earned. Drilling's paper, based on his sustained fieldwork with young urban poor in Switzerland, focuses on new schemes of capability building that aim to enlarge people's choice so that 'they could start all over again by getting out of the poverty trap.'

Reciting suffering is an important means of personal empowerment. Ikeno and Nakao recite the suffering experienced by Japanese American Atomic-bomb survivors in Southern California, who 'fell through the cracks' of two nation-states, having decided to return to the US in the hope of eventually becoming established in their 'homeland'. Withuis recites the war trauma in the Netherlands after the German occupation of the Netherlands. She suggests that uniting all survivors under the label 'victims of war trauma' and tabooing differences as an unwanted 'hierarchy of suffering' blends historically different experiences and fosters ambivalence. Paillard starts with the question 'Can one still live happily after the Chernobyl nuclear power plant accident?' and concludes that the locals have no other choice than to enjoy short-lived moments of happiness that allow escape from daily concerns, without any hope of a better future.

Furukawa ventures into the multidimensionality of happiness, focusing on traditional villages which have been split between two competing modes of governance: as minimal autonomous units under the pre-war Emperor system, on the one hand, and as resource outposts in a centralized Imperial (nation-state) system during World War II on the other. He suggests that the multidimensional state-village-family nexus was significantly reorganized during the process of postwar societal change. Through an analysis of the pursuit of happiness in Singapore, Tong suggests a hierarchy of happiness, drawing on Maslow's hierarchy of needs, arguing that physiological needs, needs for security, needs for love and friends, and needs for self-esteem are aligned in a hierarchical manner such that only after the more basic needs are met do the 'higher' needs arise. Do conducts a factor analysis of data collected in contemporary rural Vietnamese societies to elucidate the multidimensional determinants of family happiness. He found that two factors—an 'agricultural occupation' and 'the wife decides on social activities for the couple'—have negative effects upon family life, whilst eight other factors contribute positively to family happiness. He also carefully points out that there may be features of family happiness in rural areas that are quite distinct from those in urban areas, as well as differences between rural Vietnam and the modern European family.

These twelve chapters address problems of suffering in various domains of social life, and sometimes the strategies taken by actors in response to their suffering. Still, they share a view that suffering occurs in the midst of multiple intersecting, heterogeneous, and cross-cutting social circles to use Blau and Schwartz's expression (after Simmel). Belonging to one social circle renders one 'other' and 'stranger' to those of another social circle, and vice versa. And those who 'fall into the cracks' between different circles are the ones who are most likely to experience suffering. In this sense, we move on to construct a sociology of otherness or the stranger as a further step toward developing our COE program FY2003–FY2007, and will report our progress in the near future.

Kenji KOSAKA<br>Masahiro OGINO

# Part I
# Unremedied Suffering

# 1
# Hybrid Landscapes: Where Children are Bullied to Death

*Masahiro Ogino*

## Negative experience

Some of us may have experienced an event that we cannot find the words to describe, or do not want to share with others. Let us refer to such an event as a 'negative experience.' Not surprisingly, we desire to forget any unpleasant, unfortunate experiences as much as possible. However, a negative memory cannot be erased completely. In some cases, we later feel like discussing the negative experience that was once too sickening to describe. In this sense, we are ambivalent towards negative experiences.

At the core of negative experience is death and memories of the dead. For instance, Hiroshima atomic-bomb survivors talk of their experience of the disaster and describe scenes with vast numbers of the injured and the dead, from the perspective of the few who happened to survive by chance. This also applies to major disasters like the great Hanshin-Awaji earthquake. Some survivors of this disaster, whose houses had suffered only minor damage, witnessed the leveling of houses directly across the street. Through their experience of the disaster, these earthquake survivors became aware that if they had made one wrong move they could have been dead. This makes them, as survivors who shared the experience of the disaster, revere the memory of the dead and think that they must tell of their experience, if negative, so that it will be remembered by later generations.

In an event that involves a large number of victims, such as a natural disaster or war, memories of the experience can become collective due to the shared nature of the experience by survivors. However, if no one or only a handful of people shared the experience, it is difficult to understand the full-range of their feelings or to describe the experience. A typical example of this is suicide.

Most suicide victims choose to kill themselves in solitude. We can only infer the circumstances that led to the suicide from the accounts of family members, friends and others who knew the victim before his/her death or from his/her suicide note, if any. Suicide is death just the same, but unlike the deaths of disaster or war victims, it is difficult to identify the direct cause of suicide. Signs of suicidal tendencies might be apparent in some cases, but most suicides come as a surprise to the immediate survivors.

However, there is a type of suicide in which the person(s) who caused the suicide—a type of 'murderer'—can be identified through the victim's suicide note or other evidence. This is *'ijime* suicide', or suicide caused by bullying. Most *ijime* (bullying) suicide cases are discovered as such, if at all, through the victim's suicide note. Unlike a murder case, there is no clear murderer. However, the suicide victim, in his/her note, discloses the reason for his/her suicide and charges it to his/her assailants. In this respect, *ijime* suicide is characterized by relative clarity about the cause of death, which is physical and/or psychological violence enacted by others.

This can be fully understood by comparing *ijime* suicide with other types of suicide committed by junior and senior high school students. For instance, if, as was formerly seen, a student commits suicide because he/she failed the entrance exam to a high school, the high school which chose not to accept the victim cannot be regarded as the murderer. Similarly, if a boy kills himself because his girlfriend broke up with him, we cannot blame her for his suicide. However, an *ijime* suicide victim kills himself/herself as a result of suffering actual violence, racketeering and so on. At least for the victim, the assailants do exist. Still, the victim chooses not to tell anyone of the violence against him/her until he/she takes his/her own life. This is because suffering violence is a negative experience and, as such, is difficult to talk about. Only after his/her death is it found that the victim was suffering violence. At this point in time, the victim's negative experience cannot be told by anyone; it is beyond the reach of all survivors.

The aim of this chapter is to find out about the social background for *ijime* suicide as a form of death that is, as described above, extremely difficult to investigate.

## Scenes of bullying

If bullying always leads to suicide amongst a certain proportion of victims, the larger the number of bullying cases, the higher the likelihood of *ijime* suicide cases occurring. In other words, communities with a larger number of bullying cases would have a larger number of *ijime* suicide cases. However, a comparison of actual numbers of bullying cases and those of *ijime* suicide cases has found no association between them.[1] Some communities have a large number of bullying cases but a small number of *ijime* suicide victims. Others have a small number of bullying cases but a considerable number of *ijime* suicide victims. This means that *ijime* suicide occurs independently of bullying cases and that certain communities are particularly associated with suicide triggered by bullying.

In fact, a comparison of the population size of the communities with *ijime* suicide cases shows that there is a relationship between population size and the frequency of *ijime* suicide (Ogino and Yukimura 2006: 210–12). We calculated the ratio of *ijime* suicide cases to the population of the municipality where the suicide cases occurred, for the year during which they occurred. The ratio was converted to the number of cases per 100,000 persons. Based on this method of calculation, large cities with populations over 1,000,000 had 0.03 *ijime* suicide cases per 100,000 persons. Similarly, cities with populations between 100,000 and 1,000,000, those with populations between 30,000 and 100,000, and those with populations less than 30,000 had 0.29, 1.61 and 6.27 *ijime* suicide cases, respectively. This indicates that the smaller the population size, the higher the likelihood of *ijime* suicide cases occurring (Table 1.1).

What, then, are the characteristics of the communities in which bullying victims actually committed suicide? It is virtually impossible

*Table 1.1: Numbers of ijime suicide cases by population of Japanese municipalities (based on data from the Japanese Basic Resident Register Population Survey)*

| Municipal population (persons) | Number of *ijime* suicide cases | Number of *ijime* suicide cases per 100,000 persons |
| --- | --- | --- |
| <30,000 | 22 | 6.27 |
| ≥30,000, <100,000 | 40 | 1.61 |
| ≥100,000, <1,000,000 | 53 | 0.29 |
| ≥1,000,000 | 18 | 0.03 |

to investigate each and every *ijime* suicide case. I thus focus on a portion of these suicide cases with a particular characteristic: cases which involve money. Some of the bullying cases that led to the victim's suicide involved activities similar to racketeering or blackmailing. A typical example of this is the *ijime* suicide case that occurred in December 1994. The victim, a fourteen-year-old boy, explains the reason for his suicide in his quite lengthy suicide note:

> Four persons (sorry I can't mention their names) always took money from me. Today, I just couldn't find money to bring to them. If I stay alive [there would be no help] ... I killed myself because they took 40,000 from me today again. Even if I have no more money and say 'I couldn't get any money', they would just bully me and tell me to try again (the evening edition of the *Asahi Shimbun* dated 5 December 1994).

This boy is attempting to explain the reason for his suicide in the context of money. This suggests that the bullies communicated mainly through the medium of money. Friendship does not, by its nature, involve money. Indeed, the general understanding of friendship is that it develops when the potential friends do away with cash exchanges between them. Based on the view that friendship is incompatible with money, no friendship seems to have existed between this boy and the bullying boys.

However, the bullying developed in a world where the generally accepted view—that friendship is 'pure' and never involves money as a medium—does not hold. This suggests an increase of the idea that you cannot make friends without money. Another interpretation of this may be that market principles have spread into the realm of friendship and a world is being formed where friendship is a commodity that can be purchased with money. Needless to say, though, no commodity market of friendship, in a strict sense, has been formed. It may be more appropriate to say that the world of friendship is being rearranged to simulate the behavioral principles of a market economy.

Of the 142 cases of *ijime* suicide identified by us, twenty-six clearly involved money, as evidenced by the suicide note and/or other evidence. We have investigated thirteen of the twenty-six communities. Results of the investigation indicate many similarities among these communities. First, the population changes during the two decades immediately preceding the *ijime* suicide cases indicate a population increase in all thirteen communities. This is not due to the increased birthrate in these communities; rather, the construction of industrial and housing complexes had produced rapid population growth in these locales.

Population increase is not the only similarity among the thirteen communities. We have found the following common components in the scenes of the communities where the bullying victims killed themselves:

1. Mountains and forests, rivers, lakes and/or beaches: These landforms constitute the natural environment but, needless to say, this landscape has been used and modified by people.
2. Farmland: There are areas or patches of cultivated fields that were created by development projects before or after the Second World War.
3. Wooden houses: Tile-roofed, wooden houses owned mostly by farmers.
4. Old shopping arcades: These were often built before the war and are often in decline due to a lack of successors.
5. Shrines, Buddhist temples and graveyards: These communities still have shrines and Buddhist temples which used to occupy an important place in the community as well as graveyards where community members worship their ancestors.
6. Public facilities: Public facilities, such as public offices and educational institutions, are located in the central district of the community. They are reinforced concrete buildings.
7. Housing developments: After the foundation of the Nihon Jūtaku Kōdan (Urban Development Corporation) in 1955, an increasing number of housing complexes (made of reinforced concrete) were constructed. The number of rental houses constructed by the Corporation peaked in 1971. The communities are dotted with a variety of houses, ranging from relatively old housing complexes constructed in the 1960s to privately-owned condominium buildings only recently completed.
8. Factories and industrial complexes: These, too, come in a variety ranging from independent factories to industrial complexes comprising a number of companies.
9. Roadside shops: The communities have large suburban shopping facilities, such as shopping malls, supermarkets, game arcades, fast-food restaurants, family restaurants, discount electrical appliance stores and karaoke rooms.

Let us refer to the above components of the scenes as 'spatial symbols.' The spatial symbols can be broadly divided into two categories. The first category comprises symbols made mainly of natural materials. The natural environment, farmland, wooden houses, and shopping arcade buildings constructed before the war fit into this category. The second category comprises symbols made mainly of synthetic materials.

Synthetic materials became widely used after the 1970s. They are now indispensable in our everyday life. Rivers are lined with concrete embankments. Even in wooden houses, synthetic materials are used in the kitchen, bathroom and toilet facilities. Still, while the spatial symbols listed from (1) through (5) above are constructed based on the principle that the primary materials must be natural, underlying the construction of those listed from (6) through (9) is a preference for synthetic materials.

In the communities where the bullying victims killed themselves, many different spatial symbols coexist in small areas. These areas also have symbols of both the first and second categories. For example, we may find housing or industrial complexes dotted with farmland. Let us refer to this type of landscape as a hybrid landscape. The greater the variety of spatial symbols found in a scene, the more hybrid it becomes. A combination of spatial symbols of the first and second categories makes the landscape particularly hybrid.

In addition to the spatial symbols listed from (1) through (9) above, there is another spatial symbol that is an essential component of hybrid landscapes, namely, vacant lots. Let us regard vacant lots as the tenth spatial symbol constituting hybrid landscapes. Hybrid landscapes have undeveloped, vacant lots remaining after the completion of development projects. Weeds have colonized these lots. They are 'blank' spaces in the true sense of the word, in that no one knows for sure how they will be used. These blank spaces bring heterogeneity to the entire scene.

In contrast to the ten spatial symbols that are components of hybrid landscapes, there are certain spatial symbols that are incompatible with scenes of hybridity. One such symbol is skyscrapers. No skyscrapers are found in hybrid landscapes. Well-maintained parks are another component less often found in hybrid landscapes. Yet another symbol incompatible with hybrid landscapes is 'terminals.' Train or bus terminals do not exist in hybrid landscapes. Most communities with hybrid landscapes are distant from bus stops or train stations.

Skyscrapers and transportation terminals are spatial symbols that are characteristic of large cities. These components contain 'transparent spaces,' characterized by sufficiency, odorlessness and safety. Sufficiency means that people can obtain all the necessities of life. One never need starve in a big city. Shop windows symbolize material sufficiency. In a large modern city, grocery stores do not have the smell of food. In former times, fish shops and greengroceries had strong smells of the products they handled, due to the nature of these products. In supermarkets, food products are wrapped in plastic packages which shut off the products' natural smells. Odorlessness is the first requirement to show that the store has been disinfected and cleaned.

The last point about transparent spaces is the pursuit of complete safety, with surveillance cameras positioned everywhere. Some of these spaces look as though they are 'healing' spaces, giving the impression of utopia.

Transparent spaces do not have a hybrid nature, because they are dominated by synthetic materials.

## Place and body

The reason that I focus on the characteristics of the scenes in the communities where bullying victims committed suicide is because individuals do not live independently of the scenes in which they live. Landscapes are produced by the community, to which individuals cannot remain unrelated. In fact, individuals have no choice but to live in the spaces produced by the community they belong to.

Tetsurō Watsuji defines the space where an individual lives and understands himself/herself as *fūdo* (literally: culture or climate). Watsuji discusses the self which exists in the *fūdo* by taking 'cold' as an example. The cold and the self who feels it are not divided into the objective cold and the subjective self. 'When we feel the cold, our selves already exist in the outside cold' (Watsuji 1979: 12). In addition, 'the cold is experienced by "us" and not just by "me"' (Watsuji 1979: 13). Cold is felt within us or, in other words, represents the relations among us. We talk about the weather because we share the experience of feeling the cold (or heat). And, in turn, we feel that we stand on the same footing when we are in the *fūdo* of the locality, which may have strong mountain winds (*yama oroshi*) or strong dry winds (*karakkaze*) peculiar to the area. Watsuji describes this process as 'self-understanding' of the cold in *fūdo*. In this process, how we 'subjectively' feel the cold does not matter. Feeling the cold is a social process through which we take various measures, such as protection against the cold.

*Fūdo*, as Watsuji conceives it, has been engraved in history and cultivated by people. However, contemporary society does not always have this kind of *fūdo*. In hybrid landscapes, phenomena that characterize the *fūdo*, such as *karakkaze* or *yama oroshi*, become less and less significant. Once the roads have been paved, people no longer have to worry about dust. Instead, exhaust gas from cars will pollute the area and the community will face new problems, such as environmental issues. These problems are no longer caused by the *fūdo*, because exhaust gas emissions do not stem from any specific *fūdo*. Exhaust gas emissions could occur anywhere with increased automobile traffic. Exhaust gas is a product of chemical reactions of the fuel. It is a product that symbolizes the 'dominance of chemistry,' as is the case with the scenes characterized by synthetic materials.

Both hybrid landscapes and exhaust gas gradually increase and become ubiquitous. This is the dissolution process of what Watsuji describes as the historic *fūdo*. Can we solve the social problems associated with hybrid landscapes by taking measures to increase the awareness of local history and to produce a new *fūdo*? The matter is not that simple. It would not be solved simply by restoring *karakkaze* or *yama oroshi* to the scenes full of exhaust fumes.

In our attempt to understand the production of chemistry-dominated spaces, we should focus on Henri Lefebvre's description of the process through which a city incorporated rural villages in Western Europe during the sixteenth century.

Lefebvre's understanding is that a city continuously 'abstracts' the 'natural space' of rural villages. He describes the process of containment of 'peculiarity' by a 'universal existence' as the expansion of 'abstract space.' This applies to the process of the production of hybrid landscapes. This is a process through which the peculiarity of *fūdo* as defined by Watsuji is lost and scenes with combinations of different spatial symbols expand. These scenes form spaces that are abstract and lack individuality.

According to Lefebvre, when natural space has lost significance and the abstraction has reached an advanced stage, 'spatial codes' come into existence. Spatial codes comprise: (1) alphabets and vocabulary; (2) grammar and rhetoric; and (3) stylistics, each of which pertains to the components of space (Lefebvre 2000: 312). Item (1) above signifies a list of the components of space, ranging from water and air to bricks and concrete blocks, and of materials and tools necessary for the construction of the space. Item (2) indicates the arrangement of individual spatial components in a manner that ensures unity of the whole. Item (3) presents a solution on an aesthetic level which describes the harmony, order and products of the space. In short, space is encoded and treated as codes, like language. Just as language has grammar and beautiful styles, space must be ordered and arranged beautifully. Space must maintain unity and order and must be constructed systematically and presented intentionally.

The encoding of space as referred to by Lefebvre has been carried out to perfection in cities, which formed the focus of Lefebvre's attention. This was particularly the case in large modern cities. In contrast, hybrid landscapes occur in communities which have not been fully urbanized and whose space has thus not been fully encoded. As already demonstrated by statistical data, few *ijime* suicide cases have occurred in places like large cities, whose space is full of skyscrapers and is fully encoded. *Ijime* suicide cases tend to occur in hybrid landscapes where different spatial symbols coexist.

Hybrid landscapes are likely to appear during a period when the community's main activity shifts from farming to factory work and, further, the consumption lifestyle as symbolized by roadside shops is introduced. These changes occur based on the comprehensive development program formulated by each local government. 'Comprehensive development' refers to the process of encoding a space. Once a space is produced based on a certain code, the space can no longer be analyzed other than through examining how the various symbols are arranged based on the code used. However, a hybrid landscape is not completely controlled by the encoding of the space because, if so, then the landscape would not have become hybrid. A hybrid landscape is a product of incomplete encoding.

A community with hybrid landscapes contains its history in these landscapes. The spatial symbols constituting the community landscapes must have the characteristics of the times when they were produced. However, a landscape with a combination of spatial symbols produced at different times does not display its history. For this reason, a hybrid landscape lacks a focal point. A hybrid landscape only represents the two different categories of spatial symbols. These categories are divided based on the difference in materials. Natural materials give us an impression of relative 'oldness,' but not of history, which would imply a time axis. The two categories only represent a dichotomous qualitative difference between 'old' or 'new.'

In a hybrid landscape, our body does not communicate unconsciously with the space, as it does with the *fūdo* or natural space. Our body is separated from the landscape and the landscape becomes an object of appreciation as a mere presentation. This also means that our body loses a place to belong. A hybrid landscape separates the human body from the space and promotes isolation of the body. This isolation makes it difficult for some of us to communicate with others and might drive some to suicide. As discussed above, *ijime* suicide cases are associated with communities with hybrid landscapes.

## Use of former military reservations

The production of hybrid landscapes is related closely to land-use practices after the Second World War. How, then, was the postwar land development carried out? At this point, we encounter an interesting fact: the communities in which *ijime* suicide cases occurred contain, or are situated in close proximity to, former military reservations. Typical examples include: Chiran-chō (Chiran Town), Kagoshima Prefecture, in which a base for kamikaze suicide units was located; and Ami-machi (Ami Town), Ibaraki Prefecture, in which the Kasumigaura Air Base and an air force aviation preparatory school were located. Young aviators were trained at the preparatory school and departed from the suicide unit base in Chiran for their final flights, never to return alive. In addition, both communities suffered the loss of lives to suicide caused by bullying after the war.

Is it a pure coincidence that the *ijime* suicide cases occurred in the communities with former military reservations? Or is there any association between these cases and the reservations? Pondering this question reminds me of the documentary film *Bowling for Columbine* which, in an attempt to question US society's rule by the gun, features an indiscriminate shooting incident committed by two American high school students. It is known that the incident stemmed from bullying experienced by the two teenagers. The high school students responsible for the incident killed a number of students and school personnel in a revenge attack for being bullied, before killing themselves. There is a munitions factory near the high school where the incident took place. Thus, the relationship between *ijime* suicides and military facilities is also evident in the US.

In any case, former military reservations had significance at least in the postwar development of Japan. Postwar urban and economic development was not carried out haphazardly; it began with converting the former military reservations to other uses.

It is undeniable that this policy of postwar development was triggered by the occupying force's policy to 'demilitarize' Japan. However, the redevelopment of the former military reservations was instigated not only for the passive reason of complying with the occupying force's directions. It occurred because making effective use of facilities and buildings in the former military reservations, which had survived air raids, was a good policy to achieve rapid rehabilitation amid the shortage of materials. In addition, the former military reservations were located at the center of the respective communities because since before the war, a community development project had generally been carried out by constructing a military base in the community. It was therefore most reasonable to start development activities from the former military reservations. For instance, the development project of Ami-machi chose to reuse, without modification, the space that had been created in connection with the construction of an airfield before the war. In this sense, the project was an extension of the earlier development project which had constructed the military base.

In 1921 the Kasumigaura Naval Aviation base was established in Ami-mura (Ami Village, at that time). The same year, a regular bus line was introduced to Ami. In 1926, the Jōnan railway began its operation between Tsuchiura and Ami. In addition, the first paved street in Ibaraki Prefecture was constructed in Ami (Ami-machi Shi Hensan Iinkai [Ami Town History Editorial Committee], 1983). With the improvement of transportation networks and roads, the population of Ami–mura increased from 3892 in 1920 to 7964 in 1937. Conversely, the percentage of farmers in Ami-mura decreased from 93.9% in 1920 to 65% four years later and further to 52% in 1935. This must have led to a complete change in the village's environment which had previously been rural and agricultural.

Ami-machi had been developed through the operation of the military base since 1920. Through this experience, the community had accumulated knowledge of what community development is like. This means that a basic framework had already been constructed for the community to develop the former military reserves by converting them to other uses. This development was not intended simply to create material gain by reusing the military facilities. The operation of the base was the most important 'public works project.' The operation of the military base as a large-scale public works project had significantly changed the industrial and social structure of the community. This experience taught the community new methods of space-use.

The military base not only had economic ramifications but became the 'center' of the community and came to assume symbolic significance. Since its establishment, the Kasumigaura Aviation airfield had often featured as a topic of conversation as it permitted the landing and departure of foreign aircraft. In particular, the landing of the Zeppelin airship on the airfield in 1929 attracted great attention. In four days, a total of approximately 300,000 spectators gathered around the airfield to see the airship (Ami Town History Editorial Committee, 1983: 525). The airfield thus served as a tourist site as well. Needless to say, the military force of the Kasumigaura Aviation increased. By 1931, the force concentrated in the Kasumigaura base accounted for over forty percent of all naval aviation forces in Japan.

The overwhelming presence of the navy base left an imprint on the community which lingered after the war. The absence of the troops produced not only a physical absence but also a sense of emptiness amongst community residents, which was caused by the absence of the former symbolic buildings and symbolic center. It was this sense of emptiness that urged the residents to construct buildings to fill the blank space previously occupied by the troops, in order to create a new center of the community.

The former military reservations were converted to several different uses. While some were requisitioned by the US forces to be used as military bases, most were converted to farmland through the farmland development projects. Others were converted to peaceful uses, where universities and other educational institutions were constructed. These former military reservations were transformed into educational districts. After a time, housing and industrial complexes began to be constructed in some of the former military reservations. The earliest construction projects started in the 1950s, but it was around 1970 when these projects gained momentum.

By this time, the development projects for the former military reservations were almost completed. Land development projects began to expand into the areas surrounding the former reservations. *Ijime* suicide cases committed by junior high school students have occurred in these communities, which underwent considerable changes as a result of the large-scale development projects that began around 1970.

## Disappearance of death and the dead

Until the defeat of Japan in the war, the military forces and facilities had an overwhelming presence in Japan, both symbolically and physically. This was because the military served as a mechanism for controlling life and death. Max Weber understood the military as a mechanism to secure the state's exclusive authority to use force. However, this describes only half of the nature of the military. Through the conscription system, a state holds the power of life and death over its people. In particular, once war has broken out, military barracks become waiting rooms for soldiers waiting for their mission to start. Not all soldiers would be killed in action, but the mere presence of soldiers who are to be sent to the front, ready to die, gives the military facilities a special position. Through the military, a state controls not only the lives but also the deaths of its people.

Then, upon Japan's defeat in the war, this huge power mechanism, which had controlled life and death, collapsed. The resulting sense of emptiness could not be filled easily. The absence of the entire military resulted in the loss of a cyclical system which would have provided memorial services for the great number of war victims. No other mechanism was constructed to control life and death in place of the military. In fact, during the period of occupation, Japan faced a situation where the state's power over life and death was taken by another state, the US. For instance, the Shimoyama incident, in which the president of the Japanese National Railways mysteriously died, symbolized fear and anxiety arising from the fact that the power of life and death was in the hands of another country. [2]

Subsequent periods saw the production of hybrid landscapes with the progress of postwar development. Hybrid landscapes have no mechanism to control death. A community may have shrines and/or Buddhist temples, but they no longer serve as the symbolic center of the community. This has made death remote from the community residents. Death can now only be vaguely imagined. Certainly, a wartime situation is unusual, with people dying continuously. In contrast, however, our everyday world today has swept away any and all concrete images of the dead.

As Marcel Mauss (1978) pointed out, the act of exchange originally has a gift-like nature and underlying the act of exchange is the original exchange with the dead. For instance, the existence of shrines which are believed to have the power of answering prayers for good business means that there is an understanding among people that their business goes well only if they make an offering to gods. In other words, people used to believe that only after exchanges with the dead have been duly made can exchanges among the living be effectively made. The logic of giving to, or exchanging with, the dead (the logic of gift/exchange) was given priority over the logic of exchanging goods among the living, and this was how the exchange of goods was controlled.

However, with the spread of market principles, the logic of gift/exchange has declined. This has resulted in the gradual decline of the custom of modeling the exchanges among the living after those with the dead. Inevitably, our images of the dead have become less and less concrete.

At this point, let me quote another part of the suicide note written by the aforementioned fourteen-year-old who committed suicide.

> I have gone from this world. No more worries about losing money. My family will pay for food for one less person. Mum will have a good sleep in mornings.

The reason that he wrote, 'I have gone from this world,' is probably because the boy thought that he would no longer be in this world by the time his parents read this note. This can be interpreted that the boy was writing the note already as a dead person. Or rather, he might have already ceased to draw a line between life and death. For a suicide victim, there is no life or death. If alive, he/she might as well be dead. This situation causes a person to commit suicide.

Let me add another point. The boy wrote, 'No more worries about losing money. My family will pay for food for one less person.' His family was affluent. They were far from being poor and were not in a situation such that 'pay[ing] for food for one less person' would have saved the whole family. The reason why the boy still mentioned it is probably because he was no longer able to assess his own value other than in terms of money. If a person is no longer able to assess himself other than in terms of money, he/she is only one step away from being unable to draw a line between life and death. It is in a hybrid landscape where this inability is more likely to occur.[3]

How can we, then, dissolve hybrid landscapes? The only solution seems to be to create new spaces that can be shared by community residents.

# 2
# Some Thoughts on the Wartime Removal and Incarceration of People of Japanese Ancestry

*Takeo Yamamoto, Iwao Yamamoto and Akihiro Yamakura*

## Introduction

### Issues involved

In this chapter we discuss the wartime removal and incarceration of Japanese nationals and Japanese Americans in the US during World War II, because we believe that this removal and incarceration involves several serious issues with contemporary significance.

The first issue involved is that the incarceration is in direct opposition to the founding principles of the US. The Declaration of Independence states that 'Life, Liberty and the pursuit of Happiness' are among 'certain inalienable rights' endowed by the Creator. The Fifth Amendment to the US Constitution provides that 'no person shall…be deprived of life, liberty, or property, without due process of law;' this provision has served as a safety mechanism, protecting citizens from the abuse of power by the federal government. Legal historian, Gordon Woods (1969), emphasizes the importance of life and liberty in establishing the foundation of the state and the even greater importance of property to preserve both life and liberty. We can thus say that life, liberty and property—and also happiness which issues from these—have thus been the very purpose of the founding of the nation and the very founding principles of the state.

The Japanese nationals in the US and Japanese Americans forcibly removed from their residence and incarcerated in the custody of the US government because of their race during World War II were deprived of their life, liberty and property, without 'due process of law;' and a portion of them even had their lives threatened. This was the beginning of their misery and hardship.

The second issue caused by the wartime incarceration is the fact that the three branches of the US government—legislative, executive, and judicial—were all involved in depriving a particular racial minority of life, liberty and property. The Western Defense Command of the US Army with the authority of the President's executive order implemented the removal policy. The Department of War, who had misgivings about the constitutionality of the President's Executive Order 9066, consulted with the Secretary of Justice, and proposed a bill to Congress making the violation of the Army's exclusion order a misdemeanor (Grodzin 1974). Congress enacted the bill. Thus the legislative branch became a party to the executive branch's removal policy.

This was also the case with the judicial branch. In the appeal cases of Gordon Hirabayashi and Fred Korematsu,[1] the US Supreme Court not only displayed reverence to the judgment of the military authorities regarding 'military necessities' when the nation was facing a major crisis, it also granted exceptional approval for racial discrimination in times of national emergency.

Thirdly, the wartime removal and incarceration involved violations of international law. The actions of the US government were not limited to imprisoning all people of Japanese ancestry living on the West Coast of the US and placing the entire Japanese community in Hawaii under close surveillance. It also sought the cooperation of twelve Central and South American governments—especially, the Peruvian government—in kidnapping about 2000 Japanese and sending them to the US for internment; a portion of them were used as pawns in hostage exchanges for US civilians interned in Japan and Japanese-occupied areas in Asia. The Peruvian government was particularly eager to cooperate with the US government, handing over about 1800 Japanese to the US Army. As a consequence of their arrest by the local authorities and their removal to the US and internment, these people not only experienced the destruction of their freedom but also had their property, businesses, trust, human relationships, family lives and many other things miserably deprived. In addition to reports of suicides occasioned by neuroses and abuse as well as maltreatment

*Some Thoughts on the Wartime Removal and Incarceration of People of Japanese Ancestry*

*Figure 2.1: WRA relocation centers*

| Center | Date of first arrival | Peak population | Date of peak population | Date of last departure |
|---|---|---|---|---|
| Gila River | 20 July 1942 | 13,348 | 30 Dec 1942 | 10 Nov 1945 |
| Granada | 27 Aug 1942 | 7,318 | 1 Feb 1943 | 15 Oct 1945 |
| Heart Mountain | 12 Aug 1942 | 10,767 | 1 Jan 1943 | 10 Nov 1945 |
| Jerome | 6 Oct 1942 | 8,497 | 11 Feb 1943 | 30 June 1944 |
| Manzanar | 21 Mar 1942 | 10,046 | 22 Feb 1942 | 21 Nov 1945 |
| Minidoka | 10 Aug 1942 | 9,397 | 1 Mar 1942 | 28 Oct 1945 |
| Poston | 8 May 1942 | 17,814 | 2 Sept 1942 | 28 Nov 1945 |
| Rohwer | 18 Feb 1942 | 8,475 | 11 Mar 1943 | 30 Nov 1945 |
| Topaz | 11 Sept 1942 | 8,130 | 17 Mar 1943 | 31 Oct 1945 |
| Tule Lake | 27 May 1942 | 18,789 | 25 Dec 1944 | 20 Mar 1946 |

Source: Burton, J. F., M. M. Farrell, F. B. Lord and R. W. Lord (2000): 39–40.

during transportation to the US, we also have records of cases in which these people were used as forced labor while temporarily being held at a US military base in the US territory of the Panama Canal while in transit to the US (Yamakura 1996, 1997). These actions of the US government and its subsequent behavior—the kidnapping of Peruvian Japanese, the internment of civilians for indeterminate periods of time and its refusal until only recently to redress the internment—are violations of international laws such as the Geneva Convention as well as the international obligation to compensate the victims for their losses (Saito 1998).

## Contemporary significance

The wartime removal and incarceration that caused the above issues occurred more than sixty years ago. However, the present US society still contains mechanisms which can produce similar incidents.

A case in point is the current relevance of the so-called Japanese internment cases by the US Supreme Court as legal precedents. Both *Hirabayashi* and *Korematsu* decisions by the Supreme Court detested racial discrimination in singling out a particular racial group for removal and incarceration, yet practically approved the discriminatory policy as a wartime measure based on the 'military necessity' rationale. Our argument rests on the fact that there is a danger that the law in the US will become silent during wartime (see Yamamoto et al. 2001: 19; Hall (ed.) 1999: 5–6; Yamakura 2001: 45–63).

The current relevance of the internment cases is manifest by the Supreme Court's recent attempts to 'rehabilitate' these decisions by utilizing them as legal precedents to strike down affirmative action measures. As legal historian Eric Yamamoto argues, the US Supreme Court has recently started to 'reclaim the internment cases as legal authority' (2001: 21). Its 1995 decision on *Adarand Constructors v. Pena*, for example, offered the Court's 'most detailed analysis of strict scrutiny mechanics since *Korematsu*.' Its central holding is that 'strict scrutiny is to be applicable to evaluate federal affirmative action programs.' The majority opinion of *Adarand*, written by Justice Sandra O'Connor, amounted to the rehabilitation of the *Hirabayashi* and *Korematsu* decisions, whose elements of racial discrimination seemed to have been discredited by the verdict of history. O'Connor referred to *Hirabayashi*, which stated 'distinctions between citizens solely because of their ancestry are by their very nature odious,' and *Korematsu*, which stated 'all legal restrictions which curtail the civil rights of a single racial group are immediately suspect.' Claiming that the most rigid scrutiny delineated in *Korematsu* 'can sometimes fail to detect an illegitimate racial classification,' she argued that any 'retreat from the most searching judicial inquiry can only increase the risk of another such error occurring in the future.'[2] *Adarand* thus used the internment decisions as legal authority to reject an affirmative action program by the Federal Government because of its color conscious nature.

Secondly, many people today do not know the realities of what happened during the war. The wartime removal and incarceration of Japanese Americans has only recently become known both in the US and Japan, albeit among a limited number of people. There is even scant public knowledge or understanding of the kidnapping and the forced internment of Peruvian Japanese. Most people living in the US do not know the facts about forced internment—this is even the case for the offspring of people of Japanese ancestry who experienced these events. We have occasionally seen cases ourselves of the latter feigning indifference to this issue. We need a full grasp of the background, the realities and the mechanisms involved in the wartime removal and incarceration so that the 'abnormal society that ought never to exist,' which was created during World War II, will never be created again.

Ignorance and neglect can bring about tragedies. The wartime incarceration is a typical example. We have come across many instances that lead us to think that the judgments and decisions about the forced removal and incarceration and the related events occurred because of a lack of knowledge about Japanese Americans and because of a lack of effort to get to know them. We can learn many lessons—and indeed, ought to learn them—through understanding the facts. Mistakes and failures are there for us to make use of, to learn from. We ought to make the best use of lessons of the past in order to live in a rapidly changing international society.

## Purpose of the study

We will analyze the wartime removal and incarceration of Japanese who migrated to the US to find work from the Meiji period (*Issei*, the first generation Japanese immigrants), of their American citizen descendants (*Nisei* and *Sansei*, second and third generation Japanese Americans), and finally of those Japanese who migrated to Central and South America, especially Peru, for work (Peruvian Japanese). The first purpose of our study is to explore why this tragic event fell on these people. Another purpose is to consider what has been done to prevent the recurrence of this tragedy that should never have happened, and also to discuss what we ought to be doing now and into the future in this regard.

In other words, discussing these two purposes involves thinking about the mechanisms—legal, political, ideological, and historical factors—that gave rise to this abnormal society that ought never to have existed, and about the society's responses to them. It is also a matter of examining the issue of how to prevent the rise of this sort of society again.

Properly speaking, we should also include a detailed description and explanation of what actually happened and what the actual conditions were, but for the lack of space we must leave this for another work.

## Mechanisms for creating an abnormal society

### Legal framework: Era of constitutional segregation

While the Declaration of Independence states that 'all men are created equal,' the US has consistently, from the time of the founding of the nation, distinguished between 'us' and 'them' and has excluded many of the latter as 'undesirables.' Eligibility for citizenship is a good example of this. Naturalization was restricted to 'free white persons' in 1790; it was expanded to aliens born in Africa and persons of African descent in 1870.[3] In the case of 'undesirable' immigrants from Asia, the path to naturalization was closed.

How were 'aliens ineligible for citizenship' treated? Japanese in the US were excluded from mainstream society, were denied naturalization, forbidden to possess or lease land for more than three years, and segregated into ethnic enclaves along the West Coast. The segregation and exclusion of the Japanese was part of larger racist patterns in US society, where racial segregation was not only a widely practiced social custom but was also constitutionally sanctioned by official policies of the federal and state governments, beginning with the Supreme Court decision in *Plessy v. Ferguson*[4] in 1896 and ending with the decision in *Brown v. Board of Education*[5] in 1954. Within this type of political setting, employers in the US applied racial and ethnic distinctions with regard to occupations until the early twentieth century (Guerin-Gonzales 1996).

The wartime removal and incarceration was a part of the legal framework described above. It was part of the norm, never an exception or aberration from the ideals of the US at the time of national emergency. This situation was reversed only after the *Brown* decision, which struck down the constitutionality of segregated education in 1954.

### Political ideology: 'Big' government

Looking into the political ideology at the time of the removal and incarceration enables us to understand that Japanese Americans did not suffer simply as a result of anti-Japanese sentiment. The US was at that time experiencing a period of 'big' government which exercised strong intervention and control. For example, the Immigration Act of 1924 restricted immigrants to 155,000 a year, establishing quotas based on two percent of the foreign-born population in 1890. This was, it goes without saying, a consequence of policies that discriminated in favor of immigration from western and northern Europe rather than from eastern and southern Europe. That is, the state designated desirable ethnic groups for making up the members of the nation. The same act further prohibited entry of all 'aliens ineligible for citizenship.' This meant that immigration was completely prohibited for all Asians, including Japanese. This made it widely known to the nation that the state had prescribed a peculiar existence for Asians, incapable of being worthy legal members of the nation. Meanwhile, from a labor supply viewpoint, the act did not set any numerical quotas with regard to western hemisphere countries. The federal government only regulated Mexican immigrants through administrative measures. In all of these examples we can glimpse 'a vision of the American nation that embodied certain hierarchies of race and nationality' (Ngai 2004: 23).

Strong and large-scale state control is also quite apparent in the political ideology and labor welfare policies of the 1930s. US-style liberalism is a philosophy that relies on state power, supports vigorous and interventionist activity by government and aims at the expansion of government participation in and responsibility for the economy. President Franklin D. Roosevelt, in order to affect recovery following the financial panic of the 1930s, delineated his plan for encouraging a move away from an economic structure with free market principles as its highest priority towards a state-managed economy and attempted to expand the government's role in the economy (Yergin and Stanislaw 1998: xv, 3).

Moreover, these measures were supported by Americans because these were, as it were, strong measures by a powerful, reliable government in a time of national hardship. This positive evaluation of the government was part of the undercurrent that tolerated the wartime removal and incarceration.

## Limitation of liberalism: Tolerance of extra-legal measures

Liberalism is inherently a philosophy that respects the freedom of the individual. Under a state-managed economy, while the state intervenes in the economy it does not intervene in the lives of individuals. During World War II, the federal government—on the basis of reflections on the violation of the human rights of people of German ancestry during World War I—showed considerable concern for the protection of civil liberties.

This liberal political environment on the one hand and the wartime incarceration on the other should appear an odd mismatch. One key to understanding this contradiction is the limitations of the liberalism of the day. National defense is a vital matter for every country; the US Constitution contains a strong sense of national defense. Liberals thought that in peacetime—that is in normal times—it was constitutionally unacceptable to forcibly exclude a particular ethnic group solely on the basis of race, ethnicity, or ancestry. What, however, was the case in wartime?

The liberal faction tolerated the policy of racial discrimination against Japanese in the US and Japanese Americans as extra-legal measures so that they could effectively and efficiently exercise war powers of the executive branch in a case of national emergency. This policy, they reasoned, was an exception in constitutional law and lay outside the normal constitutional framework in light of the military necessity of defending the nation in a time of crisis, and the 'unique conditions' connected with the race and ethnicity of Japanese Americans. These were the limitations of liberalism that can be seen in the wartime policies that affected Japanese Americans during World War II (Yamakura 2000: 89–107).

If we were to identify two theories of liberalism, absolutist and relativist, the absolutist liberal theory does not accept the application of any restrictions on individual freedoms or rights by the state or society—under any conditions whatsoever. On the contrary, the relativist liberal theory, which prevailed during World War II, determines the amount of individual freedom and rights on a case-by-case basis in view of the greater good of the community to which the individual belongs. In times of peace, as relativist liberals argue, it is constitutionally unacceptable to exclude a particular group solely on the basis of race, ethnicity, or ancestry, but in the case of a national crisis, they accept special treatment for such groups in order to protect the nation—that is, they accept extra-legal measures that enable the full exercise of state power in times of national emergency. We can call this the limitation of a liberalism that is founded on relativism which holds that 'restrictions on individual freedom are unavoidable in order to protect the nation during wartime' (Mizuno 2005: 146–9).

## Incarceration as the peak of the anti-Japanese movement

The flow into the US of Japanese nationals looking for work came into its stride from the latter half of the 1880s, but from the outset Japanese were aliens ineligible for naturalization. Their permanent alien status naturally caused numerous inconveniences and difficulties. The most extreme case was the alien land laws in California. These laws, which ordered that land not be sold or leased to aliens ineligible for naturalization, were founded on apprehensions that agricultural land would be snatched up by Japanese who worked like workhorses from morning until sunset regardless of the day of the week. This law, enacted in 1913 with the backing of farmers and then revised in 1920, had the aim of shutting Japanese out of the agricultural industry. This was a law that had agriculture squarely in its sights, but before too long—in 1924—the so-called 'Japanese exclusion' law was enacted to prohibit the immigration of Japanese looking for work. This law was—as it were—the final and finished version (from restrictions on Japanese workers to a complete ban) of the Gentlemen's Agreement between Japan and the US (1907–1908). This agreement had its origins in the issue of the segregation of Japanese school children in San Francisco, and came to an end as a consequence of the restrictions on workers from Japan, as mentioned. In addition, the suspension of the issuing of passports for 'picture brides'[6] (see Yamamoto 1997: 33–9) symbolized Japanese-US relations which moved along in an awkward manner from the 1920s on. It was with this as background that the late 1930s arrived, full of the inevitability of confrontation between Japan and the US over Japan's advance into Asia. This is what is referred to as the imperialist war. FBI surveillance of the Japanese in the US had already begun in this period. Prior to the overt surveillance that occurred in the wartime concentration camps for Japanese Americans, covert surveillance was already being carried out. This is manifest in the fact that the arrest of the leading members of the major Japanese communities in the US occurred immediately after the attack on Pearl Harbor. Bilateral relations were thus in a delicate and strained state.

The removal and incarceration is an extension of the series of actions described above within this state of Japanese-US relations— a Japanese-US economic war. It is also related to ignorance and lack of understanding in the US of Japanese and Japanese Americans.

## Perception deficiency: Indifference, ignorance and neglect

The racial discrimination described above, in line with this kind of ignorance and lack of understanding, did not just suddenly begin in the 1940s; anti-Japanese discrimination had been brewing for many years. Among the stereotyped images of Japanese Americans were 'aliens ineligible for naturalization,' 'un-American barbarians,' 'inferior laborers,' and the like. Few Americans cared to distinguish Japanese Americans from the Japanese in Japan. This kind of negative image was linked to the amplification of feelings of fear and hostility and, ultimately, became one of the reasons used to justify their removal and incarceration.

The fact that there were newspaper articles expressing strong approval at the time that the forced internment policy was announced, and the virtual lack of any critical articles, reflects this situation. *Personal Justice Denied* (1982), compiled by the Commission on Wartime Relocation and Internment of Civilians, argues that the lack of strong counter arguments from the press was one of the factors that led the government to embark on its policy of removal and incarceration; this lack of counter arguments can be ascribed to indifference to, and ignorance and neglect of the Japanese in the US and Japanese Americans.[7]

These factors interacted with, and exacerbated, each other, leading to the wartime removal and incarceration.

## Remedies and preventive measures

Japanese Americans were placed under the exclusion orders by the US Army without any charges or accusations against them. This was a clear violation of the Fifth Amendment to the US Constitution which provides that 'no person shall ... be deprived of life, liberty, or property, without due process of law.' Let us now look at the subsequent responses to these events by Congress and the community of the victims.

### The redress movement

Firstly, in 1948, when some restoration of calm was finally achieved following the wartime hysteria, Congress released a report recommending the payment of compensation to Japanese Americans and shortly after this it passed the Japanese American Evacuation Claims

Act. This law went on to be revised in 1951 and 1956, but in any rational analysis the law did not provide satisfactory reparations to the victims. This is because it was simply limited to material loss; things such as physical hardship, mental suffering, the forfeiture of tangible and intangible profits that people had otherwise gained at the time, and the violation of their human rights all failed to be considered as objects warranting reparation. What needs to be stressed, in addition, was the lack of any discussion regarding either an apology or the mechanism that gave rise to the situation in the first place.

Around the mid-1950s the civil rights movement, led by African Americans, began to gain momentum. Then, around the late 1960s, the human rights movement began, led by Asian Americans and inheriting the spirit of the civil rights movement. It was at this time that young, third generation Japanese Americans—who had no personal experience of incarceration but who were stimulated by both movements just mentioned—became central figures in the organization of the movement to seek redress for the removal and incarceration and the movement aimed at the correction of misplaced democracy. In the midst of this linking up of the civil rights movement and the human rights movement, the wartime incarceration began to be interpreted and recognized as an urgent issue.

Subsequently—following many twists and turns—Congress became involved in this movement, and in 1980 President Carter signed a bill establishing the Commission on Wartime Relocation and Internment of Civilians. The gist of this legislation was to direct the Commission to review the policy of the wartime removal and incarceration of Japanese American civilians and the inhabitants of the Aleutian Archipelago by the federal government during wartime and to advise Congress on appropriate remedies.

We will narrow down our discussion of this law to the following two mutually related aspects: the object of the investigation and the aims of the Commission.

Initially, the legislation had no provision for a survey of the Peruvian Japanese case. When Peruvian Japanese became aware of this, they wrote letters to the appropriate members of Congress and members of the Commission, appealing strongly for an inquiry that would hear submissions on the miserable conditions endured by Peruvian Japanese as well as for permission to attend their own public hearings. The public hearings were held in eight major cities throughout the US, stretching over twenty days from July to December 1981, and over 750 people with some connection to the removal and incarceration—representing the government, the military, internees and academics—testified on all aspects of the issue ranging from the contemporary situation of the early 1940s to the realities inside concentration camps. Among these people were also internees who had been transported from Peru to the US. A total of six Peruvian Japanese were given the opportunity to testify about their internment from Central and South America. It is said that of all the statements made during the public hearings, their testimonies were among the most shocking (Higashide 1993, 1995).

This is further proof of the fact that most people, including members of Congress, had not known about these events. This also raised another problem: the issue of the violation of international law that we have already touched on. The fact that the wartime internment was enforced in violation of both domestic and international laws was brought to the public's attention by the Commission. In addition, the Commission concluded that the wartime incarceration was brought about not because of 'military necessity,' as claimed by the Department of War, but rather as a result of 'race prejudice, wartime hysteria, and a failure of political leadership' (Commission on Wartime Relocation and Internment of Civilians 1982: 18).

The second aim of the Commission resulted in the recommendation of individual payments set at US$20,000 per person, plus a formal apology signed by the President, and a resolution to promote liberty, equality and justice. In the case of Peruvian Japanese, however, there were disparate outcomes, with some people being awarded US$5,000, some US$20,000 and the claims of others remaining under dispute.

The redress scheme also included a community-based measure. The Civil Liberties Public Educational Fund was established, with ongoing support for the purpose of ensuring that the injustices surrounding the removal and incarceration are never forgotten and for public education activities and research aimed at shedding light on the background and causes that gave rise to these events (Otani 1997: 182).

From the above we see that the facts are being confronted squarely and that reparations and apologies to the people concerned are occurring under reflections about and a determination to avoid the re-emergence of an abnormal society that ought never to exist. There are also clearly ongoing efforts to shed light on the mechanisms that led to these events. However, one can also find many instances that lead to the conclusion that the above reflection and determination are not necessarily always being observed. We need efforts to preserve the memory of these traumas and soul-searching concerning the wartime victimization of a minority group.

## The Japanese American National Museum[8]

The movement to establish a not-for-profit museum, led by war veterans from the Los Angeles area who had been active members of the 442nd Regimental Combat Team during World War II, developed at practically the same time as the upsurge which led to the redress movement discussed above. Many ups and downs followed, but nurtured by this movement and thanks to grants from the state of California and the city of Los Angeles, donations from a variety of organisations and people who were affected by these events and the repeated collections of money from Japanese Americans and Japanese communities who lived through these times, the Japanese American National Museum—based in the city of Los Angeles—began its full-scale nationwide operations. This was in 1988. Its aim was to deepen understanding of diverse races and cultures in the US by informing people about the history and experiences of Japanese Americans, focusing on the topic of the wartime incarceration. In fact, in 1992 at the time of the 50th anniversary of the exclusion order, there was an exhibition of paintings on the anniversary of the wartime incarceration, called *From Behind the Fence*. This was also the year in which the museum was due to commemorate its reopening following the completion of building repairs and outfitting. In 2004 there was a further exhibition that revived the actual conditions of the removal and incarceration, and the efforts to ensure that the memories are preserved.

What has been the public response to these efforts on the part of the museum? We hear that the numbers of people coming to the museum each year are on an upward trend. When we visited the museum we met junior and middle school children being led around by their teachers—a testament to the partial achievement of the founding aims of the museum. It is the people who went through the removal and incarceration themselves who are the force behind this in their capacity as, by now elderly, volunteers. No one, surely, can fail to be moved as they solemnly relate the conditions of that time. Large numbers of people who experienced the events themselves are registered as volunteer 'guides' on the subject of the wartime incarceration. Some were the former members of the 442nd Regimental Combat Team, and others were in the 1800th Engineering Battalion, who had been in Poston Relocation center before the induction. According to one such person, the 1800th Engineering Battalion was a unique unit made up of American soldiers of German, Italian, and Japanese descent who were considered potential troublemakers. While this man was in the Army, his father was in a Department of Justice internment camp and his mother in Manzanar Relocation center, a very ironic situation (Shino).[9]

The total of donations given to the museum by government bodies, a variety of organizations and Japanese Americans, along with the sheer numbers of these people giving donations, shows that the aims of the museum's activities are being understood. We think that a common understanding of a society 'that ought never to exist' is definitely becoming more widespread.

## Looking to the future

We have, in this work, looked at attempts made to date to grapple with the need to prevent the re-emergence of a society 'that ought never to exist.' When we look at subsequent developments in international society we cannot say that the response to date has been sufficient or that the prospects for a new society are bright. What we can say is that holding an international conference on these matters is a very urgent issue. Finally, we would like to conclude by giving an itemized list of tasks that we all should strive to achieve in order to prevent the re-emergence of a society that ought never to exist.

1. Develop research and movements concerned with what we ought to do so that wars (abnormal states) do not arise.
2. Understand and recognize that the sort of society 'that ought not to exist' has existed in the past, and implement thoroughgoing human rights education so as to remove discrimination and bias in order that this sort of society will not emerge again.
3. Hold ongoing study groups regarding the Supreme Court's *Korematsu* and *Hirabayashi* precedents, and develop movements, including litigation, aimed at the repeal of these precedents. In particular, respond urgently to the use of both of these precedents in the Supreme Court's decisions in affirmative action cases.
4. Develop further the public relations efforts of the Japanese American National Museum.

# 3
# The Logic of Surveillance and the Predicament of 'the Social'

*Kiyoshi Abe*

## Introduction

The world has reputedly entered an age of globalization, yet it is clear that the 'happy global society' once so rosily portrayed has turned out to be little more than a pipe dream, even in the developed nations of the North which have enjoyed most of the benefits of globalization. Instead, the widening of the global North–South divide and the stratification of the North–South relationship, as well as the increasing inequalities which one might call North–South issues within nation-states, have now become the true face of 'globalization' (George 2004). What kind of critical intervention could sociology implement in today's 'globalized world'? In this paper, I will consider the subject of the violence which lurks in this age of globalization from the perspective of the predicament of 'the social.'

## The current status of 'the social'

### 'There is no such thing as society' and its aftermath

Margaret Thatcher, British Prime Minister from 1979 to 1990, is famously quoted as having declared: 'There is no such thing as society.' She goes on to say:

> There are individual men and women, and there are families. And no government can do anything except through people, and people must

look to themselves first. It's our duty to look after ourselves and then to look after our neighbour. (Thatcher 1993: 626)

This statement of neo-liberal political philosophy now smacks of reality not only in Britain and similarly developed nations, but in most other countries of the world. What, then, have been the changes triggered by the domination of neo-liberalism over some thirty years?[1]

Under the neo-liberal free market ideology, 'society'—which was once assumed to mediate between the nation and the individual—has lost substance. Inequalities around economic prosperity (income, assets)—one indicator of 'happiness'—are deemed to be the result of individual agents' choices and practices in the market. The implicit premise is one of self-determination, which is near-impossible. The assertions of policymakers who excessively advocate individual responsibility equate to an abdication of the responsibility to implement social security measures aimed at rectifying inequalities.

In contrast, in communitarian ideology, emphasis is given to traditions and important social foundations. From this perspective, the revival of community, made up of like-minded people who 'all understand each other well,' is deemed necessary for constituting a 'happy life' (Bauman 2001: 1–2). Here, the notion of a 'society' composed of variously differentiated individuals pales in the face of the myth of a 'community' bound together by common traditions and norms. Thus, enormous transformations are being undergone in the nature of 'society,' though in respectively divergent forms under the contrasting schemes of liberal versus communitarian. Still, any critical redefinition of the nature of 'society' itself—which has been differentiated from both the individual and the community, by the more prominent alternatives of 'individual and community'—seems to have been trivialised to a puzzling extent in both theory and practice.[2]

## Neo-conservatism and the mythification of order and morality

A third ideology, neo-conservatism, has become increasingly prominent in the political situation in recent years. Neo-conservatives advocate a return to 'morality' and 'order' in the face of social problems (a decline in moral awareness, a growing crime rate, and so on) arising as a consequence of excessive competition under neo-liberalism. The distortion of society triggered by neo-liberalism is evident behind the political trends of recent years, in which the necessity for law and order to deal with social issues such as crime is advocated and the restoration of the traditional family and community is loudly proclaimed as a remedy for the decline in moral consciousness.

Yet neo-conservatism never criticises the very foundation of neo-liberalism—individualism—which is the root cause of the 'pathology' it endeavours to address. On the contrary, it hides the essence of the problem by foisting upon people an authoritarian vision of how a 'proper' family, gender or community ought to be. In that sense, neo-conservatism operates as an ideology which affirms the present situation by obscuring the real points at issue in neo-liberalism. As Harvey (2005a) points out, neo-liberalism has forged a close relationship with neo-conservatism, which could be called a 'reaction' to the various issues to which neo-liberalism itself gives rise. It is a characteristic of the current world situation that neo-liberalism and neo-conservatism, which inherently contain mutually contradictory elements, have come to 'co-exist' based on a congruence of interest in the ruling classes of the world's most affluent and powerful nations.

## The liberal versus communitarian debate revisited

As neo-liberalism in economics and neo-conservatism in politics act in concert to increase their power, the very 'society' which modern sociology took as its primary object of consideration is plunging into a double crisis.

On the one hand, 'society,' once deemed to have its own domain distinct from either the family or the state, through all things being ascribed in principle to individual choice and responsibility, is undergoing infinite embrittlement. On the other hand, under the rise of neo-conservatism which regards traditional values and norms as absolute, 'society'—composed of diverse individuals—is made an object of control, as a risk which jeopardises the security of the community.

Simultaneously with the waging of the liberal–communitarian debate in terms of alternatives, namely 'individual or community,' or 'freedom or social order,' various attempts have been made on the political dimension to arbitrate between the two sides. Ironically, however, the perspective which questions 'the social' itself is lost from sight at that point. Young (1999) points this out in his unsparing critique of Etzioni's communitarian endeavour to strike a 'balance between individual autonomy and the community.' According to Young:

Amitai Etzioni persists in his most recent book, *The New Golden Rule* (1997), to relegate 'socio-economic factors' to a sideshow and to insist that the main route to producing a good society is the balance between autonomy and community. In this his argument inevitably counterposes the philosophies of libertarianism and conservatism, rugged individualism (neo-liberalism) and the conservatism of tradition and conformity. Social democratic ideas are left at the wayside and two right wing philosophies take centre stage as the debate of our times, with communitarianism happily providing the 'golden' promise. (Young 1999: 161–2)[3]

Under the advance of globalization as portrayed in Hubert Sauber's 2004 documentary film *Darwin's Nightmare*, which embraces the idea of survival of the fittest (Nishitani 2006), respect for diversity and uniqueness in 'society' and the importance of dialogue and combat between different entities and principles have now become difficult to maintain even as philosophies for which to strive. In this sense, the film vividly illustrates the present-day predicament of 'the social.'

## The logic of surveillance

### The post-9/11 world

What kinds of changes might have given rise to the predicament of 'the social'? What sort of circumstantial transitions can we point out as background leading to the trivialisation in people's quotidian lives of the essence of 'the social,' meaning coexistence with others and the acceptance of diversity that were previously cited as principles?

In this chapter, I focus on the 'logic of surveillance' as a key factor triggering the 'predicament of the social.' What I mean here by 'surveillance' is not merely to 'watch' a person by use of technological equipment such as security cameras. I define the 'logic of surveillance' in a wider sense, as something which encompasses the entire range of occupations which strive to comprehensively capture and control their object, including the idea of 'watching over' an other with affection and compassion (Lyon 2001; Abe 2006).

At present, what is propelling the spread of the 'logic of surveillance' is a vague feeling of insecurity and danger. In a manner supported by the nebulous uneasiness aroused by the 'deteriorating condition of public safety' and 'threat of terrorism' publicised through the media, politicians and critics loudly proclaim the need for an intensification of surveillance in building a society where people can live in safety and security. In consequence, a plethora of surveillance devices are introduced as ways and means to assure such security.

There is no need to reiterate that such a heightened orientation towards security spread on a worldwide scale in one blow after the so-called 9/11 terrorist attack (Lyon 2003). Under the post-9/11 political situation, there is even the view that guaranteeing security has been placed as a categorical imperative, being afforded top priority ahead of all other objectives.

Yet the strengthening of surveillance and security orientation is not something which suddenly emerged as a result of 9/11. The 'logic of surveillance' has indeed become apparent in recent years, but its roots can be found in the establishment period of modern society (Giddens 1985). In the process of considering the tightening of surveillance in Japan, especially, it is essential to note that the 'logic of surveillance' hidden behind the positive image of a conventional 'information-oriented society,' which sang the praises of technological advancement, was accelerated, using 9/11 as its momentum/alibi (Abe 2004).

Due to the extensive spread of the 'logic of surveillance,' a mentality that perhaps should be termed a 'culture of fear' (Glassner 1999) or 'culture of suspicion' (Lyon 2003) flourishes among the people who live there. Now, the strangers surrounding one and the world itself do not constitute a presence in which one can place one's trust without presumption, but are rather nothing but objects of anxiety and targets towards which suspicion should be directed. At the same time, with anxiety and suspicion not necessarily based on anything concrete as a background, there is a heightened trend for people to strive thoroughly to exclude the unknown and the uncertain, as typically embodied by 'others = them,' as different from 'the self = us.' In those circumstances, things which diverge from the predicted / the anticipated / the planned, no matter what, become prospective targets for elimination or control. In the present situation in which the 'logic of surveillance' is spreading, any 'event' which oversteps the self's (= our) expectations is taken to be a state of affairs to be scrupulously avoided.

## The polarization of security society

That is not to say, however, that the 'logic of surveillance' has spread homogeneously or evenly across the whole of society. On the one hand, there are some people who enjoy peaceful lives, reaping benefit from the 'logic of surveillance,' while there are others who, conversely, have their own bodies and lives threatened because of that same 'logic.' In other words, under that 'logic of surveillance,' there is progressive polarisation of social strata: one stratum being able to identify itself with the side that does the surveying; while the other has no choice but to accept itself as being on the side that is surveyed.

The great majority of people who inhabit society tend to think that the strengthening of surveillance is necessary to ensure their own safety and security. The main reason for this is that it is pleasant for one to devote oneself 'freely to one's favourite pastimes' with peace of mind, in circumstances where one's safety is assured (Abe 2006). Still, such pleasure takes shape under thoroughgoing control by means of surveillance. If we take this into consideration, then we might say that most today enjoy 'freedom inside a cage.'

On the other hand, as is typical in groups known as 'the homeless,' for people who are made the object of control by a state administration, the tightening of surveillance has no other goal but to achieve social order by nullifying those people's existence. So that no reprehensible creatures invade the parks that exist to allow decent citizens to indulge freely in doing as they like, the incarceration of homeless people in 'centres for independent living' or their expulsion outside of the 'free cage' is being attempted as a measure to address the 'homeless problem' (Yamaguchi 2006). The thoroughness of such 'logic of surveillance' goes on to divide society as a whole into an overwhelming majority of 'those who survey' and a tiny minority of 'those who are surveyed.'

Yet this is only one aspect of the divisions triggered by the 'logic of surveillance.' The assurance of security, which aims for safety and peace of mind, is sought because it is an indispensable condition for 'freely doing what one likes.' For example, we who live in affluent consumer societies accept the installation of innumerable security cameras so that we might enjoy shopping in a safe environment with reassurance. The point worthy of note here is that the gaze of such cameras is deemed simultaneously to be watching out for suspicious individuals and intruders, and to be watching over 'us' respectable shoppers. When they identify cameras in their own field of vision while strolling in a shopping mall, most people probably feel that they are being 'watched over,' and gain a sense of security. For that very reason, people are not particularly bothered by the presence of those cameras, and can enjoy their shopping.

If one follows this line of thought, one can see that even with the same 'logic of surveillance,' people have contrasting ways of identification, taking either the side of the surveyors or that of the surveyed, depending on whether they interpret 'surveillance' to mean 'watching' or 'watching over.' Most of us tend to place ourselves on the 'doing' side in relation to 'watching,' and on the 'receiving' end in relation to 'watching over.' What emerges from this is the dual nature of identification to do with surveillance. We half-unconsciously desire to watch out for dangers (shady characters or suspicious circumstances), on the one hand, while being watched over by a larger, stronger presence (typically the personalised paternalistic 'state') in our quest for solace, on the other (Saito 2004).

The simplistic division into watching and watching over, which can be sensed on a psychological level, is not so clear-cut when it comes to actual surveillance operations, however. In light of the properties of surveillance technology, it is certainly not surprising to find situations in which people who believe that they are doing the watching are actually the ones being watched, or where people who are supposed to have been watched over have actually been watched instead (the converse, though, is extremely rare). As it comprehensively captures its objects as data, contemporary surveillance is increasing its reliance upon SIGINT (signal intelligence) and COMPUTINT (computer intelligence)—which analyse digitised information—with greater rapidity than its dependence on HUMINT (human intelligence) and COMINT (communication intelligence)—which have human beings as their instrument/object. This is because all people involved are 'watched' as potential risks, and there can be no exceptions.

If we turn our attention to this point, it can be seen that polarisation in the levels of awareness of self and other in relation to surveillance is merely superficial. Today, as surveillance is tightening and expanding in a semi-arbitrary manner, those who are consciously 'doing the watching' cannot escape being exposed to the 'logic of surveillance.' Still, that slippage between the self-awareness of the parties involved over the double boundaries of 'watch/watch over' and 'those who do/ those who are done to' and the actual mode of surveillance operations is never mentioned by the pro-surveillance side, because it is only by not allowing people to be aware or conscious of such a slippage that the 'logic of surveillance' can permeate into every corner of social life.

The 'logic of surveillance,' which is advancing in a form that shares a basic commonality with the polarisation rooted in the dimension of individual subjectivity, is affecting profound changes in the very shape of society on a dimension which exceeds identification. What can be glimpsed through the gap between the image each person has of surveillance and the latter's actual substance is nothing other than the violence of 'borders' over the assurance of security. All people who live in a security-oriented society are placed in either of two categories, namely, being imprisoned 'inside a cage,' or being driven 'outside a cage.' Such selection and demarcation tends to be conducted in an extremely arbitrary manner which capitalises on vague anxiety and fear. That is precisely where lurks the essence of 'the violence of surveillance,' which cannot be reduced to issues to do with the individual, such as privacy and identity.

**'Theme parks' and 'camps'**

The advance of surveillance is supported by people who want the freedom to do as they like. The exclusion of dangers or inconveniences so as to cater to the desires of such people is a method of environmental management like that used in theme-parks. On that point, all social space these days could also be said to present a theme park-like aspect. It seems as if people desire to live in a 'free cage' in order to indulge in their favourite pastimes in a safe and secure environment.

On the other hand, those groups and individuals who are regarded as a 'threat' to public peace are placed under scrupulous surveillance and have their freedom restricted. The fundamental notion that underpins the countermeasures employed by states and administrations appears to be the idea of a 'camp' (i.e., a place of containment). The so-called 'centres for independent living' are based on policies that endeavour to contain the homeless (= non-labour force) in camps, and to return them to the labour market through training in those places. Their aim is to take those people who have fallen out of the 'free cage' and lock them back 'inside the cage.' People who consistently resist incarceration are thoroughly excluded from public space (= parks) by administrative subrogation. That means expulsion from 'the cage.'

Oddly, however, even in the midst of the sweeping enforcement of the 'logic of surveillance,' free and enjoyable theme parks are becoming increasingly similar to camps where freedom is curtailed and dwellers must endure a hard life. In both of these, environmental management is scrupulously and thoroughly implemented in order to seal in any 'alterity' which contains the potential to disrupt expectations and harmony. If there were a difference between the two, it would perhaps be that the management of bodies/spaces/environments in theme parks is done artfully, making individuals feel that they are 'free spaces,' while in camps it is carried out in a more direct and blatant manner.

Under a neo-liberal system, whether with theme parks or camps, there is never any recognition of a unique 'social significance' in the 'outer' realm of the space being managed. Indeed, this equates to 'there is no such thing as society.' It is taken for granted that no importance will be acknowledged in the ensuring of security (i.e., assurance of social safety) in the 'outer' as a policy issue. This is because expulsion to the 'outer' is deemed to be due to individual choices and responsibilities. As a result, people who are shut out of both theme parks and camps are denied the very 'right to exist' and are exposed to unadorned 'violence.'

## The predicament of the social

### The line between us and them

As the growing popularity of the voluntary community patrol movement by resident volunteers shows, people cheerfully undertake 'watch' duties in order to secure their own safety. Also, as the lack of any significant objections to the installation of security cameras everywhere in such public spaces as stations, parks and squares indicates, people yearn to be 'watched over.' Thanks to such surveillance 'from below,' there is swelling public agreement that some limitation of 'freedom' cannot be helped for the sake of ensuring safety and peace of mind. Yet it quite often happens that the freedom that is assumed here to be rightfully limited is actually 'somebody else's' freedom. After the curbing of 'my' own freedom—'I' being on the side that does the surveying—has been weighed against the 'securing of safety and peace of mind,' such curbing is not necessarily judged to be inevitable. Rather, it is the safety and peace of mind for 'us' that is pursued by unconditionally accepting the limiting the freedom of those who are on the receiving end of the surveillance.[4]

Under a surveillance-centred society motivated by anxiety about and rejection of 'them,' people increasingly strengthen their orientation towards a world (= community) composed only of 'us' who are trustworthy. In order to form a 'community' rooted in xenophobia, the presence of 'others' who differ from 'us' both externally and internally is always necessary, because we have to confirm obsessively that we are *'us'* by proving that we are *'not them.'*

> Increasingly one's identity had to be constructed by insisting on the non-identity of others. How otherwise could the neo-Nazi skinheads in Germany, wearing the uniforms, hair-styles and musical tastes of the cosmopolitan youth culture, establish their essential Germanness, except by beating up local Turks and Albanians? How, except by eliminating those who did not 'belong' could the 'essentially' Croat or Serb character of some region be established in which, for most of history, a variety of ethnicities and religions had lived as neighbours? (Hobsbawm 1994: 429)

An obsession over boundaries between the self and others, drawn by a self overcome with anxiety, is something that supports the sweep of the 'logic of surveillance' from behind. At the same time, it has a strong affinity with movements for the 'restoration of the community' and 'rebirth of the community' that are so loudly hailed nowadays. Of course, Etzioni's kind of communitarianism does not overtly champion the 'expulsion of foreigners' or 'minority discrimination' (Etzioni 2001). Still, under the post-9/11 political situation, with its spiralling levels of anxiety and suspicion, it is not rare for 'their' freedom to be sacrificed for the sake of assuring 'our' safety and peace of mind, through activities and movements in the everyday lives of community-dwellers. Consequently, it might not be surprising even if naked violence towards 'them'—those people deemed to lurk both inside and outside the 'community'—was occasionally pursued in terms of symbol, sign and utterance, rather than physically.

## Desire for expulsion of the other

In the midst of the thoroughgoing implementation of the 'logic of surveillance,' there is an ongoing attempt not merely to suppress the existence of 'them' who differ from 'us,' but also half-unconsciously to drive them out of the 'free cage' in which we live. There is, however, a radical contradiction inherent in our relationship with such others.

In the first place, it is physically impossible to spit them 'outside the cage.' Others, who have bodies of flesh and blood, would never stop being a presence 'together' with me/us in this society. Secondly, as a more basic problem, there is no predetermined boundary between others who ought to be driven 'outside the cage' and the self that should remain 'inside the cage.' Rather, as long as one discovers others who could be regarded as a menace in specific circumstances, an imagined identity consisting of a mutually-congenial 'us' is established. In that sense, threats are things which come not only from outside, but indeed are also generated from within oneself. For that reason, 'we' cannot obliterate the suspicion that a potential menace lurks in our own midst. In other words, 'we' who strive to remain 'inside the cage' are obliged to repeat a self-contradictory confirmation, through rejection of the other, by answering the question: 'Who is meant by 'us,' to begin with?'

The desire to expel the other which grows under the 'logic of surveillance' throws into jeopardy the very 'society where one can live in safety and security' for which people unceasingly hoped for from the start. That is, due to the relentless expansion of anxiety over 'the other' who is the object of expulsion, anyone (whoever they might be) who is 'together' with us must become a potential threat to the self. No association with such an other can logically create any kind of 'social relation.' The end-point of rejection of the other will probably have to be a world with 'only me,' ultimately lacking even 'us.'

The etymology of the word 'security' which is being so mindlessly pursued at present is *securus*: *se* meaning 'free from' and *cura* meaning 'care.' In other words, if security is thought of as 'a situation that is good even in the absence of any consideration,' or 'a situation where one is never bothered,' the advent of the disappearance of 'the social' at the very extremity of security, supported by the desire for ejection of the other, could even be called a perfectly natural, logical consequence. If 'society' becomes viable through the self and others interrelating not only with empathy and agreement, but also sometimes through the medium of rebellion and discord, then prisoners in the 'free cage'—who try in an animal-like manner to evade any kind of 'care' in relation either to themselves or to others and the world, while they dream of a tranquil land where they would never be disturbed—perhaps could be said to have voluntarily relinquished being a 'social presence.'

## Conditions for 'the social'

### The spirit of tolerance

Under the 'logic of surveillance,' the boundary between self and other is violently erected. In that process, even while being tormented by endless anxiety and suspicion, people are unable to escape the curse of mindlessly seeking security. In this can be glimpsed the predicament of the social, which is accelerated by globalization.

In the face of such temporal circumstances, what kind of critical imagination could sociology present? Here, I will consider the possibility of a 'logic of hospitality,' as a condition for a self/other relation differing from that based on the 'logic of surveillance.'

When 'co-existence with others' is trumpeted as a political and cultural issue in the global age, the necessity for a 'spirit of tolerance' is stressed. In continuing to live peaceably with 'others' who have a culture or religion dissimilar to their own, it is vital, so it is proclaimed, for all parties to have a spirit of tolerance that mutually respects divergent values, rather than to pit their various versions of 'justice' or 'truth' against each other. Certainly, if one looks back upon the history of the past, in which intolerant attitudes towards different cultures triggered all kinds of conflict, the assertion that endeavouring to have exchange between cultures in a spirit of mutual tolerance is indispensable in the global age is somewhat persuasive.

As previously pointed out, however, the notion of tolerance is steadfastly connected with 'Christian charity.' That concept owes its lineage to the tolerant attitude shown by Christians towards other denominations and religions.

> Indeed, tolerance is first of all a form of charity. A Christian charity, therefore, even if Jews and Muslims might seem to appropriate this language as well. Tolerance is always on the side of the "reason of the strongest," where "might is right." (Derrida 2003: 127)

The point that emerges from tolerance as the 'reason of the strongest' is that it is undeniably imbued with a paternalistic bent. The necessity for tolerance has hitherto been hailed as a charitable attitude which ought to be assumed by a father towards his children/a majority towards a minority/a ruler towards the ruled.

Such a spirit of tolerance cannot help but have great limitations in any critique of the crisis of 'the social,' because a spirit of tolerance is unable to constitute a sufficient oppositional argument against surveillance as 'watching over,' which has a similar, heavily-paternalistic aspect. Undoubtedly, a tolerant attitude might be effective to a certain degree as a protective strategy for eliminating or excluding others by means of 'watching.' As long as tolerance retains an aspect of warmth emanating from 'the strong' towards 'the weak,' however, it will always have difficulty escaping being drawn into the 'logic of surveillance' whereby 'the weak' are 'watched over' by 'the strong.' For example, in terms of sexual orientation, where a majority (heterosexuals) endorses the existence of a minority (homosexuals) and guarantees the latter's rights, members of the former group often assert that 'they themselves' have a spirit of tolerance, but one should not overlook the point that this harbours the momentum for paternalistic intervention at the same time. As proof of this, the acceptance of a minority by a tolerant majority is, in many cases, accompanied by some kind of 'conditions' (while heterosexuals may respect the rights of homosexuals as 'individuals,' they do not recognise the latter's rights as 'couples,' thus denying them the right to marry, for example).

If one thinks in this way, one perceives that it is possible for the spirit of tolerance which endorses others under certain conditions to coexist with the 'logic of surveillance' without conflict. In terms of the previous example, the acceptance of the presence of homosexuals in the name of freedom of sexual orientation easily connects with placing them under a watchful gaze which brims with curiosity about 'them' who differ from 'us.' Considering the point about the paternalistic relation towards others, one cannot anticipate overcoming the predicament of 'the social' by means of a spirit of tolerance.

## Pure hospitality

With what kind of logic, then, could we sketch the vision of a society unlike any of the present ones? Drawing on Jacques Derrida, I will consider the possibility of a 'hospitality' which differs from 'tolerance.'

According to Derrida, tolerance is nothing more than 'conditional hospitality.' As such, others can be welcomed as long as they comply with the logic upon which the self relies for its establishment.

> [T]olerance remains a scrutinized hospitality, always under surveillance, parsimonious and protective of its sovereignty. In the best of cases, it's what I would call a conditional hospitality, the one that is most commonly practised by individuals, families, cities, or states. We offer hospitality only on the condition that the other follows our rules, our way of life, even our language, our culture, our political system, and so on. (Derrida 2003: 128)

In everyday practices, the spirit of tolerance is applied to others ('them') who obey the self's ('our') rules, but others who harbour the potential to question and intimidate our selves are never invited to join 'us.' According to Derrida, however, the essence of hospitality lies in unconditionally welcoming the other, regardless of the latter's identity. In other words, 'pure unconditional hospitality' means welcoming and accepting not only those guests whom one has invited oneself, but any unexpected guests, whenever and from wherever they might come.

> [P]ure or unconditional hospitality does not consist in such an *invitation* ("I invite you, I welcome you into *my home*, on the condition that you adapt to the laws and norms of my territory, according to my language, tradition, memory, and so on"). Pure and unconditional hospitality, hospitality *itself*, opens or is in advance open to someone who is neither expected nor invited, to whomever as an absolutely foreign *visitor*, as a new *arrival*, nonidentifiable and unforeseeable, in short, wholly other. I would call this a hospitality of *visitation* rather than *invitation*. (Derrida 2003: 128–9, italics original)

With a full appreciation of the fact that a person visiting or arriving is a presence fraught with risk, and that to welcome him or her is an enormous demand, Derrida explains the significance of 'unconditional hospitality':

> The visit might actually be very dangerous, and we must not ignore this fact, but would a hospitality without risk, a hospitality backed by certain assurances, a hospitality protected by an immune system against the wholly other, be true hospitality? Though it's ultimately true that suspending or suppressing the immunity that protects me from the other might be nothing short of life-threatening. (Derrida 2003: 129)

Extending hospitality to an other at one's own risk provides the opportunity for an unplanned encounter between the self and an other. This appears to be Derrida's idea. Yet Derrida also points out that in the real world it becomes possible to be actually hospitable to an other through 'unconditional hospitality' being placed under some kind of limitation. Realistic hospitality comes into effect as a certain kind of 'conditional hospitality,' meaning tolerance. The point worthy of attention here is that the two forms of hospitality are 'indissociable.'

> These two hospitalities are at once heterogeneous and indissociable. Heterogeneous because we can move from one to the other only by means of an absolute leap, a leap beyond knowledge and power, beyond norms and rules. Unconditional hospitality is transcendent with regard to the political, the juridical, perhaps even to the ethical. But—and here is the indissociability—I cannot open the door, I cannot expose myself to the coming of the other and offer him or her anything whatsoever without making this hospitality effective, without, in some concrete way, giving *something determinate*. (Derrida 2003: 129, italics original)

In other words, the potential of 'unconditional hospitality' only becomes effective by becoming 'conditional hospitality' under some kind of system in actual society. The essence of hospitality is sought in its 'being unconditional,' but it is necessary for some kind of limits to be drawn in order for one to be hospitable, namely, to 'open the door.' Therein can be seen the paradox surrounding hospitality to others.

Interestingly, in Derrida's argument, 'unconditional hospitality' itself—a 'condition' for systematically-conditioned hospitality—is deemed (pre-)ethical, in the sense that though it is not even possible to determine whether 'unconditional hospitality' is 'ethical,' there could be no ethics without it.

> Unconditional hospitality, which is neither juridical nor political, is nonetheless the condition of the political and the juridical. For these very reasons, I am not even sure whether it is ethical, insofar as it does not even depend on a decision. But what would an 'ethics' be without hospitality? (Derrida 2003: 129)

Derrida's paradoxical positioning of 'unconditional hospitality' is reminiscent of Zygmunt Bauman's discussion around 'morality as the primary structure of intersubjective relation,' which attempts to expose the hidden violence in the modern age itself, starting with the Holocaust. In Bauman's words:

> *[M]orality is the primary structure of intersubjective relation* in its most pristine form...The substance of morality being a duty towards the other (as distinct from an obligation), and a duty which precedes all interestedness—the roots of morality reach well beneath societal arrangements, like structures of domination or culture. Societal processes start when the structure of morality (tantamount to

intersubjectivity) is already there. *Morality is not a product of society. Morality is something society manipulates*—exploits, redirects, jams. (Bauman 1989: 183, italics original)

For Bauman, 'morality,' is not something that modern society constructs as it progresses towards 'Civilization' and thrusts upon 'barbaric' peoples. Rather, it is purported to be quite the opposite, something that the societal establishes with the 'moral structure' latent in intersubjective relationships as its foundation. For Derrida, on the other hand, 'hospitality' is neither intrinsically juridically determinable nor politically selectable, but is rather a condition that makes laws, politics, and even ethics, possible. The point emerging from this is that the modes of morality/ethics variously described by Bauman and Derrida indicate a duality full of contradictions, in that while they govern the very shape of systematised society, they simultaneously are conditioned by those social systems. What we can find in common between these two thinkers who endeavour from divergent viewpoints to shed light upon the modern age is an awareness of the times which apprehends that a violence peculiar to the modern age is produced by the unilateral withdrawal of the moral/ethical domain under a social system (the societal domain).

The perspective of 'pure hospitality' or 'morality as intersubjective relation' seems to illuminate a phase of unlimited potential, brittle and ephemeral though it may be. Herein indeed lies the uniqueness of the 'event'—being with (unknown) others—which constitutes the issue in mind when Derrida advocates 'pure hospitality' as 'visitation' rather than 'invitation,' and when Bauman emphasises the importance of the sphere of the 'social,' as distinct from the 'societal.'

> Without this thought of pure hospitality (a thought that is also, in its own way, an experience), we would not even have the idea of the other, of the alterity of the other, that is, of someone who enters into our lives without having been invited. We would not even have the idea of love or of "living together (*vivre ensemble*)" with the other in a way that is not a part of some totality or "ensemble." (Derrida 2003: 129, italics original)

> [T]he factors responsible for the presence of moral capacity must be sought in the *social*, but not *societal* sphere. Moral behaviour is conceivable only in the context of coexistence, of 'being with others,' that is, a social context; but it does not owe its appearance to the

presence of supra-individual agencies of training and enforcement, that is, of a societal context. (Bauman 1989: 178–9, italics original)

Coexistence and chance encounters between the self and other in a social phase do not arise based on subjective choice. The 'duty towards the other' that Bauman discusses, drawing on Levinas, anticipates an 'I' as subject. In other words, 'I' only becomes a 'self as subject' which takes responsibility (the duty to respond) for an other by being exposed to 'your' gaze. In the case of 'pure hospitality' as well, 'I,' as host, cannot select and invite 'you,' the guest to come, in advance. The relationship between self and other through hospitality is generated from the point of welcoming another person as a 'complete stranger,' namely, a visitor who is an unknown entity surpassing our own intentions and motives. The host can only become the master of the house (a subject) by welcoming the guest. In this way, while the positioning of morality/ethics in the thinking of Derrida and Bauman is thoroughly desubjective, it simultaneously aligns with the standard of 'events' in the relationship between the other and the self.

As the two parties are of a different nature, they cannot understand each other. The other cannot be anticipated because he or she is an unknown entity. We tend to think it would be impossible to establish 'the social' between such an 'I' and 'you.' In actual fact, however, the exact opposite might be the case—perhaps 'the social' comes into being for the very reason that there is an absolute difference between the other and the self. Derrida and Bauman's ideas evoke a unique delicacy vis-à-vis 'the social' woven by the self/other relation.

## 'The communal' and 'the social'

Today, as the strange collusion between neo-liberalism and neo-conservatism is deepening, there is an increasing orientation towards a 'community' composed of 'us' who are tried and trusted. Reinstatement of the 'community,' which, at first glance, seems to emphasise traditions and norms, tends to be regarded as a solution that will counteract the situation in which people are divided under market fundamentalism, and restore social relations. As we have seen, however, the present-day community-orientation is exacerbating the seriousness of the predicament of the social, as the former maintains close links with the 'logic of surveillance.' This is because insistence on 'our' identity, backed by anxiety and suspicion, almost inevitably provokes the exclusion of 'them.' In order to guarantee the 'being together' of people who differ from each other in diverse ways without mutual negation, it is necessary, I believe, to champion 'the social' after having revealed the uniqueness of 'society,' which is distinct from the 'community.'

What enables the existence of a contemporary 'community' is the presupposition of something 'shared.' The group constituting 'us' is formed on the foundation of some kind of imagined 'commonality,' whether it be 'race,' or 'ethnicity,' or 'nationality.' In that sense, 'the communal' could be called 'a gathering of people who share something in common.'

By contrast, 'the social' is a relationship between the other and the self which begins without presupposing any sort of commonality. As Derrida says in reference to the 'hospitality of the visit' that is extended to a visitor, 'you' and 'I,' who meet through my 'opening the door,' might not share anything in common at all. If, in spite of that, we are able to accomplish something with the other on the momentum of hospitality, then herein must lie the distinctiveness of 'the social.' In that sense, 'the social' indicates 'a relationship between people who do not (necessarily) share anything in common.'

By thus highlighting the difference in subsistence structure between 'the community' and 'society,' we can more precisely depict the condition of the 'predicament of the social' that has arisen in the globalized world. The 'predicament of the social' does not mean that important social foundations are nearing crisis-point as a result of the divisions arising through the excessive competition of neo-liberalism. Rather, the essence of today's 'predicament of the social' lies in the resurrection of 'the community,' with its exclusivist and autistic nature, and the growing routinisation of elimination and expulsion of the other, with the aim of assuring 'the community's' own safety and peace of mind, as a reaction to the pathology created by neo-liberalism. Though they may appear to laud a 'spirit of tolerance,' social groups formed on the basis of the logic of community are always in danger of turning towards total rejection of the other, on some impetus. Have we not seen this time and again in history?

## Towards the horizon of 'being with others'

The 'logic of surveillance,' while supported by 'our' desire to do away with the other, endlessly magnifies the latter at the same time. In order to resist the violence latent in expulsion of the other, we now need to requestion the idea of 'being with others' which has been regarded in sociology as almost self-evident. As long as we continue to interpret our counterparts as beings whom we can select/invite/govern at our own convenience, 'the other' in its true sense will not appear. 'I' being 'together' with 'you' is something which absolutely surpasses my own selfish motives; rather, 'I' am sublimely vulnerable in the face of the event of 'being together.' The situation is the same for 'you,' too. If this is so, is not the mutual vulnerability of the subjects itself an indispensable condition in envisaging a self/other relationship devoid of violence? 'Hospitality' which harbours the potential to show up the self's vulnerability and shake its existence to its very core is definitely something to be feared. Surely, though, we can only reach the horizons of 'being together' by not avoiding such hospitality, but by opening the door (i.e., ourselves) to others.

The wave of globalization is in the process of building a world of 'the survival of the fittest,' while radically demolishing the established shape of economics, politics and culture on a global scale. In the midst of this tide, 'being with others' is swiftly and steadily being undermined from the grassroots level of people's everyday life-practices. In the face of such a 'predicament of the social,' the most vital task posed to sociology today is how to resist ongoing globalization with the aim of making 'being together in society' a reality, rather than pinning faint hopes on restoration of 'the community.'

# Part II
# 'Taming' Suffering

# 4
# Social Research/Action for Returned Filipino Entertainers
*Joe Takeda*

## Introduction

Millions of Filipinos witnessed the turn of the century not in the company of their families and friends in their motherland but with employers, co-workers, customers and strangers in any of the many countries where overseas Filipino workers (OFWs) are found. Eight years into the new millennium, an ever-increasing number of Filipinos continue to work and live away from their families, in search of gainful employment opportunities to uplift their families' economic condition and quality of life, regardless of the harsh working and living conditions abroad. In the case of OFWs coming to Japan, the majority are women working as entertainers. They work in Japan's adult entertainment industry, where sexual abuse and exploitation are institutionalized so as to continually prey upon and attack the vulnerabilities of the women. Even after they return to the Philippines, they suffer from various issues such as social stigma, mental and physical health problems, divorce and recognition of their children with Japanese male partners, and poverty (Batis Center for Women 1995).

The focus of this study is on returned Filipino entertainers. The objective of this study, however, is not simply to understand the issues faced by these women, to investigate the social structure causing these problems, or to analyze how some of these women strategically survive this harsh situation. Rather, the main objective of this study is to span the boundary between research and practice in order to empower these women by using participatory research. In conventional research, whether qualitative or quantitative, researchers are seen as experts and a superior-inferior relationship arises between the researcher and subject. As a result, more often than not, the research results are based on the perspectives and interests of researchers (Ristock and Pennell 1996). Alternatively, participatory research establishes a cooperative relationship between researcher and subject where the researcher does not play the leading role in selecting research questions or data collection/analysis but merely assists the subjects in doing so (Altpeter, Schopler, Galinsky and Pennell 1999). This enables understanding and discussion of the results in context from the subject's perspective. In other words, participatory research is characterized by collaboration between researcher and subject and the participation of all parties concerned in every process, and its objective is not the establishment of knowledge but the empowerment of the people (Sarri and Sarri 1992). This study, thus, applies participatory research to the self-help organization of the returned Filipino entertainers and evaluates its effect on the empowerment of these women.

## Returned Filipino entertainers

In 2004, the US claimed that human traffickers and bar owners have been using Japanese entertainer visas as a cover for running prostitution rings. In response, the Japanese government applied stricter visa requirements on foreign entertainers in March 2005, and the number of entertainer visas issued for Filipinos decreased from 82,714 in 2004, to 47,765 in 2005, and to only 8607 in 2006 (Ministry of Justice 2005–7). This policy change protected thousands of young Filipino women from sexual exploitation. In the last three decades, however, more than 500,000 Filipinos, an overwhelming majority of whom are women, came to Japan as entertainers, and many of them returned to the Philippines with various problems and are still battling with its after effects.

### Issues faced by returned Filipino entertainers

Filipino women entertainers are faced with many issues and problems upon their return to the Philippines. Besides the social stigma of being referred to as immoral or indecent *Japayukis* (foreign prostitutes in Japan), many women returnees have encountered intense experiences that have brought about serious psychological and health effects. The anxiety-inducing conditions of most migrants make them very prone to depression and other mental strains. In fact, medical diagnosis of women returnees showed serious mental ailments such as schizophrenia, psychosis and depression (Takeda (ed.) 2005). Various factors have triggered mental distress in these women. The most common and devastating examples of these factors revolve around family problems, psychological and emotional pains, work pressures, alcohol and drugs, and physical and sexual violence.

Many women also suffer from the pain of troubled, deteriorating or broken relationships with their Japanese husbands or partners, which often result in the abandonment of women and their Japanese-Filipino children (JFC). Major causes for unsuccessful marriages have been language barriers, quarrels and misunderstandings with in-laws, personal differences, domestic violence, and intense loneliness or homesickness, among others. In these situations, the women returnees are often faced with the hardships of coping with daily life as solo parents.

For many Filipino migrants, returning to their home country means returning to living in poverty again. Many women have endured heart-breaking circumstances and sacrifices in Japan for the fulfillment of a dream to liberate themselves and their families from dehumanizing poverty, or to maintain comfortable lifestyles for themselves and their families. However, upon their return, daily financial difficulties are constant realities for the women. As they reintegrate into their home country, the women try to cope with unstable jobs and salaries. Many find it difficult to get jobs because they lack skills and education. Most of the women are single mothers with three or four children. Because of their unstable jobs and low salaries, it is hard for the women to support their families, and this places tremendous stress on the returnees.

## Self-help organization for returned entertainers

Batis AWARE (Association of Women in Action for Rights and Empowerment) is an organization of women advocating for the rights of the Filipino women and for the protection of women migrants. The organization is composed of women with Japanese-Filipino children. Many have had failed relationships with their Japanese husbands or partners. Moreover, many have also experienced failed labor migration to Japan as entertainers. These women have experienced different forms and levels of violence. As the wives of Japanese men, they suffered abandonment and domestic violence; and as entertainers they experienced illegal recruitment, trafficking, exploitation and abuse by their employers and customers, among others.

Batis AWARE was formed to enhance the empowerment of these women. Empowerment is the process by which women gain a sense of power or capability to rise above their painful experiences and take control of their lives (Adams 2003; Gutierrez and Lewis 1999). The members of Batis AWARE began their journey to empowerment as clients of Batis Center for Women, a non-governmental organization which provides direct social services to distressed Filipino women migrants coming back from Japan as well as their children and families. Having gone through similar experiences, the women created closer ties with each other. Many activities became the setting for more than fifteen women to be together, and to share their experiences, and develop deeper friendships, which led them to the path of empowerment. Thus, Batis AWARE was created in June 1996 to further promote the rights and welfare of women migrants, most especially those coming back from Japan. Moreover, the organization is to provide assistance to fellow women in their recovery and to provide information to the public about the situation that forced the women to work abroad and the risks and realities of migrant labor, particularly in Japan.

## Participatory research as empowerment

It has been ten years since its establishment, and it is time to reflect on what Batis AWARE has achieved. This study, however, discusses not only its past and present but also the future of Batis AWARE. In other words, the main purpose of this study is to make an action plan for the empowerment of Batis AWARE by evaluating its past activities. For this purpose, participatory research, rather than conventional research methods, was chosen because the purpose of participatory research is not simply to create knowledge but to reform education and awareness and to facilitate action taken by all members of an organization or community (Hall 1981; Sarri and Sarri 1992). To put it another way, the focus is on the social or political problems faced by the organization, rather than coming up with theories. Participatory research is the process of facilitating action for social reform (Altpeter et al. 1999; Hall 1979). The process of participatory research is a repetition of the cyclical series of tasks from diagnosis and analysis of the problems to forming, implementing and evaluating action plans based on the results. The ultimate objective of this cyclical process is the empowerment of the research subjects. If the people do not gain access to the necessary information and develop the ability to understand the relevant issues through the research, and if the research does not lead to action to improve circumstances and reform the social structure, it cannot rightly be called participatory research (Altpeter et al. 1999; Gutierrez 2003). For that reason, collaboration between the researcher and subjects throughout the entire cyclical process of the research is essential.

## Overview of PLA

Participatory research has been developed in various fields and named differently in each, for example participatory action research, empowerment evaluation, feminist research, and cooperative inquiry. Among these is participatory learning and action (PLA), mainly utilized in the field of social development. Criticism of the top-down approach of specialists in developmental aid within the field of social development resulted in the spread of rapid rural appraisal (RRA) and later PLA as methods of putting community members at the center of research activities in the 1970s and later (Chambers 1997). PLA is a series of approaches, methods, patterns of behavior, attitudes and philosophies meant to enable people to share, increase and analyze information regarding their own lifestyles and circumstances so that they can construct, implement, monitor and evaluate action plans (Takeda 2005). It is the role of the researcher/facilitator to encourage participation and to facilitate the above process as necessary, but the leading role is left completely to the community members themselves.

## Level of participation

Participation by community members comes on many levels. Even in the field of development, there is a wide ranging level of participation, from passive participation where the community members listen to explanations about what is happening or has happened in their community to active participation where the community members take on leading roles in improving their community, independent of outside organizations. In Japan, the word 'participation' is often thrown about when talking about a single public hearing. In these cases, however, it is the governing body and not the community members that plays the leading role in town development. Therefore, it is important to pay attention to the way in which the word 'participation' is used.

'Participation,' as used in PLA, refers to the fair and active involvement of all concerned parties in the forming of planning and development policies as well as in the planning, analysis, implementation, monitoring and evaluation of specific development activities (Phuyal 2003). At present, many investors and executive bodies are criticized for their use of techniques labeled 'participatory approaches' in order to justify their own objectives in social development and pressure local community members into accepting their plans. However, real participation means that members of the community, particularly those who are marginalized, are able to analyze their own circumstances and use indigenous knowledge and local resources to plan a better future for the community. Simply put, the role of the outside organization must ultimately be that of facilitator and nothing more.

**Project cycle**

The researcher must first become a part of the community and build a relationship of trust. This characteristic is just like social work practice. Just as establishing a good rapport with clients is important for social work, immersion into the community is a must with PLA. Once integration is complete, analysis of the present state of affairs, the first stage of the full-scale PLA project cycle, can begin. In this stage, the people, not the researcher, take the leading role and analyze the current state of affairs in the community. When doing this, it is important that the researcher assists the people in delving into five questions, namely: 'what is good about the community?,' 'what are the community's resources?,' 'what potential does the community possess?,' 'what kinds of indigenous knowledge and technology exist?' and 'what can be improved in the community?' The reason that PLA does not focus solely on improvements is that, like the strength model, the empowerment model, the feminist approach and other approaches based on social constructivism in social work, it is not a problem-solving approach but an appreciative approach (an approach that respects the reality and capabilities of the people). The appreciative approach focuses on the positive aspects of the community, such as local resources and indigenous knowledge, thus creating a positive atmosphere among the community members, increasing their desire to participate and facilitating their existing capabilities.

In the PLA project cycle, planning, project implementation and evaluation are carried out based on the analysis of the current state of affairs, and all must be performed on a participatory basis led by the people. The people are empowered within this cycle through the sharing of information, consultations and collaboration, and the role of the facilitator is to provide assistance so that the community can exercise discretion with respect to important matters and the utilization of resources.

**Researcher standpoint**

In PLA, researchers must not be investigators but facilitators. It is no exaggeration to state that the shifting of this paradigm by researchers can make or break PLA. The role of the researcher is to facilitate the people's efforts in analyzing their own circumstances, implementing projects based on their own plans and evaluating the results. For that reason, it is important that the researcher, as facilitator, invests plenty of time, respects the participants, opens his/her heart, takes on a self-reflecting attitude and is careful not to inhibit the activities of the participants. If the facilitator's attitude is appropriate and a relationship of trust has been built with the community members, the PLA tools are highly effective and will produce better results.

**Key to empowerment**

The ultimate objective of participatory research is not to simply collect information but to empower the people by helping them gain insights and capabilities that will enable them to improve their own situations and reform society (Altpeter et al. 1999; Yeich 1996). For that reason, simply participating by providing information such as with traditional researcher-led research is not enough and will not result in empowerment (Flynn, Ray and Rider 1994). The people are empowered during the process of actively participating in the project cycle from information collection to planning, implementation and evaluation, influencing public policy decisions and achieving improvements in their community. Stated differently, empowerment in PLA is the act of turning over control of the decision-making process to the community members (Hick 1997).

It is essential to also pay attention to the relationships of power within a community in order to achieve the empowerment of the marginalized. By encouraging the participation of the marginalized, group consciousness is formed and confidence is built to tackle problems and stand up to others. Of course, just because PLA is used does not mean that the marginalized will automatically be empowered. Even if PLA tools are used, if it is the outside researcher or the persons in power in the community that gain the information, the situation of the marginalized may actually worsen. Therefore, it is extremely important who participates in the PLA process. If no consideration is given for the marginalized in society or communities, it is inevitable that participation will be centered on those with power. For that reason, the facilitator must identify the persons who are marginalized within a community and make sure the PLA process is implemented with fairness.

By using the various tools of PLA, the researcher will be able to see the relationships of power within the community and, at the same time, the people in the community will become aware of the unspoken relationships of power within the community. In particular, the marginalized themselves coming to understand their oppression and the possibility of breaking free by means of the PLA process is the key to achieving empowerment (Hall 1981, 1994).

## PLA with Batis AWARE

The application of PLA on Batis AWARE was done in two stages. The first stage is a facilitators' training for Batis AWARE officers conducted on 6–8 September 2006. Four Batis AWARE officers and one former staff of Batis Center for Women were trained to become facilitators for the second stage of the study, which was conducted on 10–13 September 2006. Those trained in the first stage facilitated the second stage, which fifteen members of Batis AWARE attended, besides facilitators. I served as a facilitator in the first stage but as an advisor/observer in the second stage to encourage active participation of the members in decision-making as well as to provide officers with chances to become empowered by serving as facilitators.

The objectives of the second stage were to assess the activities and situation of Batis AWARE for the past ten years and to make action plans for the next five years in a way that all members can participate in and contribute to. The underlying objectives, however, are to empower the participants by giving them, especially those marginalized in the organization, chances to learn and to think about the organization. Former entertainers are marginalized in the society, but even among the members of Batis AWARE, some are marginalized within the organization more than others due to their personality and lack of experience in the organization and are not able to talk bravely or share their opinions with others.

## Situation analyses over the time periods

To understand the changes of the organization over the last ten years, several PLA tools were used according to three different time-frames, specifically periods from 1996–2000, 2000–2004 and 2004–2006. According to their date of membership, members and facilitators were grouped into three, each of which was assigned to one of the time-fames.

The first PLA tool used was 'timeline,' a history of major re-collected events in the organization with approximates dates, and a discussion of what changes have occurred. This tool helps its members, especially those who joined the organization recently or those who have not been actively participating in its activities recently, to understand the organization's history and contextualize the present in comparison with its past major events. More importantly, looking at the timeline of the organization can help in recalling the effects of each event on the organization and its members. After each group created a timeline for each time period, they all shared their timelines and created one timeline for the last ten years. Through this process, they realized that two events, the decreasing number of active members over the time and the shutdown of some of their livelihood projects, were correlated.

'Resource maps' that identify the previous and existing social, human, economic, and physical resources of an organization, 'mobility maps' that analyze the participants' movements with different objectives, such as treatment, education, employment, religious activities, etc., and 'Venn diagrams' that describe the relationship between individuals, power structures, institutions and outside agencies, were also created for the three different time periods and compared. By using these tools, participants found that there are many resources, relationships, and their own programs that they have lost over the years. They discussed reasons for losses and how they suffered from these losses, and determined to regain them in order to expand the activities of the organization.

## Situation analyses by different status

It is considered that the needs and expectations directed towards the organization differ according to how much a participant is involved in the organization. For some of the PLA tools, therefore, members were divided into two groups: one with non-active or marginalized members (group one) and the other with active members (group two).

These two groups made lists of 'areas for improvement' of the organization and ranked them into a matrix. This tool is called the 'matrix ranking.' Each member ranked these identified areas according to utmost importance. The results of the ranking show that both groups found that 'livelihood' is one of the top priorities (third for group one and second for group two). 'To have more partners/donations' was ranked first for group one in contrast to group two which ranked 'fundraising' as first priority. This shows that group two, composed of active members and officers, understand that they themselves need to work for fundraising while group one, passive members, are just waiting for partner organizations to provide them with donations. Group one, on the other hand, sees the importance of unity within the organization. They ranked 'pray to God' as first; follow 'the regulations of Batis AWARE' as fourth; 'benefits for all members' as fifth; 'avoid unpleasant behavior/attitude' and 'being honest' as eighth; and 'respect for one another and the officers' as tenth. These categories were not mentioned by group two. Group one mentions these because they see the lack of unity among the members of the organization or some dissatisfaction in terms of the relationships among members. Alternatively, group two focused on more practical matters (advocacy as second and trainings as fourth). This highlighted how the members could have different views of the organization and that the members should understand where they are coming from.

After some discussion, the members of both groups have understood and respect each group's needs and have agreed to combine two lists according to their priority. To determine the top two priorities of the organization, all the participants gathered around to vote which among the pairs they think is preferred while they discuss their reasons for choosing their preferences by using a 'pair-wise ranking.' The results show that members of the Batis AWARE consider 'fundraising' and 'training' as most important for the entire organization.

By using the 'tree (cause and effect) diagram,' they further analyzed fund-raising and training as areas for improvement by discussing the causes and effects and the members' coping mechanisms and what they plan to do to respond to these challenges. This activity was jumpstarted by discussions about planning for fund-raising and training. In the succeeding discussion, it will be evident in the plotting of coping mechanisms and plans that funding is most needed by the organization. They argued that the organization will experience difficulty moving forward without funding. Everyone agreed with this observation. Training is also connected to fund-raising. Without the latter, the former is not easy to do.

## Planning

Information on the changes in the timeline, resources, mobility and relationships seen in the different periods as well as the areas for improvement and priorities was utilized in the 'Participatory Appreciative Planning Approach (PAPA),' one of the planning tools in PLA. In PAPA, participants must agree on the activities that need to be completed as the top priority of the organization, to whom the tasks were assigned, when and how it should be executed, materials needed, the challenges that will be faced in reaching them, and suggestions to solve these challenges.

For fundraising, Batis AWARE members decided to make a list of all possible funding agencies from old contacts and new ones. Moreover, they planned to continue writing proposals on other possible livelihood projects, such as a restaurant or a meat processing business. Finally, the members also hoped to find funds through solicitation and Christmas caroling in December 2006. Solicitations would be advanced through the individual approach of members in their areas of residence. As for caroling, a group of women would be organized for practice and a permit would be obtained from the town hall. The women hoped to entertain neighbors with their beautiful songs and singing, and their Filipiniana costumes.

In terms of training, the members discussed the planning of the possible projects they would like to instigate, such as the restaurant or canteen and food processing business. They would like to make use of the free training programs offered by government organizations and planned to assign members to take these lessons after funds are available to provide transportation allowances to the members. By the end of the four-day session, the Batis AWARE members became hopeful and excited to see their plans implemented.

## Implementation

Empowerment of Batis AWARE can also be observed in their organizational achievement after the session. With dedication and united effort, Batis AWARE has raised a reasonable amount of funds from their Christmas caroling and solicitation as planned during the four-day session. They were also able to obtain research funding from the International Organization for Migration and the International Labour Organization for investigating trafficking survivors. Surely, these efforts are a sign of greater success because the Batis AWARE members are not only successful in situation analyses and planning but also in their implementation.

These successes in fund-raising facilitated the realization of their long-term dream. Batis AWARE has continued pushing through with their project proposals for new livelihood opportunities for their members and has planned further to establish their own canteen. Although they have kept this idea for many years, a business opportunity finally emerged when Batis AWARE learned of an ideal property a few months after the session. To obtain funds for this endeavor, Batis AWARE has applied for loans to lending agencies both in the Philippines and Japan, and preparations for opening a canteen business as a livelihood project is underway.

## Effects of PLA on Batis AWARE members

The objectives of this study were not only to review the past activities of Batis AWARE in order to make action plans for the next five years, but also to assess how the process of PLA affects the empowerment of its members. For this, the members were asked to answer the open-ended questionnaire regarding how each member feels towards the organization, both before and after the four-day PLA session. A focus group interview with facilitators was also held after the PLA session. The data was transcribed and translated into English. Then, the data was coded for analyses and grouped into several categories.

### Rediscovery of their own strengths

Through the four-day PLA session, members rediscovered strengths within the organization. For example, one member's comments on other members of the organization have changed before and after the four-day session.

> [Before the session:] I think that because we have different experiences and status in society, it is hard to assemble the women because of our varying levels of awareness and philosophies in life... Even if there are regulations that need to be followed, we cannot avoid misunderstandings or people with ideas which do more harm than good. Although we have been through many trainings and seminars, there are still a number of women with limited comprehension.
>
> [After the session:] In the four days that we did the workshop, I saw different aspects of Batis AWARE and realized how solid this organization is. We only have a small group of members but I feel that without this group, we cannot make better plans for the future. I was surprised that more ideas come from the members themselves. Maybe because we understand each other and we know what to prioritize and what areas we need to improve.

Although she doubted the unity and integrity of the organization and was somewhat disappointed with some of the members before the PLA session, she discovered the positive attitude of other members and the importance of the members for the organization. Other members also realized how each member can contribute to the organization.

> I realized that Batis AWARE has many resources that we can tap and use to go towards progress. I found members that had many other skills that they could, and were willing to share with others.
>
> I gained a lot from my fellow members in these four days and it was very enjoyable.
>
> I was also glad to see all members participate because this is something that I did not see in the past activities that we attended.
>
> Each member can contribute and share what she has learned for the development of the organization through PLA.

These comments proved that PLA has given participants chances to learn about their organization as well as discover the strengths and passion for the organization among themselves. These insights enabled both individual and organizational empowerment, as discussed below.

**Individual empowerment**
Finding strengths among themselves helped members gain individual empowerment. Some members, who had not been actively participating in the activities of the organization, expressed their enhanced motivation and confidence in themselves as shown in comments such as 'I am now more aware of the things around me and more active in Batis AWARE' and 'Now, I have more confidence in myself.' One officer's comment made in the focus group interview also represents that the members have changed after the session and now have more confidence in themselves: 'the members began to have belief and confidence in themselves in every task and challenge they need to face.'

In PLA, all the participants, including those marginalized in the organization, can get the chance to express their opinions and to participate in the decision-making process. These experiences certainly promote their confidence and motivation for their actions toward improving their situations.

**Organizational empowerment**
Individual empowerment, enhanced motivation and confidence, further facilitates the empowerment of the organization, evident in the following comment: 'now we have a feeling of unity and respect for each other, which strengthened the organization.' Another member, who was active in the past but is currently inactive, also saw the organization differently before and after the session.

> [Before the session:] ...as time passed, I started to feel unhappy with my position [in the organization]. I felt that they [other members] were against me and talking behind my back.

> [After the session:] Batis AWARE became better thought-out and more systematic and I also learned so many things. I can now claim Batis AWARE to be *our* organization.

Although this woman had a bitter experience in the organization in the past, she sees the organization in positive ways after the session because the organization itself grew during the session. Other members also saw the improvement of the organization in terms of solidarity, confidence, decision-making, and networking.

> Not only have we felt growing confidence, Batis AWARE as an organization is invigorated.

> In the past, the members have seen the limitations and shortcomings of the organization. At present, we have already moved on because we are unified as an independent organization. The PLA methodology gave us a chance to listen and to talk...Now we have the capacity to make decisions, have integrity and courage to do so, have more networks and feel the organization becoming stronger because of our own efforts that we have not done before.
>
> The members also showed cooperation as we have come up with good plans for next year's action...it means that Batis AWARE is now moving to become a solid organization that will benefit not only me but all the persons involved in the organization itself.
>
> I felt that Batis AWARE became sturdier, stronger and more united as an organization. Our group was strengthened and renewed and I think these ties will continue to evolve in the future.

Unlike conventional research methods, in which the subjects serve only as informants, the subjects in PLA are involved in data-gathering, analyses, planning, and its implementation. Through this process, they get control over decision-making and actually take initiative for the actions to improve their situation. This causes power transfer from the researchers to the researched—especially the marginalized—enhances their confidence and motivation, and facilitates the empowerment of both the individual and the organization.

## From social 'research' to social 'action'

This study applied PLA, one of the participatory research methods, to Batis AWARE, a self-help organization for returned entertainers, not only to review their ten-years of activities and make an action plan for the next five years, but also to empower its members and the organization as a whole. Participatory research can generate knowledge that is directly relevant for practice and that spans the boundary between 'theory' and 'practice' (Gutierrez 2003). In this study, Batis AWARE analyzed their resources, mobility and networks, and prioritized areas for improvement. Knowledge generated from these results facilitated planning future actions and their implementation, which further empowered its members and ultimately enhanced their well-being. Participatory research, thus, is more than a new set of research methods or techniques. Rather, it is a systematic approach to individual and organizational transformation (Hick 1997).

Participatory research is already being utilized to improve the circumstances of and empower various marginalized groups. PLA has been mainly utilized for developmental assistance in developing countries, but other participatory research methods have been applied to various situations in developed countries as well, such as the establishment of citizen councils and community activities for drug prevention, community health, disease prevention, safe and cooperative environments, healthy lifestyles, and the promotion of improvements to medical services (Flynn et al. 1994).

Participatory research, however, is not applicable to any situation. Just like other conventional research methods, it has advantages and disadvantages. To conclude this paper, the merits and limits as well as the compatibility of participatory research are summarized below.

**Merits of participatory research**

The biggest difference between existing research methods and participatory research is that the people who are the focus of the research are not treated merely as research subjects but as participants in activities to improve their own circumstances. The researcher is a facilitator, and by shifting paradigms with respect to 'research' and 'researcher' and giving consideration to the marginalized, a bottom-up process can be established making it possible to create a project that reflects the opinions of those who are marginalized.

In a bottom-up process led by the people, more accurate and exhaustive information can be collected about the people's circumstances and, as a result, action can be taken according to actual needs. In existing research methods, researchers often overlook the indigenous knowledge and latent potential of the subjects, but the principles and techniques of participatory research help prevent such problems and failures.

Having the people take the lead in collecting information not only results in more accurate information but also increases the motivation of the people to participate in action designed to improve their circumstances based on that information and thus improves the chances of success for the project as a whole. The project cycle of participatory research does not end with an analysis of the current situation, but rather goes on to provide practical and specific guidelines for the project in order to link the analysis with planning, implementation and evaluation.

Processes led by the people do not stop with a single action or project but lead to continuous action. The process of participatory research provides an opportunity to have the people think about participation and enables them to recognize various problems as their own, based on shared awareness of the problems. Moreover, by collaborating on a single action or project, the problem-solving abilities of the people are improved, and networks with government agencies and the outside world are strengthened, bringing about lasting effects.

## Limits of participatory research

One of the shortcomings of participatory research is the time and effort it requires. If that time is not invested, it will be impossible to create a project that is truly led by the people. Therefore, along with the problems of adjusting people's schedules and recruiting assistants due to the lengthening of the project, there is also the possibility that research institutions and foundations will exhibit a lack of understanding concerning the length of time required (Alvarez and Gutierrez 2001).

When the project is lengthened, even if the people participate, there may be cases where it becomes difficult to maintain the cohesion of the community, and there is always the possibility that opinions among the people may collide. Similarly, if the people are looking for short-term benefits, it may prove difficult to work on fundamental improvements from a long-term perspective.

Secondly, if a participatory approach is used half-heartedly, such as for the simple collection of information, it has the potential to put the elite in an even stronger position rather than empowering the marginalized or to become a tool for forcing the opinions of the elite onto the marginalized (Hall 1981). In order to prevent this type of situation, the facilitator must take special consideration and use special techniques to encourage those who are disadvantaged within the community to participate and express their opinions.

Thirdly, the background and the characteristics of the techniques used within participatory research make it effective for specific communities and groups, but it may be difficult to apply the process to very large social or political systems.

Lastly, as with other so-called qualitative research methods, it is not possible to generalize the results (Alvarez and Gutierrez 2001). However, the primary objective of participatory research is to improve the situation in specific communities and to enhance their well-being, so the aim is not generalization.

## Compatibility of participatory research

One criterion for determining whether or not to utilize participatory research is to ask whether or not it matches the researcher's objectives, targets and style of relating with others (Alvarez and Gutierrez 2001). The role of the researcher is that of facilitator, and if he or she does not place value on the importance of concentrating on the process, holding open discussions and respecting the decisions that are made, it will not truly be 'participatory' research, even if the techniques of participatory research are used. Another criterion is whether or not the researcher has the ability to build friendly relationships with the participants and tolerate ambiguity as well as a flexible attitude that allows for learning from the participants.

The attitudes and interests of the community members are another criterion. Success will be evasive if the researcher is unable to determine whether or not the people understand the merits of participating in the project, have positive attitudes about cooperating and, in some cases, whether or not they are willing to undergo training in order to participate in the research process.

It is also important that the research objectives provide merit for the people and that they understand them. If the objective is simply to increase knowledge, then traditional research methods are sufficient. In order to encourage participation by the people, it is essential that action be included in the objectives of the research.

Participatory research was chosen in this study over conventional research methods not only because of the objectives of the study but also because of Batis AWARE members' high motivation for active participation and the trusted relationship between members and researcher. Without these conditions, participatory research cannot be effective. If participatory research is used for the right objective in the right conditions, it can be used not only as an investigative tool but also a very effective tool for social action for the enhancement of human well-being.

# 5
# Commercial Surrogate Mothering in India: Nine Months of Labor?

*Amrita Pande*

What compels a woman from a village in Western India to rent out her womb to a couple from the US? How does this change the way surrogate motherhood has been theorized until now? How does this enrich the literature on globalization, gender and work? My work on the new phenomenon of transnational and national commercial surrogate motherhood in India will complicate the Euro-centered literature on surrogacy by extending it beyond questions of ethics and morality. I argue that to understand commercial surrogate motherhood and to situate it within the discussions on globalization, it should be seen as an emerging form of 'reproductive labor.' The focus on 'labor' enables us to explore both the exploitative and empowering effects this kind of 'labor' has on the 'laborers.'

> Who would choose to do this? I have had a lifetime worth of injections pumped into me. Some big ones in my hips hurt so much. I feel bloated all the time. But I know I have to do it for my children's future. (Interview, Sudha, Surrogate mother, India, 2006)

> My father-in-law is very against it. But I told him it's my life I'll do what I feel is right. Right now I am young I have the health, the body and the ability to earn some extra cash so why shouldn't I? (Interview, Pushpa, Surrogate mother, India, 2006)

These narratives of commercial surrogate mothers in India reflect my contention in this paper: it is easy to assume that poor women becoming surrogates in India are unfortunate and exploited victims of globalization and new technology. It is as easy to forget, however, that most of these women *choose* to become surrogates; and some choose to become surrogates again and again. This paper will therefore focus on commercial surrogacy from the perspectives of the surrogates—their experiences and motivations as well as both the exploitative *and* the empowering aspects of this kind of work.

I realize I am venturing into contentious territory by talking about 'choice' in the context of commercial surrogacy. Unarguably, the limited range of women's economic opportunities and the parties' (couple hiring the surrogate and the surrogate) unequal social and economic positions question the voluntary nature of a surrogate's agreement to sell her reproductive labor. When a woman decides to become a surrogate so as to feed her starving child, the voluntary nature of her decision is diminished. However, by identifying commercial surrogacy as work, as an occupation susceptible like others to exploitation, and simultaneously recognizing that the workers have some agency, it is possible to identify broader strategies of change.

Much of the existing literature, almost all of which comes from the Global North, analyzes surrogacy either as a manifestation of women's freedom of choice or an example of patriarchal exploitation and men's control over women's bodies. Gender is the primary focus of analysis in this literature (Firestone 1970, Andrews 1987, Anderson 1990, Wajcman 1994, Baker 1996, Roberts 1997). Additionally, this literature is not just Euro-centered but also ethics-centered. Surrogacy is framed as a problem of white middle class heterosexual women with concerns revolving around ethics of selling 'babies' or ethics of selling 'motherhood' (Roberts 1997, Wajcman 1994). This study of commercial surrogacy in India enriches the Western literature on surrogacy by expanding it to the reality of a developing country where commercial surrogacy has become a survival strategy and a temporary occupation for some poor rural women. In such a setting, surrogacy should be seen not just as an ethical dilemma but as a structural reality. Further, I demonstrate that the Indian case requires a more complicated analysis, as not only gender but the economic class of the women, their nationality, race and ethnicity determine their rights and experiences with the surrogacy contract.

I begin by reviewing the literature on surrogate mothering in the Global North and then move on to the literature on reproductive labor, focusing on transnational care-work. Using this literature, I argue that in order to understand commercial surrogate motherhood, and to situate it within the discussions on globalization, we need to go beyond morality, laws and ethics. By analyzing surrogate mothering services as an emerging form of 'reproductive labor' similar to the care-work carried out by nannies and domestics, we can extend the existing literatures. Additionally, a focus on 'labor' enables us to explore both the potentially exploitative and empowering effects this kind of 'labor' has on the 'laborers.'

## Reproductive technology in the Global North

In the early period of the contemporary women's movement most white feminists perceived the use of reproductive technology as liberating for women—contraceptive and birth technologies could free women from the 'tyranny of reproduction' which dictated the nature of women's oppression (Firestone 1970, Wajcman 1994). 'Procreative liberty,' in this scholarship, has mostly been discussed in terms of the *right to avoid* procreation through access to abortion and contraception.

In the last few decades, however, technologically-assisted reproduction has brought another aspect of procreative liberty—the *liberty to procreate* how and when one chooses. Surrogacy is one form that these new reproductive technologies can take.

In the existing Western literature, surrogacy has primarily been framed as a problem of white middle class heterosexual women (Roberts 1997, Wajcman 1994). While defenders of surrogacy advocate this service as a manifestation of women's freedom or choice, concerns and debates have revolved around legalities of pregnancy contracts and the ethics of this practice (Andrews 1987, Anderson 1990, Baker 1996). Debates around the ethics of surrogacy are rampant in this literature and range from the view that contractual pregnancy is symptomatic of the dissolution of the American family (Ragone 1994) to the charges that it reduces women to a new 'breeder' class (Raymond 1993, Rothman 1988 and Correa 1986), one structurally akin to prostitution (Dworkin 1978), or that it is another form of baby-selling (Neuhaus 1988). It is not surprising that discussions about the commerce of love, reproduction and parenthood are inherently linked with questions of morality and ethics. Even in an age driven by technological advances and dominated by market capitalism we want to believe that some things remain beyond both markets and science, that there are some things that money cannot buy

(Spar 2006). And yet in nearly every country, eggs, sperm, wombs, infants and children are being 'sold' whether in adoption agencies or sperm banks or in the form of surrogacy services. This chapter does not attempt to resolve these moral issues, nor does it insist that this market for wombs is either good or evil. It simply argues that it exists. Whether we like it or not, there are women in India having babies for others, some on a routine basis, and some for the second time already in the two years since commercial surrogacy started in India.

It would not be fair to say that *all* the existing literature portrays surrogacy as an ethics-related problem concerning white middle class women. Some writers have cautioned against the exploitative potential of surrogacy arrangements (Raymond 1993, Rothman 1988 and Correa 1986). These scholars predicted a caste of breeders, composed of women of color whose primary function would be to gestate the embryos of more valuable white women. My contention in this paper, however, is not to depict poor rural women in India as breeders or clinics in India as baby farms. I argue that surrogacy in India can be seen as a new form of 'labor.' More specifically, I argue that commercial surrogacy is a new form of reproductive labor similar to the care-work carried out by nannies and domestics.

## What is surrogacy?

Surrogacy refers to an arrangement whereby a woman agrees to become pregnant for the purpose of gestating and giving birth to a child for others to raise. She may be the child's genetic mother (traditional surrogacy) or she may be implanted with someone else's fertilized egg (gestational surrogacy). All the cases in Anand, the Indian city in which I studied surrogacy, fall under the category of 'gestational surrogacy'—the surrogate has no genetic connections with the baby.

As an alternative means of producing children, surrogacy is an ancient practice. Throughout history, women from several cultures have used other women to bear the children they could not conceive. The surrogate was often a second wife, a concubine or a maid (Spar 2006). With artificial insemination, conception was separated from sex, making it possible for a man to impregnate a surrogate without even necessarily meeting her. In traditional surrogacy, the surrogate was also the genetic mother of the child she bore. This made surrogacy a legal and ethical nightmare—the surrogate had a greater claim on the child than the intended mother. The next step in assisted reproduction—the development of in vitro fertilization (IVF)—solved this problem.[1] Now the genetic mother (the woman who provided the eggs) could be separated from the surrogate mother. Legally, this split meant that the connection between the surrogate and the baby would be far less powerful than under traditional surrogacy arrangements. Commercially, it increased the supply of both components—the surrogates and the egg donors. Women were more willing to donate eggs if they did not also have to undergo the pregnancy, and they were more interested in serving as surrogates if the child they were carrying was not genetically theirs (Ragone 1994, Spar 2006).

The separation of eggs and wombs not only allowed the market to thrive, it also changed the market. In traditional surrogacy, the surrogate provides the genetic material as well as the womb. The adoptive parents, therefore, were more likely to emphasize the 'right' genetic makeup (race, physical characteristics, intelligence etc). In gestational surrogacy, however, the parents no longer care about the surrogate's genes (Spar 2006). Not surprisingly, gestational surrogacy also allowed the surrogacy market to go global.

Couples traveled abroad to avail themselves of services that simply were not available or legal at home (couples from Britain, Australia, Taiwan, Kuwait who could not employ surrogates at home). By the 1990s, the combination of IVF and surrogacy had created a more hospitable market for contractual pregnancy. It was now possible for a South Korean couple sitting in Los Angeles to hire a surrogate from a little village in western India.

## The field: Anand, Gujarat, India

### India and medical tourism

In the past few decades 'medical tourism'—patients going to a different country for medical treatment—has been gaining momentum across the world. The reasons patients travel for medical treatment vary, from the non-availability of that treatment in their home country, cheaper costs, shorter waiting times, to combining a tropical vacation with plastic surgery. While several countries, including Cuba, Hungary, Israel, Jordan, Malaysia and Thailand actively promote medical tourism, India is considered one of the leaders in this field; according to rough estimates, India attracted about 150,000 medical tourists in 2004, second only to Thailand (*The Economist*, 10 September 2004).

There are several things working in favor of India as a destination of medical tourism—cheap costs, a large number of doctors with degrees and training from prestigious medical schools in India and abroad, well-equipped private hospitals, and a large overseas population of Indian origin who might want to combine cheaper treatment with a family visit (*The Economist*, 10 October 2004). Additionally, the campaign has full government support. In 2004, the government launched an international advertising campaign, decided to launch medical visas for foreigners visiting India for healthcare services and declared that treatment of foreign patients is legally an 'export' and deemed 'eligible for all fiscal incentives extended to export earnings' (*CBC News*, June 2004).

## The clinic in Anand

While infertility clinics from several Indian cities like New Delhi, Mumbai, Bangalore, Pune and Anand have reported cases of surrogacy, in this paper I will focus on cases in Anand, a small city in western India. The technology needed to make surrogacy possible is available in several infertility clinics across India. Most clinics provide just the technology and require the patients to arrange for their own surrogate. Anand is the only place where surrogate mothering is becoming a routine for an infertility clinic and a new profession for some poor women. The clinic keeps a constant supply of surrogates and some of these women are going in for surrogacy for the second time in just two years.

Anand is a city of about 100,000 people in the western Indian state of Gujarat. A relatively large population of Gujaratis has settled in different parts of the world; out of the 20 million Indians spread across the globe 6 million are from the state of Gujarat, that is nearly 30 percent of the total non-resident Indian population. Non-resident Gujaratis coming to India for personal and medical visits are also making Gujarat one of the most popular sites of medical tourism in India (Bhargav 2006).

Although the demand for and supply of surrogates existed in Anand, the catalyst that made surrogacy a reality was Dr Khanderia's infertility clinic with the latest reproductive technology. The case of a woman who gave birth to her own grandchildren on behalf of her UK-based daughter in 2004 was the first successful case of surrogacy in Anand. For this case, Dr Khanderia did not supply the surrogate. The surrogate and the couple were related to each other. For her second case, Dr Khanderia convinced a forty-three year-old employee at her clinic to be a surrogate. Since then twenty women have been brought together at the fertility clinic in Anand from surrounding villages by Dr Khanderia and her staff. Out of the nineteen surrogates I interviewed, fourteen had been convinced by the clinic nurses who stay in their village or their in-laws who heard about surrogacy from these nurses. Some of these surrogates were first convinced to donate their eggs at this clinic and told about surrogacy once they came to the clinic. Only five of my interviewees had read about surrogacy or heard about it from other sources. Dr Khanderia's 'awareness campaign' has contributed significantly towards making Anand an important center for commercial surrogacy in India.

## Research method

I visited Anand in the fall of 2006 and conducted open-ended interviews with five surrogate mothers who had already delivered babies and fourteen undergoing treatment to be surrogates, their husbands and, in some cases, the surrogates' in-laws. I interviewed Dr Khanderia, the doctor responsible for bringing together these commercial surrogates. Additionally, I interviewed several couples from India and abroad who have hired surrogates and are waiting for the delivery of their child in Anand.

In my interviews I gained a certain advantage: because of my gender, many of the women opened up and trusted me. However, the class difference between us was always apparent. My appearance, my bottle of mineral water, my incessant scribbling, the tape recorder—gave me the identity of an educated, well-off woman. My single status was, however, cause of a lot of sympathy and even pity and my 'bravery' in traveling alone led to much surprise. My stuttering Gujarati was a source of much leg-pulling and laughter. I was the strange educated girl from America. My single status and unfamiliarity with their customs made them treat me like a younger person—although most of the women were either my age or younger.

## Characteristics of the women

I interviewed nineteen women who have either delivered or are undergoing treatment for surrogacy in Anand. Dr Khanderia's records indicate that, in total, there are fifty-six volunteers for surrogacy who have visited her clinic, but these women had not yet signed any contract and had not undergone any treatment. All the women are married, with children. Their ages range between twenty and forty-five years. Except for one surrogate, all the women are from neighboring villages. Eight of the twenty women said that they were 'housewives,' the others worked in schools, clinics, stores and on farms. Their education ranged from 'illiterate' to high school, with the average around the beginning of middle school, with just one interviewee having a professional law degree.[2] The median family income is about Rs. 2500 (US$60) per month. Twelve of my nineteen interviewees reported family incomes below or around the poverty line. For almost all the surrogates the US$2000–$4000 earned through surrogacy was equivalent to four years of family income, especially since most surrogates had husbands who either worked as day laborers or were unemployed.

Two of my interviewees were surrogates for 'international' couples—one for a South Korean couple settled in Los Angeles and another for an American couple from Washington. Seven were hired by Gujarati NRIs settled in the US, one by a Gujarati NRI settled in the UK and one by a Gujarati NRI settled in South Africa. The others had been hired by upper and middle-class professionals and businesspersons settled in different metropolitan cities in India.

## Surrogacy as work

### Reproductive labor as 'just another kind of work'

Many people believe that markets in women's reproductive labor, as exemplified by commercial surrogacy, are more problematic than other currently accepted labor markets. Some feminists have argued that while human labor may be bought and sold, women's reproductive labor is intrinsically not a commodity (Anderson 1990, Satz 1992, Warnock 1985). According to these views, commercial surrogacy allows for the extension of the market into the 'private' sphere of sexuality and reproduction. 'When women's labor is treated as a commodity, the women who perform it are degraded' (Anderson 1990: 75).

It is further argued that the bond between a mother and her child is different from that between a worker and his product, and that commercial surrogacy will cause parents to view children as commodities.[3] While I agree with the intuition that markets in women's reproductive labor are more troubling than other labor markets, I propose a less essentialist way of analyzing this kind of labor.

If we are able to understand how surrogates experience and define their actions, it will be possible to move beyond a universalistic moralizing position and to develop some knowledge of the complex realities of women's experience of commercial surrogacy. Further, by identifying commercial surrogacy as work, as an occupation susceptible like others to exploitation, and simultaneously recognizing that the workers have some agency, it is possible to identify broader strategies of change.

**Surrogacy and care-work**

Feminist scholarship on reproductive labor or care work done by nannies and domestic workers provides a lens to understand commercial surrogacy in India. While surrogate motherhood does not fall under the usual definition of reproductive labor used by this literature—I argue that it *is* precisely that. Reproductive labor is typically defined as activities such as purchasing household goods, preparing and serving food, laundering and repairing clothing, socializing children, providing care and emotional support (Glenn 1992).

Evelyn Nakano Glenn observed that white class-privileged women in the United States have historically freed themselves of reproductive labor by purchasing services of women of color. In doing so they maintained a 'racial division of reproductive labor.' Other writers extend Glenn's formulation of the politics of reproductive labor to an international terrain and analyze the migration of women from the developing to the developed world to take up care-work. The care-work performed by Latina, Caribbean, Filipina and South Asian immigrant women enable upper class white women to join the productive labor force. These women effectively transfer their domestic responsibilities to other women who are subordinate by race, class, nationality, and citizenship status. I argue that with globalization and ever-expanding reproductive technology, 'gestational services' need to be added to the list of care-work.

It is not difficult to draw parallels between the services provided by surrogate mothers in India and the care-work of immigrant nannies and domestic workers. The low status of 'feminized' work (like care-work) and the (often illegal) immigrant status of the nannies results in very low wage rates for transnational nannies. The exploitative potential of reproductive labor is reinforced by the belief that paid domestic work is not a 'real job.' The tasks that domestic workers do—cleaning, cooking, and caring for children—are associated with women's 'natural' expressions of love for their families. This occupation is often not recognized as employment because it takes place in a private home. Because of the private nature of work, these workers are hidden away, behind closed doors and concealed from public view. Moreover, their position as 'foreigners' and 'immigrants' allows employers, and the society at large, to perceive them as outsiders and thereby overlook the contemporary racialization of the occupation.

Similarly, in the case of commercial surrogacy the exploitative potential of the 'work' has race, gender and class undertones. None of the surrogates or their families consider surrogacy to be a kind of 'work' that the woman is doing even though all of them realize that the amount of money the woman earns through surrogacy is more than what their husbands can earn in ten years. The surrogates and their family talk about surrogacy as 'team work' totally ignoring the critical gendered nature of this work; the fact that it is *only* the woman doing all the body and emotion work.

Family members of the women—mostly their in-laws and husbands—encourage the women to take up this 'temporary' service as they believe gestation is a service that a woman is 'naturally' qualified for. Out of my nineteen interviewees, twelve had been convinced by either their sisters-in-law or their mother-in-law to get into surrogacy. In one of the cases in Anand, almost all of the women in a family have taken to surrogacy—three sisters and their sister-in-law. From my interviews and meetings with them it became evident that their parents/in-laws had nudged them into surrogacy. I visited Kundan and Manoj Sharma, the heads of this family, in their new apartment in a village near Anand. The apartment is still under construction and is being financed entirely by the money their daughter-in-law got from delivering twins for a US-based couple.

Sapna, the daughter-in-law tells me:

> My mother-in-law told me about surrogacy. She told me that it's a noble act—you'll give a child to a family and you'll be blessed for it. They used the money to build this house.

Her mother-in-law Kundan interrupts:

> The money is not that important. It's about social service. Money comes and goes but their blessings will be there for us. It will give us peace.

Sapna's father-in-law Manoj, seems to have a different perspective on this 'social service:'

> Even though everyone delivers one and *we* delivered two babies—still we got the same rate. They should have paid us more. So that's why we decided *we* wouldn't do it again. We lost our respect in society and didn't even get paid enough for it,' he says very bitterly.

Sudha, another surrogate is a scared looking thin woman huddled on one corner of the bed. She is in the eighth month of her pregnancy and has become a surrogate for an upper middle class couple from Mumbai. Her sister-in-law 'convinced' her into surrogacy. I learned later that her sister-in-law is a broker in this trade. She brings in women from villages to be surrogates at the clinic and Sudha is the fourth woman she has brought in.

Apart from the cases of exploitation by brokers and family members, the surrogates are also at a disadvantage because of their low economic class and—in the transnational cases—because of their race, citizenship and nationality. The rights of the women involved in the surrogacy cases are, to a large extent, determined by their race, class and nationality. There are no clear laws regarding the surrogacy contract and although the Indian Council for Medical Research (ICMR) has passed some guidelines regarding surrogacy, Dr Khanderia seems to be the one making the final rules. In India, the surrogate mother's right to the child is not given the same importance as in countries in the global North—she signs away her rights to the baby as soon as the child is born. This, the doctor argues, is a rule she applies to ensure that the couple that comes from abroad does not have to go through any legal trouble and the surrogates do not get emotionally attached to the newborn. By contrast, British law says that a surrogate mother can claim the baby as her own during the first two years of the child's life.

Surrogate Anjali has no idea about the money or the procedures involved in surrogacy. 'I was just told that there is no contact with anyone and it's not immoral.' Another surrogate Gauri, seems more aware but mostly about what rights she *does not* have.

> The only thing they told me about this surrogacy is that I have to keep the child inside me, rest for the whole time, have medicines, and I will have to give up the child for which I will get paid. They told me that I couldn't change my mind at the last moment and make claims over the

child—because I'll have no right. "You *will* have to give it up. If you, your husband and family are totally ready to give it up then get into this. Otherwise don't. Don't cause any problems in the middle,' they said.

Firoze (speaking on behalf of his wife Salma, who is a surrogate for a couple from Los Angeles) says,

> We were told that if anything happens to the child it's not our responsibility but if anything happens to my wife, we can't hold anyone responsible. The legal contract says that we will have to give up the child immediately after the delivery—we won't even look at it. Black or white, straight or deformed we have to give it away.

When I ask him about the money, Firoze seems confused:

> They said they will build a house for us wherever we want to get it built. They said, 'You make us happy and we'll make you happy.' Dr Khanderia has all the money that they left behind for us and she pays for the *tiffin* (fixed amount of food which usually comes in a steel box) and medicines etc out of that. I am not sure how much they have given till now.

Apart from the flexible contracts and the lower costs of surrogacy in India ($2000—$4000 compared to more than $40,000 in the US), there are other factors drawing couples from abroad. Indian medical guidelines allow doctors to implant five embryos into a surrogate mother; in Britain, because of health risks to mother and fetus due to multiple pregnancies, the maximum is two and many European countries are moving towards a single embryo transfer.

I met surrogate Parvati while she was recovering from a fetal reduction surgery. She explains the procedure to me,

> The first time they had put three embryos but they failed so this time we asked madam to plant more so she put in five embryos and three fused. I am nearly forty and was carrying triplets! Madam told us that they wouldn't get enough space to move around and grow so we had to get rid of one.

Though surrogacy is not illegal in India, it is a stigmatized profession. Most people in India are unsure as to what surrogacy entails and assume that the surrogates are involved in some sort of sex-work. Most of the women prefer not to tell their neighbors and family that they are 'renting out their wombs.' Fourteen of my interviewees had not told their parents and none of the interviewees had told their neighbors. Most said that the baby was theirs (when the pregnancy became apparent) or temporarily moved away from their village and spent the nine months in isolation and in hiding. This stigma and subsequent separation from kin and community networks imply that the women had no support system during the nine months of pregnancy. Additionally, the surrogates who decided to stay in the clinic had severe restrictions on their life. Most had minimal interactions with anyone except the nurses and other surrogates at the clinic and the doctors and nurses monitored their food, movement and lifestyle.

It would be wrong, however, to portray the surrogates as mere victims. In the care work literature, scholars have debated at length on the 'structure versus agency' question among care-workers (see, for example, Hondagneu-Sotelo 1994, George 2000, Parrenas 2001, Gamburd 2000, Hondagneu-Sotelo and Avila 2003). As migrant women take on the formerly 'masculine' role of breadwinner, they transform more established ways of thinking about gender hierarchies, personal identity, financial responsibility and women's work (Parrenas 2001, Gamburd 2000). A substantial number of studies now show that regular wage-work and improved access to other public realms has an impact on gender relations in the lives of immigrant women (Sassen 2002). Although in the case of surrogacy the income earned is temporary and for most women there is very little access to other public realms, some of the surrogates did seem to be able to use surrogacy and the money earned to their advantage.

I identified three categories of potentially empowering affects of this 'labor' on the women: changes in gender roles within the family, health benefits for the women and long-term strategic changes.

Four of the eleven surrogates were staying in the clinic either because of health reasons or because they had not told their neighbors and families and needed a place to hide until the delivery. Their husbands and children would visit but did not live with them. The other seven women were living at home but had been told not to do any housework. I was interested in seeing whether the fathers take up the housework in the absence of their wives. In all the cases house and childcare work was taken up either by a hired maid (paid for by the couple hiring the surrogate) or the woman's mother/mother-in-law. The husbands, however, had started taking care of their own needs and contributing more towards childcare.

Pragyesh, whose wife Meena has been staying in the clinic for over a fortnight says:

> Well she has been asked to just lie around and sleep. I had to learn some small things—like warming the milk and washing my clothes. Earlier I didn't bother to learn anything. I felt like it's not really my job!

The women seem to be getting more rest and nutrition than they would if they were pregnant with their own baby. One of the conditions all the couples hiring the surrogates insist upon is that the surrogates should not do any housework. The surrogates who stay in the clinic get a lunch box which is monitored by Dr Khanderia for all the required vitamins and nutrients. Others are given a list of food items that they are required to eat on all days.

Surrogate Parvati compares her current pregnancy to her earlier delivery:

> I have to stay here for a month because of the operation yesterday and the stitches but I don't mind! See I have to eat ice creams, coconut water, milk etc everyday—because of the medicines I am taking. All this costs money but then it gives me strength. I had my own child when I was very young. I didn't even know what was happening to me then. This time it is different. I've put a lot of sweat and blood in this. I have realized that once the child is out, it is *my* body that will suffer and be weak if I don't eat healthy right now.

Pushpa, another surrogate adds,

> My husband feels proud of me. Well, he should. I have earned so much money and done something that even he couldn't have.

Later in the conversation she talks about her dream to go abroad:

> You know I had always dreamt of being an air hostess. But when I saw the situation at home—with my father earning only 1500, I knew I couldn't study anymore. I just wanted to see America once, so badly. Once I got married I thought it would never happen. But now that I am planning to do this (surrogacy) for the second time, I feel 'why not'? If I can do this here, maybe I can get some job there as well, no? Will you take me? I'll pay the expenses you just have to take me with you!

Surrogacy encouraged some surrogates to take care of their health and think of their own needs and increased their self-esteem. For some surrogates the income earned through surrogacy was the first income they brought home and this encouraged them to try and find other kinds of informal jobs after surrogacy.

Another category of changes that were potentially empowering were what I call the 'long run changes'—which include expenditure on daughter's education and changes within marriage. Eleven of the sixteen women I interviewed wanted their daughters to have better education than they had when they were young and were planning to invest the money they earned through surrogacy to ensure a better future for their daughters.

Surrogate Pushpa explains,

> I wish I had studied more. But my parents were poor. I had three brothers and I told my father to not worry about me but send them to school. After all I could just go off to my husband's and in-laws' place after marriage. I want to educate my daughters very well. Right now I am young I have the health, the body and the ability to earn some extra cash so why shouldn't I? I want to leave more for my daughters than what my parents left for me. I want to make their life so happy that I go straight to heaven.

Some of the surrogates used the money earned through surrogacy as a means to get out of an unhappy marriage. For example, surrogate Savita, a woman in her late forties says

> I became a surrogate because I didn't want to be a burden on my son and nor did I want to stay with my useless husband.

Surrogate Dipali adds,

> I have been staying away from my husband for the past five years now. See, nowadays when you get married you never know whether it will last. You can't kill yourself if it doesn't work out nor can you sacrifice your children's future. With this money I want to make my own flat because I don't want to burden anyone.

Surrogacy does seem to be empowering for some women, giving them reprieve from some chores and forcing husbands to learn some household work, allowing them to take better care of their health and nutrition and increasing their self-esteem and ability to get out of bad marriages. Several of the surrogates talked about using the money to invest in their children's, especially their daughters' education—indicating a possibility of longer-term changes.

# Conclusion

This study opens up new conversations on both surrogacy and women's reproductive work by taking surrogacy beyond questions of morals and ethics—the usual focus of existing Euro-centric work on surrogate motherhood. I argue that commercial surrogacy is an emerging form of reproductive labor. Feminist scholars have already discussed how reproductive laborers, like domestic workers and nannies free more privileged women to take part in productive labor. Transnational surrogates seem to be providing a similar service.

A focus on 'work' also enables us to explore both the exploitative and empowering aspects of this kind of 'work.' As in the case of immigrant care-work, in commercial surrogacy the exploitative potential of the 'work' has race, gender and class undertones. In most cases the surrogates and their families do not consider surrogacy a kind of work the woman is doing. In some cases, the in-laws and husbands of the surrogate have control over the money earned and the women have little idea about the legal contract and how much money they are earning for the family. As in other informal work, there are both formal and informal brokers coercing the women at different levels. The in-laws often 'encourage' the women to be surrogates and in some cases brokers are taking advantage of the women's poverty.

Apart from the cases of exploitation by brokers and family members, the surrogates are also at a disadvantage because of their low economic class, and in the transnational cases because of their race and ethnicity. The rights of the women involved in the surrogacy cases are, to a large extent, determined by their race, class and nationality. There are no clear laws regarding the surrogacy contract, contracts are often informal and the couples hiring the surrogates and Dr Khanderia seem to have more control. The health and rights of the surrogates are not given as much importance as in other countries. However, the diverse narratives and experiences of the surrogates challenge the notion of poor Third World women as victims.

There are three categories of potentially empowering affects that working as surrogates has on the women. I classified these as changes within the family which included the husband's involvement with housework and childcare, broader social changes like the possibility of divorces and alternative living arrangements facilitated with the money earned from surrogacy and more rest and nutrition for the women during pregnancy.

In a country which is often associated with horror stories about people selling their organs to feed the family, women being trafficked and children being sold off by their parents out of sheer poverty and economic desperation, the story of desperate women selling their wombs seems to fit right in (Cohen 1999, Menon 2002, Scheper-Hughes 1999 & 2003). This paper, however, attempts to go beyond both sensationalist and potentially Orientalist portrayals of poverty and desperation in the Third World (Narayan, 1997). By arguing that commercial surrogacy should be seen as another form of labor, I hope to extend the western literature on surrogacy to the developing country context and to start discussions on the new types of reproductive labor and informal work that are emerging with globalization.

# 6
# Enlarging People's Choice: Reducing Ill-being by Capability Building

*Matthias Drilling*

## Prologue

While conducting our research on poverty in young adults, we had the following encounter: We met with Ms M, who had just celebrated her twentieth birthday. She had been without a job for more than a year and had to be supported by the city's welfare department. We asked Ms M if she would describe how she got into this situation, what she felt about her current life situation, and what she thought about her prospects for getting out of this dependency.

Ms M begins to tell us about her childhood: At the age of twelve, her parents divorce. Torn back and forth between her father and mother, she begins to withdraw more and more. After two years, she goes to the youth welfare office and asks to be admitted to a group residence. At the time, she tells us, she has started to use drugs. The youth welfare office also offers psychological guidance and care, and in this protected sphere Ms M manages to finish school and to start training as a hairdresser. As she now earns her own money and 'wants to start her own life,' she moves out of the group residence that also provides care. In the second year of her training, however, her scholastic deficits become greater and greater. Ms M manages to complete her training, but does not find a job. She starts to run into debt, and six months later, her landlord gives her notice on her flat. And so Ms M, who is now eighteen years old, again comes to the social welfare office. Because the flat is too expensive, she has to find another place to live. Through the social welfare office, Ms M takes a number of temporary jobs, as cashier in a shop, or as telephone operator in a hotel. No permanent job can be found, and no hairdressing salon offers further training. The young woman starts using drugs again. She often appears too late for her appointments at the social welfare office and hardly responds to work offers. Her advisor at the social welfare office punishes Ms M, after having threatened to do so several times, by reducing her welfare payments and classifying her as not able to work. A few weeks later, Ms M, who is now twenty years old, no longer comes to see her advisor. When we ask Ms M at the end of the interview what she would like for herself, she answers, 'What I'd like the most is to be a child again, so that I could start all over.'

## Introduction

At the start of the twenty-first century, Europe is faced with societal upheaval. Modernization and globalization have left the conversion from industrial society to service economy no alternative, polarizing society into rich and poor. On the one hand, there are the winners of this development who can afford a lifestyle without any deprivation. On the other hand are the young people that can only observe this increase in options without having any share in it. French sociologist Pierre Bourdieu (1999) once called this group the contrasting backdrop of society: those poor in capital that have no active shaping role in society. They occupy the spaces that are judged unattractive to other groups, such as the *banlieu* areas of low-income apartments and social housing tracts skirting the cities in France, the simply-constructed council houses in the distressed neighborhoods of Germany, and the old buildings on heavy-traffic streets in Swiss cities in need of modernization.

Today in Europe the young are particularly affected by this poverty trap. Referring to the de-stabilization of whole generations, Amato and Booth (1997) speak of a 'generation at risk.' For Germany this poverty risk can be demonstrated. The German government's second report on poverty and wealth revealed that in the year 2003 of the total of 2.81 million aid-dependent people, the 1.1 million children under the age of eighteen make up the largest group by far, followed by persons aged eighteen to twenty-four (Bundesregierung Deutschland 2005).

In the framework of the European Commission's research program, Targeted Socio-Economic Research (TSER), a research group headed by health psychologist Thomas Kieselbach, is comparing the social situation of youths up to the age of twenty-five in six countries

(Kieselbach 2000). The researchers have discovered that the increasing unemployment rate since the 1980s has had a disproportionately large effect on young people. In countries like Germany and Belgium (but also Spain, Italy, Greece, and Sweden), the result is a high risk of social exclusion. Even in Switzerland, one of the richest countries in the world, the number of people dependent on financial support from the state has risen steeply. Here, too, those affected have become younger. In Swiss cities such as Geneva, Zurich, Bern, or Basel, one out of every seven to ten young persons cannot make a living by means of their own or from their parents' resources.

## Fallacies of poverty research

For a long time, research on poverty in the affluent nations of Europe tended to be a niche area. Only since the 1990s, when the economic transformation was accompanied by a large-scale reduction of jobs, has poverty become one of the fundamental social-political challenges. Accordingly, a large number of research studies are available today. It is noticeable that in the poverty discourse, reductions were made in two central areas. The first reduction involves limiting the definition of the phenomenon of poverty mainly to economic (monetary) aspects. The second reduction is simplifying the measurement of poverty to achievements. Revising these reductions corresponds to the quest for alternative sociology that is the subject of the present publication.

In the discourse, poverty was narrowed down to monetary aspects (income) largely for pragmatic reasons. Indicators such as average or median income allow comparison among different population groups. In addition, monetary indicators can be used for international comparisons, as they are used, for example, in the reports of the World Bank.

Social scientists have been at the forefront of discussions on the problems of equating income poverty with poverty generally. Almost as a counterpoint to the resource concept described above (income), their approach, called the *Lebenslage* approach (conditions of life, or life situation, approach), is an attempt to come closer to the complexity of the poverty problem by taking further areas of life into consideration. Döring, Hanesch, and Huster (1990) write that the life situation concept examines not the available financial resources but instead the actual situation of persons, households, or groups in central areas and dimensions of life. Although no unified system of these areas of life has been worked out as yet, the following areas are often included: work (for example, employment status), education (for example, school diploma, training), living (such as size of living quarters/apartment, price of rent), and health (such as chronic illnesses, disability).

No matter whether the resource concept (income) or the life situation concept (several areas of life) is adhered to, reduction of indicators to achievements is inherent in both approaches. Guiding questions are, 'What has a person achieved?,' or 'What amount of resources does a person have under his/her control?' Accordingly, monetary income, level of training, size of living quarters, or number of friends is measured.

This narrowing down contradicts a tradition in poverty research that goes back as far as the Scottish moral philosophers of the eighteenth century. Adam Smith (1776) made the point that societies must guarantee that people can 'appear in public without shame' and that they can take part in the life of the community. Smith, an economist, wrote that in his day, men needed shirts made of linen, for this allowed them to go to church on Sunday and thus supported social integration. If integration failed, wrote Smith, the problem did not lie primarily in the level of real income or the available bundle of commodities, but instead in the lack of opportunity to act, which made it impossible for these people to attain that income or bundle of commodities (see Smith 1776). Many decades later, the sociologist Ralf Dahrendorf (1979) took up this idea in his book, *Life Chances*. According to Dahrendorf, societies obtain their quality through their ability to give people more life chances. For Dahrendorf, the opening up of chances is an expression of societal progress, for whoever gives people chances to act is creating conditions for possible happiness.

Health sociology and the sociology of education draw attention to the extent to which the question of the creation of conditions for happiness is already pre-decided in childhood. For instance, poor families limit their spending often to the detriment of nutrition, which has consequences for children's physical development. Children in poor families more frequently suffer from psychosocial problems. In families stricken by poverty, psychosocial stresses and strains are altogether higher, which also raises the risk of conflicts within the family. The connection between poverty and education is under discussion in the international studies of PISA, the OECD's Programme for International Students Assessment. Here, a close connection between school career and social origins has been found in all European countries. This is demonstrated most clearly in Germany, Belgium, and Switzerland, where children born in socially weak households have little chance of attaining a higher level of education than their parents.

## Capabilities and entitlements

Amartya Sen introduced the differentiation between achievements and capability into poverty research in order to show that social landscapes reflect only those actions that are possible under given political, social, and economic arrangements/conditions and do not reflect those actions that people, *given the opportunity, could have taken* based on their personal abilities.

For Sen, the life that we lead must therefore ultimately stand at the center of the analysis: that which we are capable of doing or cannot do and what we are capable of being or cannot be (Sen 1987). Individuals must be free to and capable of deciding to live a life in the community and deciding to live a healthy life (and the political system as well as the institutions of social policy must safeguard this freedom). Sen calls the ability and opportunity to act *capabilities*: 'Capabilities...are notions of freedom, in the positive sense: what real opportunities you have regarding the life you may lead' (Sen 1987: 36).

Therefore, what we ultimately measure about a person (according to a resource or life situation concept, for example)—whether she is rich or poor, educated or not educated, sick or healthy—is according to Sen only a current snapshot of what the person in a society at a given time at a defined location has achieved (*achievements*), and not what she could achieve. But it is precisely the person's ability to act (*capability*) that should be the subject of research and policy. Ms M, whom I mentioned in the prologue, has been trained as a hairdresser, but she finds no job. Or take the example of a carpenter who has fled Albania for Switzerland. The carpenter would certainly be able to practice his skilled trade in Switzerland, if he were not—as an asylum seeker—forbidden to work. Persons like these can come to need welfare assistance within a very short period of time, but they possess the skills that would enable them to lead a life outside economic poverty. Poverty policy must enlarge the scope for action, targeting expansion of opportunities to act; it must lead to new options for action, for example through work permits for asylum seekers, daycare entitlements, or employment guarantees for persons who have just completed training.

The analytical differentiation between *capabilities* (the ability to act and to be able to choose among alternatives, whether or not these possibilities come into consideration for the person), *functionings* (an expression of what is actually possible for the person, or what a person can actually do with his or her abilities), and *achievements* (the measurable results of the person's actions; that is, what a person has managed to do, has achieved), does not yet say anything about how the transformation of the individual dimensions is carried out. This issue is examined by Sen in his 'entitlement' concept.

According to Sen (1999), it is a person's entitlements—endowment with authorizations and rights to act, opportunities, and access—that determine the extent to which abilities can be exchanged for goods. Entitlements thus function as an intersection between the ideas people have about their lives and the actual opportunities that are open to them and the goals then realized. Of course, entitlements can change, for they are socially constituted and reproduced within a social and political process, and thus express the current status of a person within a specific society at a specific time (Watts 2002).

Previous to his studies of the Bengal famine, Sen focused his entitlement concept mainly on formal economic rights with regard to economic transactions. In *Poverty and Famines: An Essay on Entitlement and Deprivation*, Sen (1981) made a central observation: 'The law stands between food availability and food entitlement. Starvation deaths can reflect legality with a vengeance' (Sen 1981: 166). He then went on to extend his entitlement concept to include cultural and social (formal and informal) rights. While the concept of entitlement focuses on a person's legal rights of ownership, there are some social relations that take the broader form of accepted legitimacy rather than legal rights enforceable in a court. 'Extended entitlements' is the concept of entitlements extended to include the results of more informal types of rights sanctioned by accepted notions of legitimacy (Drèze and Sen 1989: 10).

## Bonding Sen and Bourdieu

Sen himself provides few empirical examples of this extended entitlement approach. For this reason I propose widening the concept by considering the ideas of French sociologist Pierre Bourdieu. Capital is central to Bourdieu's understanding of lifestyle. Capital is accumulated labor in its materialized form or in its incorporated, embodied form (Bourdieu 1983). It is capital that structures society and adjusts this structure. Following Bourdieu, individuals stand in a constant exchange of capital and competition over capital, whether in the form of transfer of property rights, through the acquisition of educational 'goods,' or through the exchange of time or attention.

In addition to economic capital, Bourdieu's forms of capital include *cultural capital* and *social capital*. For Bourdieu, cultural capital is the culture that people are provided with through their parents and social surroundings starting at birth, and that they pass on as their social inheritance. But cultural capital also includes all the certificates and diplomas that people earn throughout their educational careers. Bourdieu defines social capital as the aggregate of the actual or potential resources that are linked to membership in a group (Bourdieu 1983: 183). By social capital Bourdieu does not mean only membership to relatively loose and terminable unions such as groups, associations, or political parties, but also considers the family or ethnic group as non-terminable relationships.

Let us now put the thoughts of Sen and Bourdieu together (see Figure 6.1). The capabilities of a person are based on the person's endowment with economic, cultural and social capital, and the ratio of the kinds of capital in the mixture (the structure of capital), and on access and rights to offer these endowments for exchange, under the given current economic and social conditions on the various material (exchange entitlements) and non-material markets (extended exchange entitlements). The endowment with capital and the structure of capital allow a person to have goods at his/her disposal, to be entitled to certain claims, or to have access to capital. Resulting from this endowment, exchange relations are analyzable physical and mental spaces of capabilities.

This partition then also determines the position of an individual in society and results in a polarity: on one side are people who can largely freely decide what kind of lives they want to lead, because they make sufficient income but also because they have the corresponding cultural and social capital at their disposal, which they trade for goods (and accumulate). On the other side stand people who can choose among a clearly smaller number of alternatives (at a lower level) in order to reach their goals.

Understood in this way, poverty can take on various forms (economic, cultural, and social poverty), and life situations can take on different states (well-being, scarcity, poverty). Exclusion is understood as a combination of economic, cultural, and social poverty that does not come together suddenly and without cause but

*Figure 6.1: Spaces of capabilities*

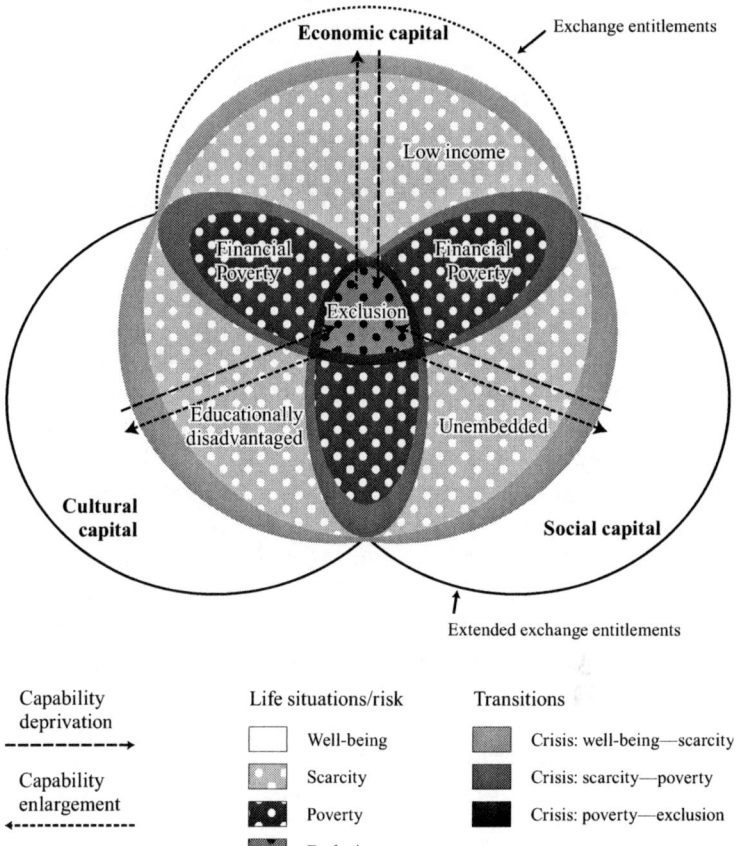

instead develops out of preliminary stages of deprivation and crisis. In accordance with Sen's dynamic view, capability deprivation is a process in the course of which the capability to act is lost. It should be noted that both Sen and Bourdieu increasingly observe such deprivation processes in modern societies. Impoverishment processes are therefore in no way only 'pockets of deprivation in a small number of places' (Sen 1992: 114).

For both Sen and Bourdieu, the power factor is decisive regarding the stability of this inequality model. Sen indicates numerous times that the poor (but also women generally) are denied access to authorizations and rights to act. Bourdieu shows that it is not only economic power that plays a role here but also the power of social 'distinction' (social subjects distinguishing themselves by the distinctions that they make): people can close access to options to act also artificially through processes of social closure.

## Happiness, ill-being, and capabilities

At this point I do not want to examine the debate in the literature on the measurability of capabilities (see Alkire 2002). Instead, my objective is to engage in further discussion of sociological research that I find fruitful.

In his book *A Sociology of Happiness*, Kenji Kosaka (2006) recently proposed a shift from consideration of increasing well-being to consideration of reducing ill-being. With Kosaka's definition of ill-being—'the deprivation of life opportunities' (Kosaka 2006: 7)—the discussion can be connected with the capability concept, the more so as Kosaka demands that we give up pure utilitarian analysis in favor of focusing on capabilities and their dynamics: 'the state, in which all human beings' capabilities are satisfied, at least above the minimum level, is well-being and the state in which they are not satisfied is ill-being' (Kosaka 2006: 15). In the model of spaces of capabilities presented in the present paper, Kosaka's understanding corresponds to the stages of 'well-being' and 'exclusion,' and the model indicates that there are two processes that must be considered: capability deprivation is the process from well-being towards ill-being/exclusion and capability enlargement is the process from ill-being/exclusion towards well-being. This understanding supports Kosaka's statement that well-being and ill-being/exclusion should in no way be viewed as inseparable (Kosaka 2006: 18).

The change in perspective called for by Kosaka is extremely enriching, especially because he asks for identification of processes of capability enlargement (in order to prevent ill-being). This expansion is valuable for micro-sociological studies particularly, for we very often observe that people that can be objectively considered poor do not feel poor subjectively at all. Or, in other words: what is relevant for the ability to act is not simply the resources available objectively (or, in the terminology used here, the endowment with capital) but also that which a subject perceives to be resources/capital.

Health sociology makes this discrepancy between objective situation and the individual's feeling a topic for discussion under the concept of 'coping.' Although Ms M has no income, she stays at her apartment, which for her provides identity and identification with 'normal' life. Even though Ms M is poor and is actually dependent on social welfare, she no longer comes to see her advisor at the social welfare office and thus goes without financial support. People actively seek ways in which to create coherence: coherence of their actions, actions that will make sense, be feasible, and be understandable.

But what possibilities exist for reducing ill-being through enlargement of capabilities? Based on what has been said so far, we can conclude that this process can be described on two levels: first, at the objective level of measures by the social welfare state, which are meant to promote the vertical mobility of a person towards a higher social status, and second, at the subjective level of the single individual through producing coherence. My thesis is that a process in the direction of well-being is optimized only if both levels can be successfully joined very closely. That is, the entry of Ms M in a re-employment program will only show successes if Ms M sees the program as holding new chances to act. These chances can be economic (a future job becomes more likely), social (Ms M gets to know people who are in the same social situation), or cultural (Ms M can acquire a training certificate).

What chances to act open up for young adults that receive social welfare assistance? Ms M was one of 1123 young adults that we considered in the framework of our poverty study on young urban adults (Drilling 2004). The results of the analysis of welfare case files and the interviews that we conducted with the young adults led us to the hypothesis that during the period of receiving assistance and services from the welfare system, young people's capabilities in fact improve little.

The failure of the welfare system is due partly to the young adults' endowments with capabilities when they enter social welfare and partly to the way in which the social welfare department has shaped the process of capability enlargement. Our analyses have shown that already prior to entering the welfare system the young adults are affected by a multitude of scarcities—economic (growing up in a poor household, no financial resources, no income), cultural (no or low-level school diploma, dropping out of school, little language competency, limited residence permit), or social (lack of a network, growing up in a children's home). In this respect, we can speak of a *baseline vulnerability* of the young urban poor that frequently reaches back into childhood.

The young people attempt to cope with their situation and, already prior to entering the welfare system, develop strategies for expanding their ability to act. One common strategy is to take on practically any possible kind of work in order to get the money to acquire new entitlements. But moving to the city also serves to widen young people's pool of decision alternatives. Besides this, for a number of young people the dysfunctional coping strategy of retreat into drug abuse has become established.

The entry into the welfare system is the most important coping strategy that all of the young people share: through financial support as well as welfare services, they hope to gain access to the regular labor market but also to gain entry into education and training establishments through access to sources of financial aid.

Welfare, however, hardly takes note of this subjective situation. Its task according to the law is to integrate the young people as quickly as possible into the labor market. All efforts are accordingly focused on employability. From this unsuccessful coherence between objective and subjective situation, processes of capability deprivation arise. In particular, collective descent processes take place.

1. Disqualification for labor market institutions (the young adults have not contributed enough to the system to be eligible to receive unemployment money).
2. Increasingly precarious economic situation through atypical work history and high rotation rate (even trained workers find no qualified jobs—this is destruction of cultural capabilities; frequent pattern of going on and off welfare).
3. Devaluation of educational capital through many years of not working in one's trained occupation ('entitlement failure').
4. Debt and collection processes: as their financial situations become increasingly precarious, young people economize, especially on their living arrangements (in cases where the young adults have already lived in residential areas for a long time, this is tantamount to social uprooting and thus destruction of social capital).

What are the indicators for a grave deprivation situation in which a person's capability is so severely restricted that we can speak of exclusion (see Figure 6.1) or ill-being (Kosaka 2006)?

First, it was found that an increasing habit of drug abuse as a strategy of coping with deprivation has a dysfunctional character. After a time of heavy drug abuse, the young adults are no longer willing or in a position to take on responsibility, they lose the ability to structure their days, they can hardly be integrated into the primary labor market, and they lose their jobs quickly. At the same time, they view increased drug use as a way out of this dilemma.

Second, and affecting young foreigners, a process of descent is caused by receiving welfare and justified by migration policy and it can lead to an exclusion situation—namely, through threat of deportation in cases of persisting welfare dependency. Any persons who receive written notification from the state in which they live that they are no longer desirable due to transfer spending are being excluded on the part of the government authorities—whether this procedure is justified or not.

In this way, welfare works counterproductively with regard to enlarging capabilities. For some of the young people, *exiting the welfare system* is a strategy for ensuring capabilities. These young people discern no advantages in financial support from the social welfare state that prioritizes economic independence above all other forms of help. In these cases, no coherence is created between state social support based on the objective situation and the needs of the young adults based on the subjective interpretation of the situation.

Other young adults remain in the welfare system but make hardly any effort to meet the set requirements. Although their advisors at the social welfare office always draw their attention to their poor prospects for the future, they seek out closeness with other young adults in the welfare system. They move into share-accommodation with them or meet them at public places. These places provide a common everyday culture, and a group feeling becomes configured that creates identity. Despite their objective situation of deprivation, the young people have the feeling that they are among people that share the same fate. In these cases, too, there is no coherence between state social support and the young adults' individual needs.

## Conclusion

Martha Nussbaum (2000) examines the lives of Indian women and shows clearly that processes of capability deprivation can affect people who are actually 'innocent' (they are female by birth). Kenji Kosaka (2006) takes up this discussion when he speaks of the innocent people that died during the Vietnam War. I do not want to give the impression that the same kind of innocence applies to the young urban poor that stand in the foreground here. Nevertheless, we must ask ourselves: What influence does growing up in a poor household have on young people? Could they have prevented the flight out of Yugoslavia and the loss of all of their possessions? What influence did they have on the fact that their education and training are not recognized in Switzerland? What part do young people play in the fact that after they complete training, no employer wants to hire them?

Recently in our modern welfare states we are seeing processes of social, cultural, and economic descent that are *collective* in character: they impact all young adults, independently of gender, nationality, or other variables. Neither the politicians nor the welfare system are finding appropriate answers. In contrast, successes like steady employment or training often have to be realized *by individuals*. On the basis of this discrepancy, I posit *individualized ascent within collective descent processes.*

Amartya Sen's demand that capabilities must stand at the center of the analysis must be met by the political system as well as the institutions of social policy. Only in this way can we guarantee that people get the chance to decide to live a life in the community and to decide to live a healthy life.

Against that, the predominant goal in the current practice of social policy is 'employability.' As we have seen, however, reducing ill-being means more than economic integration. When poverty is understood as the loss of economic, cultural, *and* social capital, and when the endowment with capabilities and the structure of capital open up a field of options within which a young person can build up capabilities, then we need to rethink the strategy of social policy. A new strategy is needed that takes into consideration social and cultural integration that is oriented to biographies and that attempts as early as childhood to support the development of capabilities. From the perspective of the capabilities approach, this must be connected with stronger cooperation among welfare institutions, family, school, and the young people themselves. Otherwise it is very difficult for the young adults to create coherence of their actions—actions that make sense, are feasible, and understandable. Nussbaum's (2000) terms for these capabilities include 'affiliation,' 'senses,' 'emotions,' or 'practical reason.' Only in this way are young people capable of dealing with questions regarding their futures, appropriating the world, dealing with the contradictions of modern societies, and finding adequate answers to these conflicts. Only in this way do they succeed in finding a place in society they can identify with and that allows them to take responsibility.

Sociological research on poverty that seeks not only to describe the processes of poverty but also to map routes out of impoverishment can encourage, and in the optimal case help to model, the shift in the social political strategy towards reducing ill-being through capability building mainly through micro-sociological, biography-oriented studies.

## Acknowledgements

I express my sincere gratitude to Dr Dorothee Schaffner, who is one of my colleagues and an excellent researcher in educational science, for her kind exchange of views with me on the young people who are facing multiple problems. Thanks are also due to Professor Kenji Kosaka for the discussion at the conference on social capital in Malta. I wish to thank Ms Ellen Russon for translation and editorial work on the earlier version of this chapter.

# Part III
# Reciting Suffering

# 7
# Aging Japanese American Atomic-bomb Survivors in Southern California: A Case Study

*Kayoko C. Nakao and Satoshi Ikeno*

## Introduction

Earlier historical events surrounding Japanese Americans abound with lessons in US immigration policy and welfare. Such events include the mass relocation of Japanese Americans from the West Coast to internment camps during World War II. Little has been documented, however, about the sizable number of Americans of Japanese ancestry in Hiroshima when the atomic bomb devastated the city on 6 August 1945. Following the end of the war, some of those American Atomic-bomb survivors, or *hibakusha*, chose to recover their American citizenship and returned to the US with the hope of establishing themselves in their homeland.

Their life in America continued to be filled with hardships, however. Radiation exposure caused them unknown ailments and physical fatigue. Psychological distress kept troubling them, especially for those who survived while others perished. Socially and politically, they were estranged even from the Japanese American community, where the majority shared 'the camp' experiences. Both the American media and the public remain oblivious about the fact that the atomic bomb attacked thousands of Americans, conceivably because they were 'Japanese' Americans, who were once seen as the enemy (Sodei 1978; 1998). According to a 2006 report, there are 920 *hibakusha* in the US today with an Atomic-bomb Certificate from the Japanese government (Hiroshima International Council for Health Care of the Radiation Exposed, 2006).

Given that Japanese American A-bomb survivors are a particularly vulnerable aging minority group, we believe that it is vital to understand their sociopolitical profile and their life experiences to date. Acknowledging the risk of generalization from a small number of subjects, the purpose of the current study is to document the socio-historical background of Japanese American A-bomb survivors and present some of the prominent issues facing them today. In the following, we first discuss our study design and procedure, as well as offer justifications for the current inquiry. We then present our findings, drawing illustrative comments from the interviews.

## Study design and procedure

For our inquiry, we first conducted an intensive information search about Japanese American A-bomb survivors and reviewed documentation in both English and Japanese. Our search found radiation research had proliferated in the post-war period, while there had been an incremental increase of A-bomb survivor lawsuits in Japan and pertinent newspaper articles in media archives. Under these circumstances, a case study approach would provide the best opportunity to obtain a pertinent line of information including the socio-historical background of Japanese American A-bomb survivors and help to refine the future data collection plans in both content and procedure (Yin 1994).

### Data collection procedure

To obtain the socio-historical profile of aging Japanese American A-bomb survivors, we agreed that the survivors' personal accounts would be equally as valuable as documented records. We sought the possibility of conducting interviews with Japanese American A-bomb survivors. Convenience and geographic proximity drove our case selection. We contacted two *Kibei-Nisei* Japanese American *hibakusha* or American-born-Japanese-educated A-bomb survivors. Mary was a seventy-four year-old and George was a seventy-six year-old A-bomb survivor from Hiroshima. In addition to the interviews, we collected data from multiple sources including the government printings and media data archives. We were also offered copies of personal documents kept by the interviewees, including newspaper clips, government reports, newsletters from A-bomb survivor support organizations, and announcements about assistance programs for *hibakusha* overseas.

## Interview processes

We adopted the life-course perspective to develop our interview questions. We took this approach to organize both interview questions and findings because of the significant interdependent nature of national decisions, community movements, and individual life experiences. The life-course perspective emphasizes the importance of taking into account both individual and social levels of influence for explaining later life outcomes (Dannefer and Uhlenberg 1999; Elder 2007). To capture the broadest range of information possible, we decided to focus on individual life experience in the interview with Mary and the community history with George. Tables 7.1 and 7.2 provide topical areas of the interview questions.

When making an appointment, we catered to their preferences for time, place, and language. Mary and George each chose a place where they could secure their privacy. Mary's interview took four hours and thirty minutes while George's took three hours. The main spoken language was Japanese, but English was spoken at times depending on the context. Prior to the interview, we explained the purpose of our study and obtained verbal permission for tape-recording. Because we were informed that their previous experiences with investigators, including researchers and journalists, were distasteful at times and left them with a feeling of exploitation, we provided our resumes and offered to provide them with their interview transcripts, to which both expressed their interest. We also prepared a box of Japanese sweets, which is a traditional practice of courtesy in Japanese culture. We wrote a thank you letter to each of them after the interview was over. The whole interview procedure took place between February and March 2006.

## Analyses

First, we put relevant socio-historical information in chronological order to understand the connecting events over time. Second, referring to the early steps in analysis of qualitative data explicated in Miles and Huberman (1994), we coded the interview transcripts by ATLAS.ti 5.0 (ATLAS.ti GmbH Company 2004), using a provisional code list

*Table 7.1: Interview guide: Topical areas for life review*

| Topical areas | Descriptions |
|---|---|
| Background questions | Demographics<br>Race and ethnicity |
| Growing up | Family (Parents, grandparents, siblings)<br>Community<br>Schooling/Education |
| Adulthood | Work<br>Marriage<br>Family and children<br>Military participation |
| Later years | Health and well-being<br>Retirement<br>Grandparenting<br>Caregiving |
| Capping questions | Overall, what would you say were the HARDEST times in your life?<br>Overall, what would you say were the BEST times in your life?<br>Is there anything else about growing older that you think younger people should know? |

Notes:
1. These topical areas were organized in chronological order during interviews.
2. This table was created based on a handout in a Community Health Science Course at UCLA in Fall 2003, taught by Steven P. Wallace, Ph.D., School of Public Health, University of California, Los Angeles.

developed based on the conceptual frameworks. This process did not exclude adding emerging codes to the list. Third, we compared the provisional and emerging codes to find any patterns and reorganized all the codes in order to identify more fitting patterns and sequences of life experiences. Finally, we exemplified ongoing challenges by drawing some illustrative comments from the interviews.

## Findings

In this section, we first offer findings from documentation. The first half of this section provides an overview of the pertinent socio-historical context surrounding Japanese American A-bomb survivors (Table 7.3). The second half presents interview findings (Table 7.4), drawing illustrative comments from the interviews. The comments

*Table 7.2: Interview guide: Topical areas for organizational history*

| Topical areas | Descriptions |
|---:|:---|
| Organizational profile | Mission<br>Goal(s)<br>Location |
| Membership profile | Size<br>Gender<br>Age<br>Ethnic make-up |
| History of the organization | Inception<br>Central players |
| Projects | Purposes<br>Past accomplishments<br>Ongoing projects<br>Future projects |
| Organizational challenges | Human resources<br>Finances<br>Interpersonal relationships |
| Prospective changes | Goals<br>Projects<br>Expected challenges |

Adapted partially from Netting, Kettner & McMurtry (1998).

were originally made in Japanese and have been translated into English by the authors.

## Documentation findings

### Prewar period 1885–1941

One of the fundamental questions about Japanese American A-bomb survivors may rest on the association with Hiroshima. The answer lies in historical evidence that Hiroshima produced the largest number of immigrants in Japanese immigration history (Sodei 1978; 1998). Soon after the Japanese government instituted the immigrant worker system to Hawaii in 1885, an increasing number of Japanese began crossing the Pacific Ocean. By 1936, 73,763 Japanese living overseas were from Hiroshima, of which 26,403 headed to Hawaii and 22,604 to the US mainland (Hiroshima Prefecture 1938; Kodama 1992). This first wave of Japanese immigrants at around the turn of the twentieth century—so called *Issei* (first generation)—held Japanese education

*Table 7.3: Abbreviated chronological table: Historical events 1868–2005*

| Year/Date | Events |
| --- | --- |
| 1868 June 19 | A British ship *Sai-oto* with 153 unofficial Japanese immigrants (*Gannen-sya*) arrives in Honolulu, Hawaii |
| 1871 | The Hawaii-Japan Treaty of Amity and Commerce is signed |
| 1885 February 8 | The first 944 officially organized immigrants (*Kan-yaku Imin*) arrives in Hawaii on the Japanese ship *City of Tokyo* (220 were from Hiroshima) |
| 1886–1894 | 26 ships with 29,069 officially organized Japanese immigrants arrive in Hawaii |
| 1894 June 15 | The last 1,491 officially organized immigrants depart from Japan for Hawaii |
| 1898 | The US annexes Hawaii |
| 1907–1908 | Gentlemen's Agreement is formalized to halt the migration of Japanese laborers to the United States. Women are allowed to immigrate if they are married to US residents ('Picture brides') |
| 1913 May 19 | California Legislature passes a bill prohibiting aliens from owning land |
| 1915 | A total of 59,591 overseas Japanese come from Hiroshima by 1915 |
| 1920 | Referendum placed on the ballot in California to deny Japanese the right to lease land; soon followed by Washington, Nebraska, Texas, and Nevada |
| 1924 | Revision of the US Immigration Act comes into effect (Asian Exclusion Act), rendering aliens ineligible for citizenship |
| 1925 | Japanese government established a provision of the law of nationality (dual citizenship until 20 years old) |
| 1929 January | Japanese Ministry of Foreign Affairs estimates 30,000 Japanese Americans living in Japan for family reasons or education |
| 1936 | Total 73,763 overseas Japanese come from Hiroshima by 1936 (26,403 in Hawaii, 22,604 in the mainland US, and 11,956 in Brazil) |
| 1941 December 6 | President Franklin D. Roosevelt (FDR) launches a project (Code name 'S-1') to develop the atomic bomb |
| 1941 December 7 | The Imperial Japanese Navy attacks the US fleet at Pearl Harbor, Hawaii |
| 1941 December 8 | US declares war on Japan |
| 1942 February 19 | FDR authorizes Executive Order 9066 and 120,000 Japanese Americans are relocated to 10 camp sites; their classification is changed from 'Aliens ineligible for citizenship' to 'Enemy aliens' |
| 1942 June | Manhattan Project begins |
| 1945 Spring | Special intelligence squad is established in Hiroshima and many *Nisei* women are mobilised to intercept short-wave messages in English |
| 1945 July 16 | Trinity, the first detonation of an atomic bomb, Alamogordo, NM |

| | |
|---|---|
| 1945 August 6 | The first atomic-bomb is dropped on Hiroshima (Uranium-235 produced in Oak Ridge, TN) |
| 1945 August 9 | The second atomic-bomb is dropped on Nagasaki (Plutonium produced in Hanford, WA) |
| 1945 August 15 | Japan surrenders and the Allied Occupation of Japan begins |
| 1946 May 8 | General Headquarters (GHQ) is ordered to compile a list of all Japanese Americans living in Japan |
| 1947 | New Constitution comes into effect in Occupied Japan |
| 1947 | Atomic Bomb Casualties Commission (ABCC) established in Hiroshima & Nagasaki |
| 1948 | *Kibei Nisei* returning to the US reaches its peak |
| 1952 | The Allied Occupation of Japan ends |
| 1952 April 28 | Peace Treaty comes into effect |
| 1954 March 1 | Fallout from a US hydrogen bomb test at Bikini Atoll contaminates Lucky Dragon No.5 (*Daigo Fukuryū Maru*), a Japanese fishing boat |
| 1954 | Movement against Atomic and Hydrogen bombs gains widespread support in Japan |
| 1957 | Atomic-bomb Survivors Medical Care Law is enacted in Japan |
| 1957 | *Kibei Nisei* in Southern California reached 3,000 |
| 1965 August 6 | A '*Hibakusha* Friendship Group' meeting notice appears in local newspapers in Southern California |
| 1965 August 12 | First meeting of *Hibakusha* in America |
| 1968 | Atomic-bomb Survivors Special Measures Law is enacted in Japan |
| 1971 October 13 | Committee of Atomic Bomb Survivors in the US (CABSUS) is formed |
| 1972 October | Son Gin Doo files a case to receive a *Hibakusha* ID card in Japan |
| 1972 | HR 17112 to provide medical aid to *Hibakusha* is introduced in California |
| 1973 | HR 17112 is reintroduced as HR 2894 in California as an ammendment to the Disaster Relief Act |
| 1973 | Northern California Committee of Atomic Bomb Survivors is established |
| 1973 December 2 | SB-15 to provide medical aid to Japanese American *Hibakusha* is introduced in California |
| 1974 May 14 | A public hearing is held by the Senate Health and Welfare Committee |
| 1974 June 2 | Senate Finance Committee hearing is held in California |
| 1974 July 22 | Japanese Ministry of Health and Welfare issues Directive No. 402 stipulating that survivors lose their rights to payments if they move out of Japan |
| 1975 | Radiation Effects Research Foundation is established (Former ABCC) |
| 1977 March | Team of doctors from Japan arrive in the US for medical examination of A-bomb survivors living in the US |
| 1978 | Son Gin Doo, a Korean atomic bomb survivor, is granted the right to obtain a *Hibakusha* ID card, resulting in the issuance of ID cards to overseas *Hibakusha* |

Continued...

Table 7.3 continued

| | |
|---|---|
| 1978 March 31 | US Congressional hearing is held in Los Angeles, California on Japanese American *Hibakusha* |
| 1994 | Atomic-bomb Survivors Relief Law is enacted in Japan |
| 2002 | Kwak Kwi Hun, a Korean atomic-bomb survivor living in Korea is given a health allowance (back payable to 1997, due to a Hiroshima local government regulation limiting retroactive penalties to a five-year maximum) |
| 2005 | A Japanese American *Hibakusha* qualifies to apply for *Hibakusha* benefits from overseas |
| 2007 | Three Japanese Brazilian *Hibakusha* are deemed to have the right to receive the health allowances retroactively for the period prior to 1997 |

Sources: Hiroshima City (2006), Hiroshima Peace Site (2001), Hiroshima Prefecture (1972 and 1988), Kodama (1992), Kuramoto (1999), *The Rafu Shimpo* (1946), Takeda (1929), The Atomic Heritage Foundation (2007), The United States Strategic Bombing Survey (1946), Tule Lake Committee (2004), major Japanese newspapers for lawsuit information and personal communications with interviewees.

and culture in veneration. Many therefore sent their American-born children to Japan for schooling (Takeda 1929), which consequently led to more than 30,000 *Nisei* (second generation) and *Sansei* (third generation) crossing the ocean by 1929. One archival record shows that Hiroshima welcomed 4,805 of those American-born descendants by 1929, of which 3,803 were of elementary school age (Takeda 1929; Sodei 1978). Upon the outbreak of the war in 1941, however, these American-born descendents lost their social and political ties with their country of birth, resulting in the renouncement of their American citizenship.

**August 1945**
Once the war started, people were called up to work in the Japanese military operations at various stages. Japanese Americans were no exception; some were drafted and some were engaged in the services to provide different types of physical labor. On the morning of Monday, 6 August 1945, people in Hiroshima were either already at work or en route (Hiroshima Prefecture 1988; The United States Strategic Bombing Survey 1946), including school age children who had been mobilized to work for the city's major renovation project. Immediately after the A-bomb exploded at 8:15 am, the conflagration swept through the city, yielding a huge exodus of survivors, mostly injured who were seeking help. However, thousands of people were streaming back to the city as soon as the conflagration calmed down, searching for

relatives and friends, and assessing the extent of their property loss and damages (Hiroshima City and Nagasaki City 1979; Hiroshima Prefecture 1988; The United States Strategic Bombing Survey 1946), which consequently exposed them to high doses of residual radiation. The immediate death toll varies between 64,600 and 282,000, depending on the literature, due to a substantial loss of records (Gensuibaku Kinshi Nihon Kyogikai Senmon Iinkai 1961; Hiroshima City and Nagasaki City 1979). The exact number of casualties among Japanese Americans remains unknown. The second atomic bomb was dropped in Nagasaki on 9 August leading to the surrender of Japan on 15 August.

**Postwar period**
Although the war was over, the quality of life remained relatively poor in post-war Japan under the Allied Occupation led by the US. In February 1946, hundreds of *Nisei* appealed to the General Head Quarters (GHQ) office to return to their homeland (*The Rafu Shimpo* 1946; Sodei 1998). In early May 1946, GHQ ordered the Japanese government to compile and submit a list of all Japanese Americans residing in Japan during the war, those who were naturalized Japanese citizens and those who served in the military or government operations (Sodei 1998). This was to consider the re-acquisition of their US citizenship, and it is estimated that more than 3,000 Japanese Americans had returned to the US by 1948. The number of returning A-bomb survivors in this group is unknown.

It was not until the 1960s that a group action was initiated by A-bomb survivors in the US (Kuramoto 1999). In August 1965, an announcement about a small friendship group meeting appeared in local bilingual newspapers in Los Angeles. Group membership grew gradually, but their activities hardly extended beyond companionship (Kuramoto 1999; Sodei 1978, 1998). Aiming to become more effective as a political group, the group was formalized and became the Committee of Atomic Bomb Survivors in the United States (CABSUS) in 1971. For the first group action as CABSUS, they lobbied the US Congress and the State of California to provide medical assistance to A-bomb survivors in the US. The bill never passed the state level, defeated by assembly members with anti-Japanese sentiment (Kuramoto 1999; Sodei 1978, 1998), which was aggravated by the misconception that the US had provided medical treatment through the Atomic Bomb Casualties Commission (ABCC) in Hiroshima and Nagasaki, which was, in fact, exclusively for radiation research. In 1978, the bill was finally introduced for legislation and two congressional hearings were held in Los Angeles. Yet, the bill was not well received in Washington DC, due to strong opposition from various sources including the WWII veterans and others with different political interests. Thus, the bill never reached the full Judiciary Committee and yet again it eventually died (Sodei 1978, 1998).

**Political movement to help A-bomb survivors**
While the Japanese American A-bomb survivors were individually coping with hardships in the US, the anti-nuclear movement broke out in Japan in 1954, following a deadly accident of twenty-three Japanese crew members on a fishing vessel named the *Daigo Fukuryū Maru* (Lucky Dragon No.5). They were trapped by the radioactive fallout from the US Hydrogen Bomb test at Bikini Atoll. This nationwide anti-nuclear lobbying ignited another national movement that called attention to the needs of silently suffering A-bomb survivors in Japan. As a result, the A-bomb Survivors Special Medical Care Law was enacted in 1957, which created the A-bomb Survivor Certificate that would provide free medical treatment for the certificate holders under the Japanese healthcare system. The certificate would be issued as long as an A-bomb survivor met the prerequisite of having three witnesses who could testify that the applicant was in a specified area within two weeks of the detonation. In 1968, the A-bomb Survivors Special Measure Law was enacted that would provide financial assistance to the certification holders. However, the provision of the programs did not include the survivors living overseas, such as those in Korea, Brazil, and the US. In 1994, these two laws were amended and integrated into the A-bomb Survivors Medical Relief Law, yet the provision remained fairly exclusive of the overseas survivors.

**Brief history of lawsuits by overseas A-bomb survivors**
Given abiding discrimination by the country of residence in the support programs, the A-bomb survivors living overseas began taking action to bring justice. In October 1972, Son Gin Doo, a Korean A-bomb survivor, filed a lawsuit against the Japanese government at the Fukuoka Local Court, claiming his right to receive the Certificate. In 1978, the Japanese Supreme Court granted his claim, which accordingly deemed any overseas A-bomb survivors to be qualified for the Certificate. Four years prior to this Supreme Court decision, however, the Ministry of Health and Welfare issued Directive No. 402, stipulating that survivors would lose their rights to payments if

they moved out of Japan. This proviso instructed local governments to remove any records of A-bomb survivors from the payee list once they left the country. This practice lasted until a lawsuit by Kwak Kwi Hun in South Korea, who demanded the financial assistance regardless of his country of residence. When the Osaka Local Court ruled in his favor in 2002, it finally abolished the stipulation of the Directive. Nevertheless, benefits prior to 1997 were not paid due to a local government prescription for a five-year maximum on any retroactive rulings. In 2003, a Japanese American A-bomb survivor filed a suit, demanding that the government grant her application for financial assistance from her country of residence. The Hiroshima Local Court ruled in the plaintiff's favor and survivors living overseas with the Certificate no longer had to fly to Japan for the application procedure. In 2007, the Hiroshima Local Court ruled in favor of three A-bomb survivors in Brazil who had sued the Japanese government to retroactively make payments of their health allowance prior to 1997, finally rendering the prescription ineffectual for this type of benefit.

## Interview findings: Emerging topical area

### The A-bomb experience

Our analysis revealed the A-bomb experience as the central and emanating phenomena in the life of aging Japanese American A-bomb survivors. The effects of the A-bomb were many-sided, being particularly noteworthy in terms of biomedical, psychological, and social aspects of their well-being in old age. To exemplify the multifaceted and life-long effects of the A-bomb, we will draw on the interviews with Mary and George. Mary went to Japan in 1937 when she was five years old, upon her father's decision to return to Japan for his children's education. Mary became a naturalized citizen of Japan during the height of militarism, due to her father's concerns about her security. Although she escaped from the direct attack of the A-bomb, she was exposed to radiation when she went into Hiroshima city in search of her sisters and friends three days after the detonation. She began telling her A-bomb experience with the death of her older sisters.

> The hardest time in my life was, well I think it was the deaths of my two older sisters. The immediate older sister and I were always together as if we were twins. So, after she died, I felt as if I lost a half of my body. I lost my appetite and I couldn't eat. I guess that further weakened my

Table 7.4: Provisional and emerging topical areas

| Provisional Codes | Reorganized Codes |
|---|---|
| *Life-course perspective* | *A-Bomb* |
|   Demographics |   Experience |
|   Society level |   Health effects |
|   Community level |   Psychological effects |
|   Family level |     Loss and grief |
|   Individual level |     Survivor guilt |
|   Coping |   Social effects |
|   Race/Ethnic identity |     Social support |
|   Growing up |     Survivor group |
|     Family |   Government assistance |
|     Community |     Problem |
|     Schooling/Education |     Lawsuit |
|   Adulthood |   Spirituality |
|     Work | |
|     Marriage | *War* |
|     Family and children |   Concentration camp |
|     Military participation |   Military operations |
|   Later life |   Discrimination |
|     Health and well-being | |
|     Retirement | *Immigration* |
|     Grandparenting | |
|     Caregiving | *Education* |
|   Hardest time in life | |
|   Best time in life | *Language barrier* |
| | *Personal belief* |
| | *Message to younger generations* |
| |   Criticism of the young |
| |   The importance of peace |

health at that time. Food would go bad very quickly in summer, because there was no refrigerator or icebox. Although food was awfully scarce then, we had to dump the meals because no one would eat (in my family). We just cried every day.

My oldest sister was working for the military. She was called up to work in the special intelligence squad to intercept short-wave messages in English. She, of course (as American-born and educated in the US) had a good command of English. Many *Nisei* women were in the squad. They were working in shifts and my sister was on duty that day.

Looking back, I think she was prepared for her death. The day before she died, she was with our Mama in the backyard. She was opening her mouth and showing her teeth to Mama. I asked them what they were doing, and then Mama said, "Your sister is asking me to remember where her teeth are capped with gold." "I heard a story of a mother in Tokyo who was able to find her dead son because she remembered where his teeth were capped. So, I want you to remember that I have two capped teeth, here and here. If something happens to me, say being bombed and dead, I want you to find me because I want to come back and be with you, Mama," my sister said. "Come on, don't even think like that. The building you work in Asano Park is much sturdier than our wooden house, you know," I said to my sister.

Indeed, her work place was located in the old and beautiful park, built of very sturdy structure, but the A-bomb shattered it just like that. When the bomb hit, six *Nisei* women workers were trapped underneath the broken structure. The surviving soldiers stationed there pulled up the structure and told them to escape. "Hurry up! Run! Hurry up! Run!" But their hipbones were broken because the structure was too heavy, so they couldn't even crawl out. Then the fire was coming close, and the soldiers had to give up and leave.

On the night of August 6th, Mama went to Hiroshima to look for my sisters, but no one was able to go into the city. Next day, early in the morning, she went back to the city and reached the park. She walked around to search for my sister, and she met a soldier who said he knew where my sister was. He took Mama to the place and pointed the burned structure, "Your daughter is underneath this," he said. "How do you know?" "Your daughter was the only one who was crying for you 'Mama help, Mama (*Mama tasukete, Mama*).' Others were saying, '*Okāsan* (Mother).'" The soldier pulled up the burnt structure, and Mama saw my sister lying on her stomach. Because she was quite burnt, there was almost nothing remaining, except a small part of her forehead with some hair. Her lunchbox escaped the fire and it was just by her side. The soldier told my Mama that she could not take all of her daughter's remains because they were going to cremate the victims all together. So, Mama picked up my sister's forehead and hair and put them in her lunchbox. Mama took my sister home in the lunchbox.

Mary explained the tragedy in extreme detail, indicating the intensive and vivid memory of her loss and grief that she had experienced more than sixty years earlier. Notice that the story was originally her mother's. The vividness of her mother's experience, grief, and loss were transcended to Mary, and her mother's life experience eventually became hers. The mother-and-daughter's story not only showed the profound and lasting grief of the surviving family members, but also revealed the intergenerational transcendence of experience and emotion. Her mother's psychological pain was bequeathed to young Mary, and she held it throughout her life-course.

**Survivor guilt**
Mary also expressed what Lifton (1968) called 'guilt feeling as a survivor' in relation to the loss of her other sister.

> On the day of the A-bomb, I was supposed to go for work as a student volunteer in Hiroshima city with my immediate older sister. In the morning, we went to the station together to catch a train, but it was behind schedule because of a small bomb dropped in the neighborhood prefecture. We waited for the train, then, all of sudden I felt a headache. So I said to my sister, "I think I want to go back and stay home today because I have a headache." "You always have a headache and I think it will go away by 10 o'clock just as usual. So, stay with me and let's go (to work) together," she said. "No, no, today's is different. I think I am going home." "Then leave your 'can' for me," my sister said. Each of us had a tin can of roasted soybeans, a common emergency food for children to carry around at that time. "You can get more from Mama when you get home." "No, I won't leave this to you because this is mine and I will eat it for my lunch when I get home." And I went back home. ...Oh, I don't know how much I regret this afterwards. The A-bomb hit Hiroshima as soon as my sister's train got into the city. I don't think she had time to eat her soybeans before she died, but I lamented: why didn't I give my can to her? I blamed myself for a long time, really a long time.

Mary also described the surroundings in extreme detail such as the station and the trains she saw on her way back home. The narrative of the episode flowed smoothly and was highly pictorial, suggesting Mary had rehearsed the scene over and over again with her guilt feeling as a survivor attached to it. Coupled with the fact that she lost two sisters simultaneously, her mother in grave remorse, and diminished health effects because of radiation, questions arise about how Mary coped with these multifaceted burdens given that she was only 13 years old at the time of tragedy.

**Aging effects**
Besides psychosocial effects of the A-bomb, the interviews revealed the gap between the government assistance for A-bomb and the needs

of aging Japanese American A-bomb survivors overseas. Under pressure from the A-bomb survivors overseas, the Japanese government implemented several enterprises. Currently, there are three major programs: the Travel support program, the Medical support program in the country of residence, and the Information provision-based program (Hiroshima International Council for Health Care of the Radiation-exposed 2006). The travel support program provides travel expenses for survivors if the local government deems them eligible for the Certificate or recognizes their need to receive medical treatment in Japan. The medical support program has two sub-programs: the Medical Expense Support Program and the Medical Staff Dispatch Program. The Medical Expense Support Program subsidizes the medical expenses up to 130,000 yen (approximately US$1,150) per year for A-bomb survivors overseas with the Certificate or those with the statement of eligibility for the Certificate. The Medical Staff Dispatch Program provides health consultation by sending A-bomb disease specialists to survivors' countries of residence. Every two years, the medical team visits several major cities in the US such as Los Angeles, San Francisco, Seattle, and Honolulu. This program also provides on-site training of A-bomb medical care to physicians and nurses overseas and training for physicians from overseas in Japan.

**Healthcare needs with age**
George pointed to critical issues and immediate needs such as an increasing conundrum facing aging Japanese American A-bomb survivors, resulting from the gap between the current support program and their increasing healthcare needs. In addition, the financial burden among aging Japanese American A-bomb survivors increased due to the expensive medical costs under the US health care system.

> As we got older, the benefit of having the medical team becomes more and more obscure. Every two years, the medical team comes to the US and provides health examination. The function is primarily to provide medical checkups, not treatment. They cannot treat patients in the US because of the law.
> In addition, the current assistance programs won't do much for those whose health is severely debilitating. Some of the aging survivors are too sick to fly to Japan (for medical treatment or anything). Medical care costs really a lot here in the US. There are some people who got $10,000 or $20,000 bills. So, if there is no limit for the financial assistance for medical care, just like those survivors living in Japan,

the A-bomb survivors with severe health status could be relieved from financial burden.

Mary talked about the difficulty with her functional mobility due to her declining health as she bacame older. She has developed a back problem that makes it difficult for her to make long-distance trips. Although Mary has her Certificate, there is an increasing challenge for her to use programs such as receiving treatment in Japan.

> I cannot take a trip to Japan anymore (because it is a long distance flight). They say they would provide the trip for receiving certificate and medical treatment in Japan, and I could probably use a wheelchair to move around, but it won't reduce the flight time. You have to carry your luggage and push the wheelchair... It is not easy. It is not easy anymore with my age and health.

Finally, the last aging-related issue mentioned was about program application procedures. For example, it has been increasingly taxing for non-certified holders to find witnesses because an increasing number of witnesses are dead. And the application procedure for the Certificate is nonetheless strict; the survivors have to fly to Japan to receive the Certificate.

## Discussion

Our study unveiled the intricate sociopolitical and historical profile of Japanese American A-bomb survivors. They took sociopolitical group action against their country of birth in the 1970s, which in fact had to do with infringing on American patriotism. In addition, the study revealed the survivors' real-life challenges that have been increasingly multifarious with age. Over the years, their biomedical problems were joined by long-lasting psychological anguish, which has been aggravated by the reluctance of the welfare state of Japan toward the war victims, particularly those living overseas. It appears that, while the issues became intensified with age, the cracks they have fallen through became deeper and broader. Understanding their current health and well-being would inform the future research and policy implementation, so that it would reduce the gap between the current assistance programs.

Because they are an extremely vulnerable population in various ways, we need a well-planned study design and procedure to reflect the needs of Japanese American A-bomb survivors' voices as much as possible. To do so, it is critical to work together with them in designing a study and use research to advocate the intensity and magnitude of their multifaceted issues as an extremely marginalized group of older Americans. To this end, we contend that the future study will play a significant role to promote their well-being in old age.

## Acknowledgements

Support for this study was provided by a grant from the Kwansei Gakuin University 21st Century COE (Center of Excellence) Program 'The Study of Social Research for the Enhancement of Human Well-being,' Nishinomiya, Japan. Generous cooperation was provided by North America A-Bomb Survivors Association (Hiroshima-Nagasaki), Los Angeles, CA. We conducted original research at the UCLA Research Library (Special Collections) and Biomedical Library in Los Angeles, CA, and Hiroshima Central City Library, Hiroshima, Japan. Portions of this data were presented at the 54th Japanese Society for the Study of Social Welfare, 8 October 2006, Saitama, Japan, the 2006 International Conference for Social Work in Health and Mental Health, 14 December 2006, Hong Kong, China, and the 6th Annual Hawaii International Conference on Social Science, 31 May 2007, Honolulu, Hawaii.

# 8
# From Victims Divided To Victims United: The Politics of War Trauma in the Netherlands, 1945–1980

*Jolande Withuis*

## Introduction

During the German occupation of the Netherlands, which lasted from May 1940 to May 1945, about 225,000 citizens lost their lives (of a population of almost nine million). Among the dead were 102,000 Jews and around 7000 members of the Dutch resistance. After the liberation approximately 4500 surviving Dutch Jews and 8500 Dutch political prisoners returned to their country. This chapter analyses the post-war histories of the 13,000 survivors from two perspectives, firstly through the rise and success of the concept of trauma, and secondly in terms of the rise and decline of the Cold War. These two perspectives, though seemingly far apart and associated with different disciplines, are in fact connected. I demonstrate this connectedness by presenting the parallel histories of Dutch medical-psychological theory and practice in regard to the consequences of concentration camp imprisonment, and of the Dutch camp survivors in the context of post-war political developments. Those two histories visibly intersected in 1972.

## 1972: The 'Breda Three'

The year 1972 was pivotal in the culture of WWII memory in the Netherlands. Early that year the Roman-Catholic Minister of Justice decided to release from prison the last three German war criminals: Kotälla, Fischer, and Aus der Fünten. His determination to release these so-called 'Drie van Breda (Breda Three)'—so named after the city in which their prison stood—caused a storm of anger, especially among members of the former resistance and among surviving Jews.

Their protest began as a political protest. The minister was accused of being insufficiently aware of the political dangers of his policy with regard to the growing neo-Nazi movement in the German Federal Republic. Soon, however, the debate moved to the damage his decision might do to the well-being and mental health of the victims of the sinister trio. Release would harm the survivors' health.

As a result of the fast-growing anger about the possible release, a special parliamentary hearing was organized. At this hearing a long line of spokespersons from Jewish and resistance organizations evoked the gruesome images this subject brought to the survivors' minds, the nightmares still haunting them, and the suicides attempted by comrades. It was clear that release of the Breda Three would aggravate this suffering. Parliament was also addressed by several psychiatrists. Just like the victims' organizations, they warned Parliament that the release of these criminals might be too heavy a burden for their patients to bear and for war victims in general. The only speakers in favor of release were lawyers and probation officers. They underlined from a humanitarian perspective how bad the prisoners' situation was and argued that keeping them imprisoned no longer served any reasonable purpose.

Not only was this parliamentary debate the first ever to be broadcast live on national television, in the same week the documentary drama *Begrijp je nu waarom ik huil?* (Do you now understand why I cry?) was shown on television. Both had a deeply emotional impact on their audiences. *Begrij je nu waarom ik huil?* shows a therapeutic session of a former inmate of the German concentration camp Sachsenhausen with Professor Jan Bastiaans, a psychiatrist who in those days was becoming famous for his treatment of war victims. Under the influence of the drug LSD (which Bastiaans used as a therapeutic medium) the patient remembers his camp experiences and achieves an emotional catharsis.

After all these demonstrations of the intense grief experienced by war victims, public opinion shifted dramatically and political opinion soon followed. The minister was forced to abandon his plan.

The affair of the 'Drie van Breda' illustrates a radical change in the Dutch culture of war memory. Until then terms such as 'post-concentration camp syndrome' or 'war trauma' were simply not part of the Dutch social vocabulary. The year 1972 witnessed the medical and public discovery of the phenomenon that a victim can suffer from the psychological consequences of a tragic experience as many as twenty years after this experience occurred. Now widely known as Post Traumatic Stress Disorder (PTSD), this newly recognized phenomenon was then named 'late psychological consequences.' Relatively new also at this time were psychiatrists supporting war victims. Only three years earlier, when the imprisoned war criminals had also been a political issue, mental health professionals had argued in favor of release, saying that hate hurts those who hate and that victims' resentment would create more unhappiness among victims than the possible shock of deporting the three to Germany.

In the years following 1972, the post-concentration camp syndrome became common knowledge. It became clear that more people than anybody had realized were suffering from the symptoms of this syndrome. Victims, professionals, the public and the media became convinced that long-term war damage was widespread and propagated this new knowledge. Soon also an explanatory theory emerged: the disorder was the outcome of the lack of state care in the immediate post-war years and of the conspiracy of silence between 1945 and 1970. The myth was created that until the seventies nobody had ever known that the fear, the hardships, the threats and the loneliness of the long stay in a concentration camp or the loss of loved ones by genocide would take their toll even after a quarter of a century.

## Mental war damage 1945–1980

This myth lives on to this day, but a myth it is. In actual fact some psychiatrists immediately after and even during the war predicted probable 'mental war damage.' In the development of medical theory and the prevalence of war-related health complaints four periods can be distinguished:
1. 1945–1948: return from the camps; early understanding of possible psychological consequences.
2. 1948–1968: relative silence on WWII; low prevalence of psychological war disorders.
3. 1968–1980: discovery of post-concentration camp syndrome; growing number of patients.
4. 1980–2005: trauma culture: ever more people identifying themselves as being 'traumatized.'

For my purposes here I divide the third period in two parts, 1968–1972 and 1972–1980, and only briefly discuss the fourth period, from 1980 to 2005. I describe the mental health developments not as a patient or therapist, but as a historical sociologist. Medical science does not develop in a laboratory or social vacuum. A long-term sociological analysis should demonstrate dynamics and processes that are impossible to perceive by those personally and directly involved in the process: in this case patients and therapists. Such a sociological analysis may appear over-critical, cold and detached. However, analyzing the rise of 'trauma' as a social and historical process does not deny the existence of war trauma, nor does it intend to trivialize suffering.

My research into psychiatric thinking is grounded on a broad base of medical and psychiatric literature. Amongst other things, I analyzed sixty volumes of the *Maandblad Geestelijke volksgezondheid* (MGv) (Monthly on Public Mental Health). This monthly journal was conceived by doctors and social workers involved in the rising mental health movement during the war years; it was initiated in the autumn of 1945 from the conviction that when the war was over, extra care would be needed. The monthly was written and read by professionals such as psychiatrists, psychiatric nurses, social workers and policy makers, and it presents contemporary insights into the broad field of social psychiatry and mental health. Just counting pages regarding WWII is revealing, evident in Table 8.1.

Contrary to what one tends to expect, the attention paid to the psychological war damage does not show a decline from fierce beginnings towards zero in the end. In the first years MGv spent almost one-third of its pages on war-related problems. This was followed by a considerable drop in WWII coverage during the fifties and early sixties. Attention revived again between 1970 and 1980.

The sharp decrease during the fifties is similar to developments in the numbers of WWII books published and monuments built. In the

*Table 8.1: Editorial pages about WWII in MGv (%)*

|           |       |
|-----------|-------|
| 1945–1946 | 32%   |
| 1947–1949 | 6     |
| 1950–1959 | 0.3   |
| 1960–1969 | 0.3   |
| 1970–1979 | 3     |
| 1980–1989 | 1.5   |
| 1990–1999 | 0.8   |

initial post-war years a considerable number of books, brochures and autobiographies about the camps was published and read. As to monuments, so many ideas were submitted to the municipal and national committees running this department that government put a stop to it. By 1948 the public had had enough. The predominant feeling was that the subject of 'war' should be brought to a conclusion. In the mid-sixties interest grew again, an important impetus being the moving study on the persecution and destruction of the Dutch Jews by historian Dr. J. Presser. Also between 1960 and 1965 a long television series on the war years, *De bezetting* (Occupation) was broadcast, which kept Dutch families glued to their more and more prevalent television sets (the proportion of households with televisions grew in those years from 25% to 68%). From then on, interest grew. In 1995, half a century after the liberation, the fifth of May, 'Liberation Day,' officially became a National Holiday—a decision many victims experienced as a late victory over the governmental negligence from 1945 on.

## 1945–1948

What, then, were the contents of the early post-war warnings for psychological war damage?

In 1946 Jewish psychoanalyst Jaap Tas (Tas 1946), who had himself survived Bergen-Belsen, published a perceptive article on the effects of concentration camp imprisonment and on what might be the (possibly long-term) psychological consequences of such an experience. Fundamental in his view was the inability of sufferers to express emotions like fear of death and anger about humiliation, and the fact that this necessary repression lasted for a relatively very long time. Contrary to 'normal' war trauma, this repression was not alternated with periods of relaxation and pleasure.

WWI had shown that a short intensive experience of fear or shock, like being shot down as a pilot, was less harmful in the long run than the seemingly endless, powerless, fearful waiting in the trenches. The experience of intense powerlessness, as it turned out, was one of the major factors that caused psychological damage. Tas' plea illustrates that before 1945 there was no such thing as an accepted medical or psychological theory that endeavored to understand the impact of the concentration camp experience. Comparing these new experiences with the medical knowledge of WWI, Tas felt obliged to convince his readers that imprisonment in a concentration camp, though being a situation without armed conflict, might be a serious threat to one's mental state.

Tas also predicted that the atmosphere into which the survivors returned would be decisive in terms of their later well-being. In this regard he shared the disappointment of the surviving Jews—their homes robbed or taken by others, their jobs gone, and their culture and social environment destroyed. Most survivors had to find out for themselves if their families were dead or missing, and had to rebuild their lives while they received almost no care and were not made to feel welcome. One of the measures Tas suggested was large-scale availability of psychotherapy. This was not realized. Psychotherapy in 1945 was an unusual, unknown and scarce treatment.

A second important author was Dr Eddy de Wind, a physician and psychoanalyst like Tas, and a survivor of Auschwitz. During his career de Wind would write many articles on psychological war damage. In his first article in 1949, 'Confrontation with death,' he thoroughly examined the differences regarding inner experience and lasting psychological damage between concentration camps designed as punishment and camps designed for genocidal extermination—death camps. In the first category, the chance that prisoners would die was great and the prisoners certainly were aware of it—all around them their friends were dying. However, one could try to behave sensibly and to make the most of any opportunity, such as avoiding the quarry and trying to get a job with a roof over your head or with some extra food.

In contrast, the extermination camps were intended solely for the destruction of those who arrived there. According to de Wind the human mind cannot cope with such knowledge. Realizing this reality, de Wind explained, meant insanity or regression to mental childhood. This regression—'going back' to an early phase in psychological development—means living in a state of being in which one no longer calculates any future, but just survives by the minute and by the day. At the same time, however, to survive one should not give up hope and stop caring, as this means certain death. Trying to survive requires a two-way mental habitus: regression on one side, and constant alertness on the other. After their liberation those who had escaped the gas chambers faced the mental task of recovering from this regression. Such a recovery demanded immense personal care, attention, and professional therapists who were capable and willing to descend into imagining the hell that their patients had actually lived in. None of these were available.

Not writing in any post-war Dutch periodical but nevertheless remarkable in his sharp foresight of possible health damage was military psychiatrist Joost A.M. Meerloo (1903–1976). In the early war years Meerloo, who worked for the psychology department of the war ministry, published a book and several articles on the psychiatry of war and peace. In 1942 he fled to England, where he was one of the authors of the UNRRA (United Nations Relief and Rehabilitation Administration) report of June 1945 on the expected 'Psychological problems of displaced persons' (UNRRA Inter-Allied Psychological Study Group 1945). He also wrote a military report in Dutch in which he warned that the 'lost psychological balance' would prove a larger problem than the physical damage. Regression, vulgarization, feelings of inferiority and distrust, feelings of superiority, cynicism and nihilism were among the possible psychological outcomes of the war years. Meerloo particularly pointed out the burden that the lack of privacy in the camps put on psychological well-being.

If authors like de Wind, Meerloo and Tas had insights like this, why did care fail and why did public and medical interest in this group so urgently in need of help disappear?

It is important to realize that the victims, and most of all the Jewish victims, often kept silent, not only because their stories frequently were not welcome, but also because their stories were too gruesome to tell. Many victims tried not to remember, and to resume their lives: family, children, and work.

At that time the mental climate was totally different from what it is now. Dutch society was not yet permissive and affluent, but ascetic and austere. Though the liberation had caused joy and spontaneous festivities, individual happiness was no common goal as it is nowadays. The reconstruction of the fatherland required work, not reflection. Silence was golden. It was considered brave to declare the past a closed chapter. Expressing complaints was certainly not considered proper conduct. Psychoanalysis was an avant-garde treatment, known only to a small elite sector of the population. The popular thought was that one was either sane or insane and the insane belonged in asylums. To 'be treated' belonged to that stigmatized world of insanity.

Society was not yet secularized. Priests and clergymen still deeply influenced personal life, and Christianity was still a powerful influence on government. Dutch mental health care in those days was divided along religious lines. After the war it was feared that moral decline and social chaos loomed in these milieus. Would it be possible to discipline the wild unkempt hordes returning from the camps and from the resistance where men and women had had to make their own decisions? Even some of the most law-abiding parts of pre-war Dutch society had acted against the German occupiers and had lived in a state of lawlessness. The supposed threat to the supposed natural male authority received special concern. During the years that men had been in hiding or deported by the Germans, women had acted as heads of their families. In the eyes of the rising profession of social workers, family relations had become abnormal and pathological.

Liberals and social-democrats were also touched by this moral panic. Society had to be disciplined and normalized. 'Reconstruction moralism' was also no stranger to psychiatry. In these first post-war years one could roughly distinguish two perspectives. Doctors who had themselves survived a camp or had been in hiding tended to be more concerned about psychological damage and personal unhappiness than about moral decline and social chaos. On the other side, professionals and spiritual leaders were afraid that society would not succeed in returning people to normality.

The first approach focused on damaged individuals, the second on society as a whole. Stimulated by the fact that by then a new war had started (the Cold War), the latter won.

## 1948–1968

I will address the influence of the beginning of the Cold War on this development later, but the shift to social normalization was also an outcome of former psychiatric opinions. Analyzing contemporary publications one notices how fear of social unrest gained priority over concern about damaged individuals.

Unlike Germany and Great Britain the Netherlands did not participate in WWI, so Kriegsneurose (shell-shock), was not a Dutch disease. In connection with insurance pensions, however, the Dutch medical world during the thirties was aware of the debates about the psychogenesis of this disorder and had discussions about 'traumatic neurosis'—the phenomenon that people do not recover from work accidents, for instance, even when their physical health is restored. Could fright, shock, powerlessness or confrontation with death by themselves cause illness and inability to work? Two central issues from this pre-war debate returned in the post-war medical thinking on war trauma: *ziektewinst* (secondary gain) and *premorbide persoonlijkheid* (pre-morbid personality).

The first dilemma, secondary gain, concerns the question as to whether immaterial and material attention (such as pensions and treatment) might keep patients ill. The psychodynamics of secondary gain differ from malingering (a malingerer is not ill, secondary gain is illness caused by social arrangements that make it more comfortable to stay ill than to take up daily tasks again), but the two are often mentioned in the same breath. In combination with the above-mentioned moral panic, the concept of secondary gain led to the conclusion that 'spoiling' people would confirm their neuroticism and maladjustment.

The second pre-war concept to be continued after 1945 was so-called pre-morbidity; this concerns predisposition and is a classic issue indeed. The central question here was: Is it possible that dramatic events or stressful periods would cause damage in a person who before the event had been a healthy, non-neurotic, stable adult personality? This in particular was a problem for psychoanalysts, as according to classic theory, neurosis is rooted in childhood. How to relate camp experiences to oedipal conflict? In those years the concept was still war neurosis, not yet trauma or post-concentration camp syndrome.

During the fifties and early sixties dominant medical opinion held that those who did not recover from their wartime experiences had been vulnerable before the war. Their symptoms were not caused by the war but expressed pre-existing neuroticism. In daily medical practice the concepts 'secondary gain' and 'predisposition' were often tainted with arrogance, paternalism and distrust. Many medical practitioners lacked knowledge about what some of their patients had gone through. However, their conclusion that most war victims would recover without special attention was confirmed by the fact that few patients still seemed to suffer from war illnesses. A relative outsider could believe in good faith that war victims had recovered. This statement, to be sure, neglected complaints like sleeplessness, nightmares and mild or severe obsessive behavior, but in those days complaints like that were privately borne, suffered in silence and more often than not accepted as peculiarities one lived with. Victims were not aware that others suffered similar complaints, or that one could ask one's doctor for help.

## 1968–1972

As statistics show, this situation changed radically at the end of the sixties. Regrettably I do not have data on the health of Jewish survivors. In the law on which I base my information—the 1947 law on war pensions, WBP (Wet Buitengewoon Pensioen (Law on Extraordinary Pensions))—only resistance fighters and their next of kin were entitled to allowances. Jewish victims deported because of their 'race' and not because of resistance activities did not qualify. We therefore have no statistics on their health.

The WBP awarded pensions to widows and children of resistance fighters who had been killed. Between 1947 and 1970 about 90% of the pensions went to these relatives. In addition, pensions were given to resistance fighters who, because of illness after the war, could not earn a living. Although it may seem heartless that in 1947 the former resistance achieved a pension only for 'themselves,' history offers an explanation for this outcome.

During the occupation years one major concern was the fate of the children and widows if resistance men were killed. Most of these men were not soldiers. They received no wages for their activities against the German occupation and in peacetime earned their living with normal jobs. To make it possible for these men to participate in the resistance, others would have to take care of their wives and children, even more so if they died, were arrested or went underground.

To this end a very clever support structure was set up to provide for the families of resistance fighters during the war. At the same time, the Dutch government operating from exile in London promised that no family should worry about the future. Post-war Dutch society would gratefully take responsibility for the next of kin of all those who fell fighting for their country.

And so it was. In the autumn of 1944 foremen of the Dutch resistance founded the 'Stichting 1940–1945' (Foundation 1940–1945) that would take care of invalid comrades and the next of kin of those who had died. Immediately after the liberation money was raised through public collections, legates, voluntary extra work, profits from published autobiographies of ex-political prisoners, and a gift from the Queen. Further, the Stichting brought heavy political pressure on the first post-war governments in order to achieve the WBP and played a large role in the grounding of the law's juridical philosophy. The WBP law was based on the philosophy of 'fictional state employment.' The resistance fighter or his next of kin got a pension as if he had been employed as a civil servant during the war; he was supposed to have been under contract with the state. Following this philosophy, the funds necessary to pay WBP pensions largely came from the state.

In 1945 the Stichting also started some clinics where former resistance fighters could regain their health. Most illnesses of the men and women of the resistance were due to camp life, for instance tuberculosis and hunger oedema, but in cases where no clear physical disorder was established the ailments were nevertheless assumed to be physical. Psychological disorders in this rather masculine milieu were not considered—not by the patients themselves, but even less by the resistance elite, afraid as they were of social chaos and of spoiling people into lasting maladjustment. The prescription was: get back to normal. In accordance with the following WBP statistics, the clinics were closed around 1950.

The graphics on the numbers of applicants for a resistance pension follow the same pattern as discussed above in relation to monuments and publications. In the early fifties the number of new applications declined so sharply that government considered discontinuing the WBP arrangement. The sick had recovered. Then, quite suddenly, from the end of the sixties onwards large numbers of new applicants knocked on the doors of the WBP. Whereas in the twenty years between 1950 and 1970 approximately 6000 new clients requested a pension, in the following ten years some 8000 members of the former resistance applied. With a rapidly decreasing population, the number of applicants almost tripled.

A WBP pension is not supposed to be a compensation for hardships; it compensates for loss of earning capacity due to invalidity as a consequence of resistance activities. To be entitled, one must be ill and the illness must be caused by the war. My data show that a quarter of a century after the war many people became ill, or thought of themselves as ill, as a consequence of their wartime activities.

What then were their ailments? Almost all problems were psychological. Some doctors tried to distinguish different forms of psychological consequences, such as psychosomatic and psychogenic impacts. However, it proved impossible to use this precise classification in medical practice. Most of the complaints were vaguely somatic without discernible physical substrate. Eddy de Wind, one of the first to observe the mysterious wave of new patients, introduced the generic title 'late consequences' (de Wind 1966), to stress that the new patients seemed to have been functioning well for some twenty five years.

The fact that no clear physical cause could be established in most of the new cases caused problems in the medical examination procedure prior to the granting of a WBP allowance. Conflicts arose about the question as to whether or not these psychological handicaps were caused by the war. After all, if the patient had always been weak, he was not entitled to apply for a pension.

This suspicious approach, however, and the accompanying concepts of pre-morbidity and secondary gain, were fast becoming socially unacceptable. Times were changing. Patients not only grew in numbers but also in assertiveness. They started protesting against the often very long and bureaucratic admittance procedure and against what they considered the arrogant, ignorant and insensitive attitude of the medical examiners who decided on 'their' WBP entitlement. The protesters had the wind of democratization in their sails. More than before, authorities felt obliged to listen. Victims more and more were considered worthy participants in the debate about their treatment. Organizations were set up as well as pressure groups demanding faster procedures, higher pensions and broad admittance criteria. Further, the patients' protests won support from some doctors who were willing to support their patients when they appealed negative WBP decisions. These doctors confirmed that more former camp prisoners and former members of the resistance had breakdowns, and—an important additional note—that these were patients who had successfully rebuilt their lives after the war. They blamed their colleagues for their lack of understanding of the 'post-concentration camp syndrome.' They presented as new medical insight that their patients' breakdowns were the late consequences of their war experiences followed by hard work and deep silence after the war.

Quite a fundamental result of this development was that it became taboo to look into the pre-war medical history of patients or to consider the possibility that a pension might prevent recovery. In the light of the growing number of new patients, the lack of evidence-based medical theory on their ailments and the general feeling that these victims had long been neglected, the most humane medical practice then seemed to be to throw the concepts of pre-morbidity and secondary gain on the social and scientific rubbish dump. Though it was rarely possible to prove any hard causal relationship between health complaints and war past, it was considered inappropriate to burden the victims with the task of proving their case or going through lengthy and demanding appeal procedures. More often than not this first generation of patients felt ashamed about their symptoms, and furthermore, had they not suffered enough during the war?

In 1971 the law was adapted to the new practice that the burden of proof that one's ailments were caused by the war no longer rested on the plaintiff. The burden of proof was reversed: from now on, when a person who could prove that s/he had been a member of the resistance developed health problems, these problems, whatever their nature, were assumed to be caused by the war.

Contrary to usual assumptions and pretensions, I do not consider this psychiatric paradigm changed the pure result of medical 'progress.' The social, political, cultural and mental revolution of the sixties steered medical opinion about the possible consequences of war. The medical turnabout also expressed itself in the conviction that the late consequences were due to decades of lack of 'recognition.' Whereas doctors, the resistance elite, and the public at large around 1950 assumed that attention would result in psychological weakness, in 1975 a lack of attention was assumed to be the cause of psychological weakness (which was no longer labeled 'weakness' but was transformed into 'disorder'). This theory caught on—the victims, the public, the medical and psychological professions, and last but not least politicians, all took to it.

In her dissertation on the 1972 affair surrounding the 'Breda Three,' historian Hinke Piersma (2005) shows that in 1972 the new responsiveness to victims, and to the recently discovered KZ (concentration camp) syndrome, influenced the decision made by the Dutch Lower House to not release the infamous Three after all. Nobody wanted to be accused of repeating earlier wrongs. Nobody wanted to be accused of a prolonged lack of attention for wartime suffering.

**Victim organizations 1945–1972**

In 1972 developments in the medical-psychological approach toward the health consequences of the war visibly crossed the post-war social and political history of the war victims. The case of the 'Breda Three' illustrates how interwoven these two seemingly separate fields became.

One of the reasons the opposition against the minister's plan won was that the minister found himself opposite a united front of resistance fighters and Jewish survivors. Until then no such united front had existed. The victims had been divided for many years.

Since the war a gap had existed between organizations of the former resistance and the Jewish survivors. Immediately after the liberation, ex-resistance fighters established associations to organize reunions and to lobby for pensions However, the most important of these post-war organizations excluded Jewish members who had not been active in the resistance movement. For instance, a condition for membership of the Association of Ex-Political Prisoners (Expogé), a large organization with strong political connections founded in September 1945, was imprisonment. This imprisonment had to have been punishment for resistance activities; Jews who had been deported 'solely' because of their being Jewish were excluded. The Jewish survivors as Jews lacked this kind of politically influential organizations and strong pressure groups.

Besides the gap between Jewish victims and resistance, the Cold War produced intense hostility among the former resistance members themselves. The optimistic feeling of 1945 that the pre-war religious, political and class distinctions would disappear in the new Netherlands thanks to the togetherness of the war years, rapidly melted away. The communists, who had met with goodwill after the liberation because of their courageous resistance to the Germans and their big losses, became the new enemy around 1948. For Expogé the fight against communism became an important goal; an initial step in this endeavour—following the 1948 coup in Prague—was the expulsion of the many communists from the organization. From 1949 onwards, former concentration camp inmates belonging to the Dutch communist party (CPN) or any of its front organizations could no longer be members of this association of political prisoners.

On the list of communist front organizations the so-called 'camp committees' figured highly. Contrary to their image, these *amicales* (as they are internationally called) were in no way simply supportive clubs of fellow sufferers. They often had hidden political goals. Former prisoners fought bitterly about the camp remembrance. Some committees became bulwarks of communist political manoeuvering; the communist victims linked the remembrance of the camps directly to their actual political struggle against the Dutch government. Even the firmly anti-communist Dachau committee could not obtain Expogé support for their efforts to make the former concentration camp Dachau (situated near Munich in the western part of Germany) into a place of remembrance—so risky did the organization think it was to start an amicale. Communists, Expogé feared, would take over and abuse the camp remembrance for their own political purposes. Better no monuments and reunions of former camp inmates at all, Expogé decided, than running the risk of supporting a front organization.

Especially distrusted by the government and by the non-communist ex-resistance was the Netherlands' Auschwitz Committee (NAC) that started in 1956. The Polish government took the initiative to start an

Auschwitz Committee and the NAC board indeed consisted mainly of communist party members. During the Cold War the Jews, one might say, fell between the cracks. On the one hand Expogé fought communism (and considered the NAC to be communist) and fostered its active resistance identity (as opposed to Jewish victimization). On the other, communist ideology saw capitalism as the enemy and included Jewish victims among all victims of Nazism, denying that there was anything special about this group.

While communists during the Cold War saw capitalism as a first stage of fascism, their counterparts (and former camp-mates) in Expogé saw communism as a new form of totalitarianism. Both conflicting sides of the former resistance defined the Cold War within the frame of WWII. For Expogé, as it defined itself during the fifties, WWII had been a war against totalitarianism and now a new totalitarian threat had to be confronted, a threat Dutch communists were part of. The communists in their turn stated progressively that WWII had essentially been a war against communism. The two contradicting views of the former resistance thus mirrored each other. Both groups emotionally and cognitively continued WWII.

To formulate it in another way: during the coldest Cold War years WWII was defined within a political paradigm. In this political paradigm victims could be enemies. The perspective on the violence of 1940–1945 was not psychological but political. At the same time— and this is a remarkable finding—nobody in those years appeared to be suffering from war trauma.

## The development of a war welfare policy, 1972–1980

Between 1948 and 1972 victims were deeply divided. However, in the seventies the landscape of the Dutch survivor organizations radically changed. The clash between the war victims and the Minister of Justice around the 'Breda Three' was in fact the first occasion when Expogé, NAC and the communist resistance acted together. From the seventies onward communist and non-communist, Jewish and non-Jewish survivors found common goals. Their united performance resulted in new forms of cooperation that in later years strongly influenced government policy on issues concerning WWII, especially regarding war criminals and government provisions such as pensions and mental health care for war trauma victims.

To give one striking example of these changes, during the sixties the NAC, still under suspicion of being a front organization, demanded that invalid or ill Jewish survivors should be entitled to a WBP-pension. This claim was still rejected as late as 1968. After 1972, however, when the Cold War ebbed away and the concept of post-concentration camp syndrome became widely accepted, the NAC became a respected committee. The claim for a pension now got the support of the former resistance and in 1973 a new law was passed (the 'WUV') that entitled Jewish war victims to a state pension.

After decades of bitter hostilities, this psychological approach of the past brought about a new unity among the former resistance and among resistance organizations and Jewish organizations. Seeing each other as victims suffering from trauma transcended former disagreements. 'Aren't they victims as well?,' asked the president of the non-communist Buchenwald amicale rhetorically.

During the parliamentary debate on the Breda Three the minister could not help but notice the change in atmosphere, and realized that this unwelcome development was brought about by the sudden massive realization of how many people still suffered from their wartime experiences. One of his attempts to hold to his plan to release the three German prisoners was the strategic offer to start a special war trauma clinic. This proposal was rejected; or, more precisely, the offer was insufficient. The victims, supported by public opinion impressed by the victims' testimonies, asked for more: they wanted the clinic and they wanted the minister's plan abandoned. The proposed exchange was rejected. The victims claimed both and achieved both—and even more. Within months after the debate the construction started of the specialized war trauma clinic. The clinic opened in the same year the WUV was introduced, which also granted pensions to people who had been interned in the camps in the Netherlands' Indies during the Japanese occupation and who had returned to Holland during or after the Indonesian struggle for independence. Last but not least, in 1984 a law granting compensation for so-called 'civilian war victims' was enacted.

From the seventies onwards psychological war damage became a national issue and an important target of governmental policy. A war welfare department was set up, a help-desk installed, mental health professionals were informed about war trauma, brochures and books were published, victim groups were initiated, pilgrimages to the camps by victims and their families were funded, et cetera. Psychotherapy for the first and second generation war victims was paid for by the government, and psychotraumatology developed into an accepted medical discipline. Further, the governmental promise that no war criminal would be released without the consent of the victims rested on the assumption that release would aggravate their traumatic pain.

When the American Psychiatric Association recognized PTSD as a disorder in 1980, this decision was warmly welcomed by Dutch war professionals, who long had wrestled with the question as to what to call the new war illness. 'War neurosis' was taboo because it was not a neurosis, that is to say: the cause of the disorder was clearly not located in childhood experiences. 'Post-concentration camp syndrome' failed because many kinds of war victims had never been in a camp. The new official disorder united all the victims and seemed to end, once and for all, the old debates on predisposition and secondary gain.

War trauma and trauma in general became basic social knowledge, a development stimulated by the fact that the Dutch government founded a sizeable apparatus to propagate these new medical insights. Mental weaknesses that once had been private and shameful disrespect now became public and even respectable—on one condition, the suffering should be caused by a respectable trauma like 'the war.'

## Conclusion: Distinctions lost

Relating the four periods I distinguished in medical-psychological thinking on mental war damage to the social history of the victims and to the political, cultural and mental changes since 1945, we find some striking correlations.

### 1945–1948
- National reconstruction
- No Jewish organizations; strong, rather masculine resistance organizations taking the initiative to care for their invalid companions and for the widows and children of the dead
- Stigma on psychological disorders; fear of maladjustment, spoiling and social disorder among mental health professionals and among the resistance elite; the early understanding of possible psychological consequences disappears; no visible or expressed psychological complaints

### 1948–1968
- Cold War, relative public silence on WWII
- Fierce conflicts between the communist and the non-communist members of the former resistance; large gap between resistance and Jewish survivors
- Low prevalence of psychological war disorders

**1968–1980**
- End of interior Cold War; growing interest in WWII; mental and cultural changes towards democratization, emancipation, expression of emotions
- Diminishing of conflicts among the resistance and of gap between resistance and Jewish survivors
- Discovery and public knowledge of post-concentration camp syndrome; growing number of patients; new laws, new provisions

**1980–2005**
- Culture of trauma: DSM recognition of 'PTSD'; more and more organizations of all kinds of categories of (war) victims; ever more people identify themselves as being 'traumatized.'

The early post-war concern about individual psychological damage disappeared as the Cold War reigned and the victim organizations split along the political lines of the Cold War. Recognition of possible psychological trauma re-appeared as the Cold War ended and victim organizations were again on speaking terms. Or, putting it another way, seeing war survivors as victims of psychological damage reinforced the lessening of hostilities that came with the decline of the Cold War.

Both developments together brought about a new unity amongst victims, and this unity—though never free of tensions and always fragile—in turn strengthened the tendency to define survivors primarily as victims of trauma. More than that, it swept away meaningful differences in war experience, background, world view and degree of suffering.

The results of my research show that the former hostilities softened not only because of the decline of the Cold War but also as a result of the fast development of a trauma culture in the Netherlands. As much as politics had divided ex-prisoners, psychology united them and offered opportunities and common goals in demanding provisions for their welfare.

The fragile unity of the survivors, which was shattered soon after the war, was revived thanks to the psychological outlook on the past. WWII was transformed from a political issue concerning totalitarianism (in which former communist prisoners were seen as future enemies), into a psychological issue in which all political prisoners, resistance fighters and Jewish survivors (and other, new, victim groups) were the possible or even probable victims of traumatic stress. This brought material as well as immaterial profits: victims could feel progressive and liberal in overcoming their distance towards the former communist resistance and were collectively rewarded with ample provisions.

The concept of PTSD stimulates this mutual 'recognition': are we all not suffering from the same disorder? The Dutch model of war welfare policy stimulated a victim unity that neglects or even denies real differences. Distinctions were lost in a compelling atmosphere of mutual recognition (and as a consequence of rivalry at the same time). Uniting all survivors under the label 'victims of war trauma' and tabooing differences as an unwanted 'hierarchy of suffering' blends historically different experiences. The late discovery of war trauma in the Netherlands was an ambivalent process of recognition and denial at the same time.

## Acknowledgement

Translation of this article was made possible by financial support from Vertaalfonds KNAW/Stichting Reprorecht.

# 9
# Can One Still Live Happily After Chernobyl?

*Bernard Paillard*

> All men are looking for happiness. There is no exception, whatever the way they are attempting to use. They all aim to reach happiness (...). This is the reason for all of their actions. Even for those people who decide to hang themselves.
>
> Blaise Pascal, *Pensée, 181*, (2004 [1670])

April 26, 1986: the date still haunts one's memory as the largest industrial disaster of its kind. Some would even measure other accidents, past, present or future, against it, even if, for some others, the Bhopal disaster (3 December 1984), that caused the deaths of 15,000 people and had long-term impacts on a further 500,000 people, represented a more considerable disaster. In the collective psyche, the Bhopal disaster has been replaced by the Chernobyl one which, taking place only two years later, has now become the ultimate symbol of an apocalyptic-scale catastrophe presenting all the characteristics of absolute evil. To be sure about it one only needs to check the Internet where numerous French websites give frightening statistics: 9,000,000 victims;[1] Hundreds of thousands of recorded deaths, with many more expected in the years ahead;[2] Huge increase in the number of unexplained deaths whose causes/symptoms have often been explained due to exposure to high radiation; A never before seen increase in the number of children with malformations or even genetic mutations;[3] Some geographic areas have now become No Man's Land for the coming hundreds, if not thousands, of years.[4]

In such a situation, one could rightly wonder if it would not be considered insulting to ask if people living in these territories could actually enjoy any time of happiness in their daily life. They must all be in constant pain, and if one had to think of a sociology type to describe life there, the sociology of sadness and despair would be the first to come to mind.

Those French Internet reports, however, are not representative of most online reports written about Chernobyl. English language reports posted online, for example, do not focus as much on those cataclysmic views. When reading detailed reports of the UN's International Agency for Atomic Energy (IAEA) or the UN's Scientific Committee on the Effects of Atomic Radiations, one will find a much less pessimistic view. Both organizations register lower numbers of deaths and expect fewer in the future, as well as lower numbers of illnesses. Daily life there does not seem as apocalyptic as described online, even if people have to face, without doubt, economic, social and psychological hardship.

Some people would consider the measures that have been taken to keep people away from their lands ridiculous, asserting that, except in a defined 'No go area,' one could perfectly live in such a world, even knowing the likely risks of contamination, and one could even expect to have a little happiness, too. Consequently, a sociology of this happiness could even be analyzed. Is such a controversial idea sustainable?

## Itinerary in contaminated zones

When I first visited Narovlia, one of the most contaminated areas of the Belarus Republic,[5] in June 2000 I did not have a clue how people were living there. One of my colleagues who, some years earlier, had traveled to a less contaminated territory, had told me of his experience and I was expecting to see a plethora of children and people presenting symptoms of numerous illnesses. My initial expectation therefore was a very pessimistic one and was reinforced by my first visit to the forbidden zone, seeing abandoned houses, gardens, uncultivated fields and deserted forests, making me even more apprehensive of what I would discover. All were symptoms of an invisible evil, as obvious as if there were those yellow signs with a black symbol usually used to signal nuclear sites: beware—nuclear risk. Words such as 'cancer,' 'leukemia' or 'thyroid'[6] were coming almost obsessively to my mind, to such a point that I could imagine seeing a child with leukemia. He had such short hair I believed he had had chemotherapy.

# Can One Still Live Happily After Chernobyl? 143

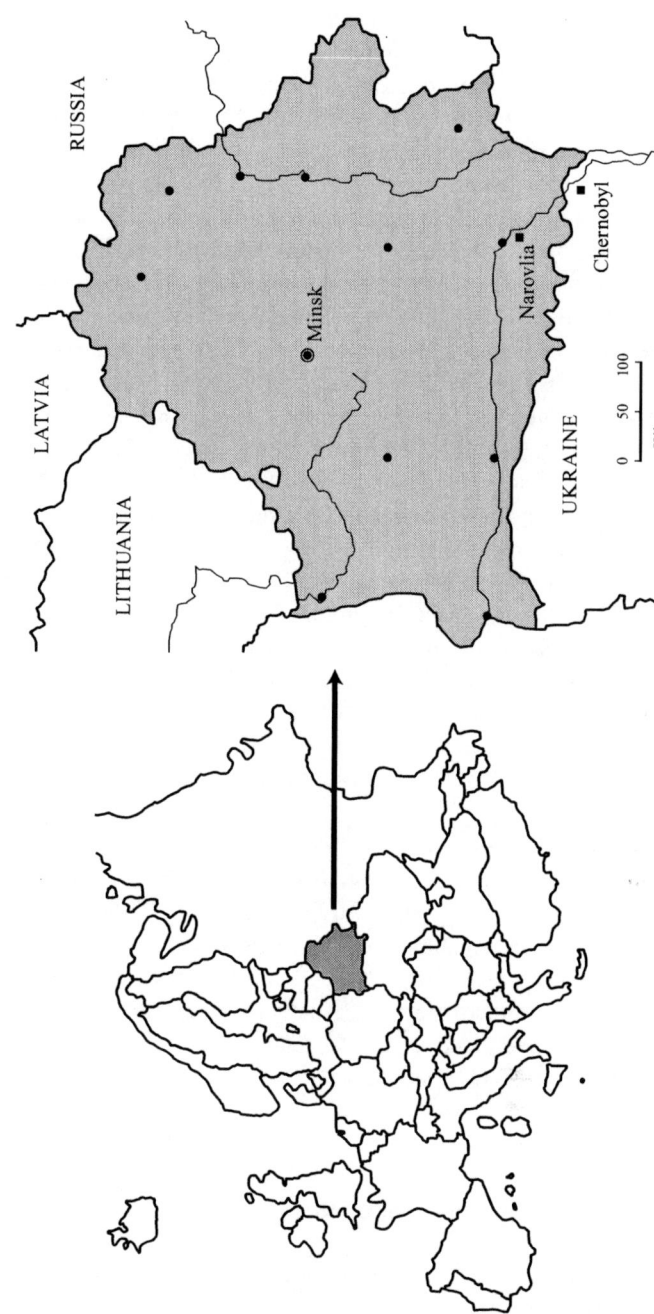

Figure 9.1: Geographical location of Belarus, Narovlia and Chernobyl

It was truly easier to interpret everything through this pessimistic lens; even the happiest behaviors, such as scenes of vodka drunkenness which could be interpreted by some as signs of immense despair, or others, more jubilatory, as manifestations of a will to forget radiation. Others could have simply seen those as proof of an ordinary active social life that keeps going even if located in a risky environment.

After having made myself more familiar with daily life in Narovlia, I had to acknowledge that the thirst for life and its numerous pleasures had not disappeared. Young people loved going out and dancing to the sound of Belarus' 'techno' music and, like many others of their age in the West, smoked pot. Women were pushing prams while playing with their babies. Some were even meeting for a meal at a restaurant on 8 March, a holiday celebrating Belarus's women. Between two meals or two vodka shots, all of them were singing or dancing.

Dancing and singing, supposedly the 'trademark' of Slavic people, was obviously still practiced, the same way as activities so typical of their culture, like winter fishing expeditions during which men can remain several hours near the hole they made in Pripyat's ice,[7] thanks to the long metallic hook they use to break the ice. While fishing in Spring or Summer, fishermen use their catch for their own consumption or to make a wood-fired bouillabaisse that is eaten on the spot. On days off, such as 9 May, the day the Red Army defeated the Nazis, family picnics take place along the river or in gardens near the city, before the whole family attends celebrations organized by the authorities. During holidays, some school children are dispatched to some European countries, thanks to a non government organization called Chernobyl's Children. Wealthier families will often go to the Black Sea in Crimea for their holidays while those who cannot afford holidays remain in their house and enjoy Summer there. These occurrences are proof that the vision of a dark and sinister post-Chernobyl era does not stand up under closer examination: there is life, happiness and *joie de vivre* in Chernobyl and the people even make a harsh everyday life easier to bear.

## General outlook

### A worrying national conjuncture

The people of Narovlia are living in one of the most contaminated areas (between fifteen and forty $Ci/km^2$ and sometimes even more[8]); the city and the nuclear plant being only about seventy kilometers

*Figure 9.2: Levels of contamination, from darkest to lightest shade*

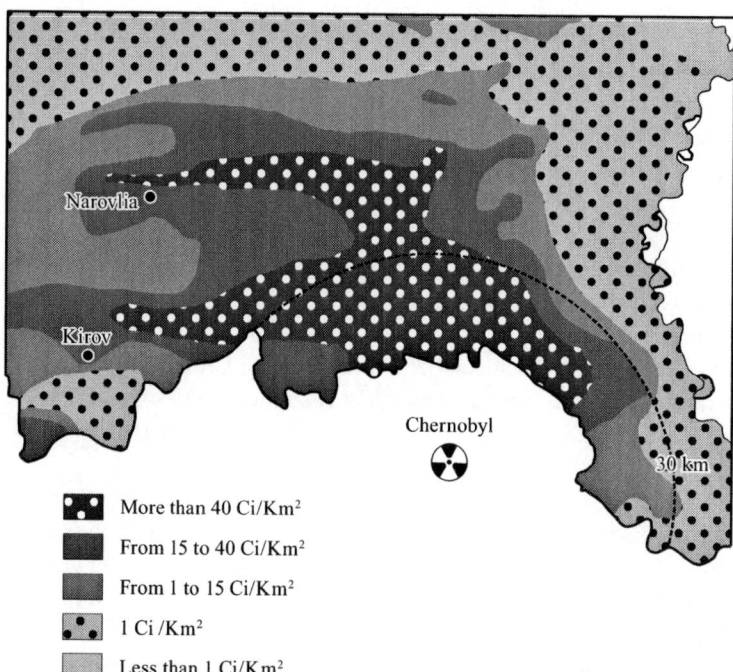

away from each other. This whole area, which represents a triangle measuring approximately forty kilometers at its base and seventy kilometers in height (160,000 hectares), is mostly centered on agriculture and forestry industries. But about one third of this ground has been included in the so-called thirty kilometer perimeter (in which all human activities have been banned) while two-thirds of the rest of this zone are still contaminated. Thirty-six villages were evacuated soon after the accident and the population as a whole was expected to be relocated to 'clean areas.' This decision, taken by Moscow at a time when Belorussia was still part of its empire, has never been implemented. Such a massive relocation implied building new cities from scratch, the creation of new economic zones, and last but not least, a sanitation and social system—all things the tormented USSR, on the verge of collapsing, could not (or did not want to) implement.

Consequently, after the USSR collapsed, the newly independent Belarus republic had to face the consequences of this disaster alone. In 1991, a law was passed classifying the national territory in five areas according to their contamination: less than one $Ci/km^2$, from one to five Ci/km² (29,000 km²), from five to fifteen Ci/km² (10,000 km²), from fifteen to forty Ci/km² (4200 km²), and forty and higher Ci/km² (2200 km²). This classification was used to help define and check levels of radioactivity and set a surveillance standard, and also to grant different advantages to locals.

People living in 15 Ci/km² contaminated zones, as was the case with Narovlia, have been relocated to non-contaminated areas. They were granted priority when applying for positions and were entitled to free healthcare if their pathologies were recognized as consequences of radioactive fallout. While waiting to be relocated, they were granted further advantages: wage increases, free food for school children who were also entitled to two month-long trips out of the contaminated area (and cared for in specialized facilities) and holidays in a foreign country, as well as a regular health check (once a year for the whole population, twice a year for children). Finally, the whole territory was under radiological watch.[9]

All of this is expensive: the cost of damages for the Belarus Republic over the next thirty years has been estimated at US$235 billion, thirty-two times the 1985 Belarussian national budget. This global cost is the sum of the loss of agricultural production and forest exploitation. This figure also takes into consideration additional amounts of money spent on healthcare for locals, on the reorganization of, and support for, the agriculture sector, for soil decontamination, radiological watch, building new infrastructure and accommodation, providing compensation to locals and so on.[10] All of this has been implemented by a highly centralized state which is very reluctant to accept outside aid and which leaves very little or no room for private initiatives.[11]

As a result, the Belorussian Republic's 1996 GDP represented only sixty per cent of its 1991 GDP. Its national economy, based on the socialist division of production, had to find new foreign markets to sell its industrial production and to create new consumer goods.[12]

## A deteriorating local situation

Decisions to evacuate populations from the Narovlia District taken in 1991, were postponed in 1996 as the state became overwhelmed with demands for relocation. Radioactivity measurement standards were also changed and, as a result, Narovlia lost its priority status. In 2001, only inhabitants of the thirteen villages closest to the exclusion zone were entitled to apply for relocation, representing 629 families, or a total of 1239 people. This represented less than two persons per family, most of them being old and not willing to leave the village where they were born anyway. What would these people who had spent their life in the country do in big cities? They knew that their new life there would not be easy, as proven by formerly relocated people who returned to their village to tell about their bad experience but had therefore lost the right to be relocated again.

Since 1986 however, about 15,300 people (or a little over half the population) have relocated. This demographic hemorrhaging has had a tremendous impact on the regional and local economies, making life harder for the 12,500 people who remained and have to survive in a deteriorated economy with fifty per cent of the land of this mostly agricultural district (including the best lands near the Pripyat river) now unable to be exploited and only seven kolkhozes (collective farms) still in use (compared to fifteen before the accident.)

As agricultural production is decreasing, its cost is constantly rising due to the expensive measures needed to deal with soil pollution. There was firstly a need to register the different fields and their level of contamination while hiring radiological experts who people call 'radiologists.' The lack of specialists in other fields (agronomists, veterinarians, agricultural technicians and so on) has had an impact on the production itself, its output and the quality of agricultural products. The district is now 'in the red.'

Another major resource is the forest industry, but in this case too, most of the wood cannot be sold, putting more financial pressure on the region. Forest management has become a specialized area and qualified specialists as well as loggers are bitterly absent, because, even in the case of contaminated forests, one has to remain vigilant against bush fires that could, through ashes, concentrate radioactivity and be blown by the wind. In order to partly protect them from radiation, workers take short shifts, wear special protective clothes and, in the most contaminated areas, 'decontamination rooms' have been built, as even forests out of the excluded zone are under strict watch.

Dealing with this issue has been made even more difficult due to the lack of local qualified workers, engineers and managers who have all left. Measures were taken to retain or attract young educated and dynamic populations but they all failed.

The first people to make the move into the area, however, were not the expected specialists but victims of wars or those coming from poorer parts of the former Soviet Union who were attracted to the area by the various promised incentives, such as low-rent accommodation, free food for children and other advantages. Nowadays some villages are full of migrants originating from Kazakhstan, Chechnya, Russia and Siberia. Some people unable to adjust are facing issues typical to other migrants: marginalization, family breakup and divorce, social instability, alcoholism, etc.

The first issue, consequently, is one of public health. Families most at risk of propagation of contamination are usually the poorest and most marginalized, those whose family cell has been broken, those who are victims of psychological and moral suffering. Some of these families are said to be sometimes completely opposed to medical staff and the care they provide, to the point that sometimes, material support and food assistance is provided by schools that dress and feed people as well as prescribe medicines. In some far away places, distant from urban centers, schools may be the only bulwark, the last refuge for children living in absolute poverty.

If marginalization can increase the feeling of indifference to the sad reality of contamination, other issues can also help explain such indifference. The most obvious one is the general poverty, whether among the rural population (people working either in fields or the forest industry) or the retired workers who are only surviving on their homegrown vegetables, fruits and some hunting. These are all foods which, in addition to the absorption of cow milk, are responsible for the propagation of radioactive contamination! On top of this, teenagers with their traditional divergent attitude give way to a situation in which taking risks become a daily routine (the classical phenomena of 'relapse'[13]).

## Daily duty

Such a broad description nevertheless gives an idea of the depth and complexity of crises finding their origin in the Chernobyl accident. Local authorities (co-op and union managers) not only have to face the lack of a skilled workforce and of expertise but are also facing local traditions: there are numerous stories of workers in Kolkhozes who do not show up and instead go to pick mushrooms and blueberries they will sell at markets to make extra cash. If they are lucky, they could manage to earn as much as a full month's wage in one day. Their harvest is often sold to itinerant sellers who come 'en masse' from the capital city 400 kilometers away.

In all these rural areas there is still today a very strong underground economy of fruit picking, hunting, fishing and even cattle grazing, all of which are most likely to end up in local market stalls and therefore not likely to be detected by the State's anti-radiation watchdog. Consequently, locals in rural areas are being fed radioactive food coming directly from their own backyards. This can only increase their own level of contamination as well as that of their relatives.

## Hygienic consequences

In Narovlia, of a total population of 12,500, 137 people have been registered as suffering from Chernobyl's fallout: thyroid cancers, leukemia and heart conditions. This figure is based on administrative criteria. The census records people who suffer from illnesses atypical for their age group or sex. There is a lack of global epidemiologic studies, however, which could define the different types of illnesses and classify them by group. The general sanitary situation has deteriorated since the end of the USSR due to a serious lack of doctors, proper equipment and medicines. Another startling fact is the increasing development of tuberculosis, a sickness that is usually recorded in poor countries. For now at least, cancers and heart-related diseases are limited to the oldest sector of the population but one can expect the number of young people who will develop thyroid cancers or immunity deficiencies will soon be on the rise. In fact, it is already starting to happen. To make matters worse, alcoholism is also increasing.

## The State and its population

The State only has what one would call a 'primitive' approach to the problem, limiting its action to avoid further contamination of the food-processing industry and only producing edicts in the form of recommendations or advice. It mostly legislates only on the acceptable level of radionuclides and declares precautions that are to be taken when dealing with different situations. It reminds its people where to pick, or not pick fruits, with anyone caught breaking the law likely to be fined the equivalent of nine months' wages. But there is no real repression and there is no real effort toward prevention either: no newspaper ads or TV commercials, no education seminars. Even if there is some discussion about radiological risks as part of the school curriculum, our observation was that it remained purely theoretical.

This lack of a culture of prevention is the best proof of the bureaucratic approach adopted to deal with the consequences of the

Chernobyl accident. Each has its role: the State, through its different layers of bureaucracy, has the duty of ensuring that contamination and its consequences are minimized. The people have the duty to respect laws, rules and regulations. This clear separation is obvious through the whole administrative chain: information and analysis are being sent from the local level and climb up the ladder, rung by rung, to the capital, Minsk. From there, directives and rules which must be obeyed are simply sent in the opposite direction.

The fact that the current regime is presidential increases the 'vertical effect' of the decision-making process. Alexander Loukachenko[14] can directly intervene in local, even minor matters. In Narovlia, he overturned the refusal of local authorities to accept the settlement of Kazakhs in the exclusion zone. Following the same strategy of grassroots involvement, he accepted the demand of Kirov's inhabitants to remove the checkpoint at the exclusion zone's entrance and, in order to demonstrate his desire to help locals, he even gave them a small school bus with a sign that read 'Gift of President Alexander Loukachenko.'

# Daily greed

### Looking backward: Lost happiness

This local situation helps explain the general unhappiness and despair of people there, as Chernobyl symbolizes the breach with what has now often become an idealized past. Idealizing the past is a recognized trend among communities going through difficult times. In Narovlia, however, this tendency is even stronger as the population is rather old. The oldest people remember a time when the district was known for its dynamism, its living standards and enthusiasm, due to the reconstruction efforts following World War II:[15] the construction of new high-rise buildings and housing commissions surrounded by public gardens, the creation of new factories[16] and villages, the increase in size of agricultural areas, mechanical improvements in agriculture and the development of the forest industry. Some still remember, with tears in their eyes, that Narovlia used to be a summer holiday destination where even Russian holiday-makers would come. One also remembers scenes such as gardens full of summer tents and cabins, of summer activities such as sailing, cruising, fishing or swimming in the Pripyat River,[17] sporting events, dancing parties and so on. 'I will only believe in Narovlia's revival when I see tents in the park again,' a local told us.[18]

What holiday-makers coming from cities are missing the most are these small pleasures found in simple activities such as walking in forests while collecting mushrooms and all sorts of berries, activities that have all been banned. The manager of the District's 'Education Committee' told us of his disappointment when, for the first time after fifteen years, he dared to return to the forest where he used to pick mushrooms. He found plenty at the spot he used to find them, each one more tempting than the next. But after a quick check, they were all contaminated. 'Life will never be the same again!' he said, with tears in his eyes. Now retired, the man has left Narovlia.

There used to be life and happiness in pre-Chernobyl Narovlia. There used to be opportunities for young people, some of them hoping to get a position, a better life working for the nuclear plant that was supposed to be extended with an extra three reactors. The nuclear plant was the 'lighthouse' of the region, and the city of Pripyat was the place where workers and their families lived. It was therefore a feature of modernity. There used to be a twice daily service between Narovlia and Pripyat, and it is to Pripyat that people living in Narovlia would look, rather than Mozir, which was closer but offered fewer opportunities.

## A hard life and a missed past

Nowadays, one cannot travel to Pripyat anymore: there is no shuttle service by boat or bus. The road is closed and access to the Ukraine is now cut by barbed wires and watch towers. Narovlia, which used to be a city for travelers, has now become a dead-end; an appendix; a place at the end of the world.

The city, that once was supposed to be evacuated, has not seen any material improvement in its living conditions, whether in infrastructure, equipment or housing. All have slowly deteriorated. It is only due to the forced 're-population' policy that Narovlia rediscovered some of its lost past and beauty. The hotel has undergone renovations, renovated shops are now better provisioned, the only restaurant has upgraded its cellar and even has a jukebox, there are sun-umbrellas under which one can sit while eating ice creams. The whole city is slowly becoming a place of relaxing holidays and leisure, and now even has a certain '*joie de vivre*' reminiscent of the pre-Chernobyl-era.'[19]

Even though life seems to be slowly starting again in Narovlia, locals are struggling to make ends meet. Some are missing the old times when wages and pensions were paid on a regular basis, when the post-war economic boom offered opportunities for a better life. At that time, one was proud to be part of such a strong empire, of such a military and industrial power. The depressed mood is even stronger when one thinks that the country has now become isolated and has to adjust to the market economy system, with Russia refusing to grant it a preferential deal for oil and gas. Overwhelmed by these issues, some are now idealizing the Soviet past.

**Looking inwards**

The renewal of cities has had little impact on the countryside. The Narovlia district still comprises approximately thirty-five villages in which 3500 people live, 2500 of whom survive near the exclusion zone. These abandoned villages, with their struggling economies, have no future. Isolated from the district's main town, they seem barely alive. On top of the soil contamination and the increasing age of the people, direct consequences of post-Soviet reforms are also hitting hard. If these reforms have not fundamentally changed the collective system of agriculture,[20] the need to become profitable has made the weakest kolkhozes more vulnerable.

The Kirov kolkhoz, which is hemmed-in by the forbidden zone, has trouble providing its employees with regular wages, with some receiving about US $15 a month. A little more than 400 people are still living in this village, where the main street leads to a dead-end. The small 'isbas' with their fruit and vegetable gardens surrounding the house, have been built one next to the other for over three kilometers, which does not make the neighborhood very welcoming as many of these houses have been abandoned and are likely to be demolished in the near future. Businesses have not been upgraded; there are no parties, no young people, and no life. The village is not even connected daily with Narovlia anymore.

If one compares this to the period before 1986 however, this village was the symbol of these new structures implanted in the middle of recently cleared forests, with its own decentralized administration. The 1200 inhabitants could then enjoy a school, had their own municipal room, a dedicated youth center and even their own small hospital.[21] The beauty and enthusiasm of local women contributed to the city's reputation as 'Little Paris!'

Nowadays, in the middle of winter, the village looks sinister. Winter is cold, snowy and often foggy and lasts about six months, everyone staying in their home, living on tins and garden vegetables. Some are becoming depressed while others, under the constant influence of alcohol, forget to start their fires or feed their children. Old people do not leave their houses anymore. Forgotten because they are isolated, people are isolating themselves to forget.

## One constant worry: Deteriorating health

This feeling of isolation has been reinforced by the constant worry that parents have for their children. Numerous babies born soon before or after the accident have contracted thyroid cancers and their health is slowly deteriorating. This is the case in Belarus where, due to the poor health system, medical follow up that would not be an issue elsewhere is hard if not impossible to access.[22] Worried parents are trying to detect any symptoms of sickness in their children as their constant watch can help to record symptoms that have never been researched. Without giving credence to the official view that people are now 'Radiophobic'[23] there is a constant apprehension that simply feeds anxiety. The unknown world of atoms and radiation is most often associated with people's fear of the atomic bomb and the constant suspicion of radioactive contamination 'from the outside,' that leads to almost immediate death, and contamination 'from the inside,' that slowly weakens and attacks the body. Even the outside world, such as water in fountains and lakes, or surrounding forests, presents as a constant source of fear, a menace that is initially invisible and unnoticed. The fear of contamination has now been integrated in stories parents tell their children about the dangerous unnatural environment that surrounds them. Parents, mostly those in cities, adopt habits they want their children to also follow, such as never going for a walk in a forest or a swim in a river. Whether these risks are real or imagined, contamination now symbolizes the limited universe in which locals can live and it has become their prime concern, ahead of any other material concern or their constant fear of the future.

This fear, however, is not felt the same way by everyone. It varies according to age, sex, knowledge and whether one comes from the country or city. The fear can be constantly felt or may sometimes disappear and even be forgotten for a while. Homeless people for example, who are more worried about their daily survival, are not as preoccupied. But this fear often leads to all types of sicknesses, social emptiness and, to put it simply, absence of a future.

## A worried youth

Teenagers, especially in the countryside, cannot think clearly about their future. Their isolation, the absence of local meeting places and leisure activities, as well as local jobs, all make them think about moving elsewhere, anywhere else. Even more now that, thanks to the non-governmental organization Chernobyl's Children, most of them have had a taste of and visited a foreign country (trips to Italy, Germany, Belgium, Luxemburg and some to the United States). They have all seen wealth and economic development, in sharp contrast to what they know at home. Their overseas trips have fed their desire to become part of the consumerist society and the easy life that their European *alter ego* are enjoying, such as music and clothes; all the things they cannot access in Belarus. These 'eye-opener' trips, that make teenagers think of their own situation at home, have become a serious concern for the State, with President Loukachenko moving in October 2005 to limit them.[24]

In order to keep its young people in the territory and convince others to move there, the State has taken measures to make access to universities and jobs easier. Grades required to be accepted at university are lower if one decides to work on the contaminated territory.[25] Youth can be given jobs with responsibilities and instant 'upward mobility,' as well as numerous material advantages, including free accommodation. Most people who accept such arrangements however, usually see them as temporary postings, helping them to more quickly climb the professional ladder before being sent to more promising regions. For them, as for most young people, the future is anywhere but here. Is this brain drain, however, the symbol of an aspiration to happiness?

## To escape misfortune

### To forget

If, for some, there is no other solution than attempting to escape, how do people who actually stay manage to protect themselves against defeatism?

In *Civilization and its Discontents*, Freud wrote that 'What one names happiness, in the most restricted meaning of the word, results in some sort of sudden satisfaction of bitterly felt needs, and remains, due to its nature, an episodic phenomena' (1989 [1930]). He added,

'Mankind usually attempts to restrict his/her pretensions to "happiness" (the same way as the principle of pleasure, which morphed under the outside world's pressure to a more modest principle, the one of reality) and one sees him/herself happy to have avoided unhappiness and sufferings; for a general rule, attempting to avoid suffering makes the attempt of reaching ecstasy irrelevant.' Consequently, if one follows this idea, one can still experience happiness, even after suffering the disastrous consequences of Chernobyl!

Attempting to escape from unhappiness could be the key. So what are the prospects for people living in Narovlia?

## Can Chernobyl be dissolved in alcohol?

Freud had seen in the consumption of drugs, one of the illusory solutions to escape unhappiness. In the case of some people living in Narovlia, this is obvious; their daily consumption of vodka is enormous, as evidenced by what one can see by simple observation. Each Saturday, before midday, one can see men holding each other in an attempt to hide the fact they are already drunk. On days off, meals are frequently interrupted by successive toasts in which even some women partake. Winter adds to the isolation due to the city's location in making drinking alone more acceptable. But, can one say that Chernobyl has some responsibility for this behavior? It seems more likely that this attitude is a reflection of ancestral behaviors, even if some used to say that alcohol was a good medicine to help cure radiation. Post-Soviet alcoholism finds its roots in communism's alcoholism, which could also be related to the time of the Czar's oppressive powers. Alcoholism is related to a society in which economic hardship and social instability are growing together, in parallel with a loss of familiar landmarks and lack of socialization.

## Habituation: Forgetting sorrow

The concept of habituation used in psychophysiology and cognitive psychology seems to apply to the case of Chernobyl: twenty years after the explosion, locals have been getting on with their life as they do not actually directly feel the effects of radiation. If one, however, feels worried, he/she may not actually think about leaving this high risk area. Having been acclimatized to the risk, people have been almost getting on with their normal daily lives. This general attitude of 'quiet survival' is usually more characteristic of older people.

Having to struggle with daily life, they seem to underestimate a danger that seems less real than sicknesses they are already experiencing, or that will not change much about their approaching death anyway. Some other people are reacting the exact same way as, for example, people who have come to the region willingly: those who came back to their village of birth after being relocated by force, those who escaped from areas where there was a more imminent danger (war, starvation) and those, who, finally, are wanted by police and found a safe haven in this removed region.

**Escaping the daily blues: Life's small pleasures**

This attitude of living with daily danger leads to a refusal to follow recommendations made by authorities, such as strict enclosure of some areas, recommendations on gardening and agriculture and rules on the levels of acceptable food contamination. General cooking recommendations have been made, such as for the garden, not to use ashes as fertilizer (as it actively concentrates radio-elements) and to use phosphate complements abundantly instead. Washing some types of food in salted water before cooking is also recommended, and people are also advised not to eat any raw or grilled food and are advised to buy food in state-managed supermarkets.

Unfortunately, not everyone follows these recommendations, as this recommended decontamination process make food particularly flavorless. Furthermore, as illustrated in the example of mushrooms that people are forbidden to pick,[26] such customs have been part of ancestral traditions for family meals. These are seen as social occasions and so it is hard, if not impossible, to avoid serving them or eating them.[27] Finally, mushrooms added to different winter meals are among the small extras people can still afford in times of hardship. Banning their consumption would be attempting to go against tradition and ways of life deeply rooted in rural as well as city-style traditions.

Chernobyl has not changed food habits or other moments of happiness in life: family feasts (births, weddings) and days off, meetings and evenings among friends, meals at restaurants, nights out among teenagers, holidays, gardening, picnics and barbecues, fishing or hunting trips, fruit picking,[28] in fact, all activities that make time off work relaxing. One also has to add to this list the 'Russian Bath' (*banya*) which, following the example of the Finnish Spa, remains a strong tradition.[29] The *banya*, a small wood structure built at a distance from the *isba*,[30] is a place for families or friends to gather on Saturdays in summer or winter. During winter, between two hot baths, one would crawl in the snow or jump into a hand-made hole in the iced river. Bathing is fundamental to social as well as family life, not to mention hygienic. People meet in the small room which is used as an entrance, in the changing room when resting between the two baths or while eating a snack with a drink of vodka, beer, kvass[31] or fruit juice.[32] Singing also remains a pleasure one can still afford.

The pleasure of singing has not ceased. Even if Chernobyl has had a tremendous impact on this practice, the main reason behind its current demise has more to do with the number of people that are moving out of Narovlia than anything else. One of the first victims of such moves has been the well-acclaimed Kirov choir that had no choice but to dissolve due to the departure of numerous singers. Schools, however, are attempting to preserve the choir tradition and perpetuate singing traditions: children are taught at an early age the entire register of Russian traditional songs, coming from Belarus as well as the Ukraine. Even in Narovlia, an arts and cultural centre is teaching classical music (piano, violin) as well as how to play traditional instruments.

## One escape: Nature

Music, singing and dancing are, for most, the remaining pleasures of a blinkered life. Some prefer finding refuge in nature, the other main component of Russian culture. Nature and its pantheistic cult coming from old Slavic traditions have remained preponderant in oral tradition, popular history and traditional songs, despite successive waves of Christianity. Surviving communism, some aspects were absorbed into days of celebration of the communist area, as for example, Women's day[33] (8 March), a public holiday that symbolizes the approach of spring, and the end of World War II ('the Great Patriotic War') celebrations on 9 May[34] which, with snow melting all around, symbolizes the actual start of spring. On that day off, families go for picnics and barbecues and spend evenings in gardens as mosquitoes are not yet out. This is the beginning of a communion with nature which will only weaken with October's first snowflakes. Winter will make some happy, as for example, fishermen who can spend days looking into their ice holes.

Because of the 'Post Chernobyl Blues,' some find in nature's generous and beautiful gifts a mere consolation. Beautiful to contemplate at the beginning of Spring or during its flamboyant Autumn, one could think that even Chernobyl did not manage to change the natural spring of life still present there. This need for nature makes some ignore the ban and go for walks into the forest to pick mushrooms and wild berries, to hunt, to admire its beautiful landscapes or just to have a quiet walk and find that little bit of psychological strength they need.

One can therefore say that Chernobyl has not killed nature as a place for rest and relaxation.

**Ordinary happiness or an end of utopia**

Can all the facts described above qualify as proof of happiness? Probably not if one considers happiness as a constant state of felicity, something Freud, and most other philosophers, considers impossible. For Kant (1969 [1785]: 131–2), happiness, this 'imaginary ideal,' is only a vague concept that,

> even as Mankind has the desire to reach Happiness, no one can actually define in detailed and coherent words what he/she desires or want...He/She is unable to define with certainty what would make him/her definitely happy.

Happiness would therefore be relative to situations as well as people. Depending on one's sensitivity, happiness would only be a feeling taken from past experiences, allowing each of us to find *times* of happiness. These short-lived feelings, related to ephemeral pleasures, would help people to withstand hardship and tough conditions.

There is therefore no doubt that one can experience happiness even after a disaster such as Chernobyl. Precarious experiences for people living there could be qualified as 'ordinary' happiness as ethno-methodology would call it. Such a possibility, leaving the metaphysical perspective aside, forces us to admit we must consider the need for a history, a sociology, and maybe even an anthropology of happiness.[35]

However different, according to cultures and civilizations, conceptions of happiness and ways to express it have widely evolved through history. While two main traditions (one from the Occidental World, one from the Oriental World) have symbolized the concept of happiness, a more recent, materialistic one has now gained ground throughout the world, thanks to the expansion of the industrial revolution and the development of industrialized society. Aided by a consumer-focused capitalism (see Lipovetsky 2006), the ability to own and use manufactured goods has become through the last century the prime focus of modern society. In parallel to the development of individualism, a new mythology has now taken the lead. Stoked by the mass media, this mythology has exacerbated the ideals of material well-being, the focus on personal development, the promotion of childish and feminine values, as well as the cult of sexualized love (see Morin 1962).

Such a utopia was diametrically opposed to the one from Soviet societies. If communist idealism was focusing on the development of productive forces too, individual consumption was not the main engine of it, as everyone had to sacrifice everything as well as his/her own life to establish socialism, which was the ultimate goal. Socialist ambitions of creating a 'New Man' had nothing to do with the contemporary westernized and individualistic humankind of our societies. As this Western consumerist vision of society could be described as a utopia in the process of being progressively achieved, the Soviet societies' concept remained a vague utopia whose announced accomplishment was indefinitely postponed in time. Being future-focused, this utopia had in its favor the mobilizing strength of all endless and impossible-to-achieve tasks.

As the communist dream had already suffered setbacks due to decades of privations and authoritarianism, it finally collapsed with the Chernobyl disaster. As acknowledged by Mikhail Gorbachev himself, this also put in motion the slow process that would lead, five years later, to the collapse of the USSR.[36] Even if the Belarus President is attempting to keep afloat a Soviet-age economic and political system, this is no longer supported by the communist mythology.

The Occidental ideal of consumerism is constantly expanding to such a point that, as seen earlier, Alexander Loukachenko is now attempting to limit its influence over the youth by promoting his own nationalistic ideology. This new doctrine he elaborated aims to oppose everything he has opposed: Marxism, capitalism and conservatism. Mixing different streams of thought (pan-Slavism, Sovietism, orthodoxy) it outlines the exceptional destiny of the Belarus nation, and of its leader, the only strong bulwark against aggressions originating from the Occidental world or even from Russia. These principles, even if taught in schools as well as in factories of more than 150 employees, do not have the same mobilizing power as the communist ideology. As a pragmatic vision rather than theoretical one, it does not provide masses with a *raison d'être*, a vision for the future.

Foreign to the daily life of people living in contaminated territories, this doctrine cannot provide them with any hope for a better life. They therefore have no other choice but to enjoy short-lived moments of happiness that allow them to escape their daily concerns, without any hope of a better future.[37]

# Part IV
# Multidimensional Happiness

# 10
# Village and War: Unit of Well-being in Japan under Imperial Rule

*Akira Furukawa*

## Introduction

This chapter intends to discuss the continuity and separation of Japan as a nation and its villages and households, through describing and analyzing how these villages faced World War II. I intend to focus on how, in historical terms, the well-being of the nation's villages and individuals were connected with, and separated from, each other. I also focus on the relationship between the well-being of villages and that of individuals in the socio-historical context of World War II.

The development of capitalism in modern Japan since the Meiji Period (1868–1912) has seen rural village populations used as a spare source of labor available on demand. This is evident in the history of local policy adopted by the central government, through which villages were transformed from independent livelihood organizations to the lower branches of the government. Specifically, Japanese villages have experienced a total of three major consolidation programs in the Meiji, Showa (1926–1989) and Heisei Periods (1989–). These programs significantly changed the village framework as an administrative unit. Villages were also deprived more and more of their independent financial bases during the consolidation process.

This was particularly so during the Sino-Japanese War and the Pacific War, which broke out in 1930 and 1941, respectively. During these wars, villages served as a significant source of soldiers, fuel and food for the wars and of women, children and elderly people who were engaged in the production of these supplies. Then, once the country entered the process of post-war democratization, villages were condemned for providing labor and supplies for the wars. The idea was that these village efforts served as a hotbed of grassroots fascism which, in turn, provided foundations for the Imperial system of Japan. From the way Japanese villages have been treated, they may seem to be nothing more than the central government's lower branches, always buffeted and exploited by the government's macro-policy.

What, though, does this history look like through the eyes of these villages? How has this process of modernization been experienced by villages that have constantly been affected by population mobilization and have also been, in organizational terms, forced to become the lower branches of the government? How has the relationship between the central government and villages changed during the process of their transformation into the lower branches of the government? Furthermore, what social relationships have been changed in what ways within villages?

For the purpose of this chapter, I define the Sino-Japanese War and the Pacific War as the peak of the movement to transform Japan into a nation-state, which had been in process under the Imperial rule since the Meiji Period. Japanese villages provided foundations for this movement during these war times. I would like to analyze the villages' experiences by studying minute changes in their daily life as described in their own records.

## Village and the state

In the argument about villages and war, it has been understood that villages, which supplied a workforce in response to the national mobilization, provided foundations for grassroots fascism in direct cooperation with the central government. This is the context in which the reforms of rural villages during the post-war democratization have been understood. In this understanding, it is considered self-evident that the wartime government and villages formed a continuity. It is also understood that this continuity had arisen before the war from the relationship between the central government and villages in the context of national policy, and that the wartime continuity of the government and villages existed as a continuation of this prewar relationship. At the same time, urban dwellers' nostalgia for rural villages resulted in secondary, village-like unions in cities, such as graduates' associations or associations of people from the same village. It is believed that these village-like unions provided certain principles that governed Japanese society, making the country easy to incline towards imperial order and supporting the creation of the national mobilization program (Kamishima 1961).

'In this country, fascism started off by using a specific social class (rural middle class) as the basic driving force of the movement. Fascist forces established organizational units by organizing rural villages and attempted to organize the entire country based on these prototypes' (Fujita 1996: 174). In terms of historical understanding, the above perspective about the continuity of the central government and villages before and during the war can be said to be virtually a common view. However, with the enactment of the National Mobilization Law in 1938 as a turning point,

> a labor shortage in rural villages resulting from conscription and draft …brought about, in almost no time, a tendency for solid independent farmers to change into small or medium parasitic landowners, resulting in rural communities being further divided and reduced in size. Rural villages thus had relatively more and more "selfish" families, which caused gradual breakdown of the purely Japanese traditional local system. The continuity [of households and traditional local system] with the central government was about to be severed. Thus, in all parts of Japan the concept of state was lost in the air. No matter how seriously the general public might have believed in the state under imperial rule, there was no state in their actual life. (Fujita 1996: 191)

Fujita goes on to argue that, with the year 1938 as a turning point, a major rift occurred in the continuity between the state and villages (households). Fujita argues that the complementary relationship (familism) between the Emperor and the public in the previous state under imperial rule was reduced to a mere formality. This led, Fujita says, to the expression of selfish desires in villages which were now cut off from the imperial system (Fujita 1996: 192–3).

There is no point in building a loose argument on the continuity of the state and villages here. However, with respect to the common view that villages provided foundations for grassroots fascism, it should be accepted that several reservations are necessary with regard to, at least, the times to which this view applies. Furthermore, when, according to Fujita, a rift occurred in the continuity between the state and villages (households), we must question what was happening between the state and villages (households). Fujita continues his argument, saying that the rift which occurred in Japan under imperial rule, where there was no concept of homeland apart from the imperial control system, went on to create the political environment of post-war Japan. During this process, Fujita says, villages (households) that had been cut off from the state under imperial rule changed into a system of selfish desire that simply showed 'insensible response to ever-changing external conditions' (Fujita 1996: 193).

As a common practice in the history of thought, linking Kamishima's and Fujita's arguments is an understandable attempt to view the discontinuity between prewar and post-war Japan in terms of the rift between the state under imperial rule and villages (households) during the war, instead of in terms of Japan's defeat and post-war reforms by the GHQ (Allied Occupation Force's General Headquarters). However, what was actually happening in villages? It is necessary to analyze this based on everyday life situations instead of from the broad view of the history of thought.

## Historical changes in national control and villages

Before analyzing historical materials, let us take a general view of the historical changes in national control and villages, while mentioning special characteristics of Japanese villages.[1]

A village had always faced the necessity of providing total control of its villagers' business, livelihood and beliefs. On one hand, this was intended to control any deviations from the village's internal code. On the other hand, this was because a village as sub-society often had to make its decisions and act upon them against a backdrop of tense relations with the outside world. For this reason, a village had been formed so that it would function as an autonomous organization. The village's representative, whose designation changed from *shōya* to *sonchō*, *sōdai* and then to *kuchō* and so on, held meetings to discuss matters for the whole village. At these meetings the village made its decisions.

Under the shogunate system, most villages ran their agricultural (business), religious and administrative organizations as one body (Furukawa 2004). The separation of these organizations seems to have started from the change of villages' administrative organizations into something more like lower branches of the central government, due to the local community improvement movement and repeated changes in the local system under the Meiji government; the change of *kannushi* (shrine guardianship) into a full-time occupation; and the organization of agricultural activities into productive cooperatives

(Ochi 1974). The total management of agricultural, religious and administrative affairs in a village was forced to be separated gradually. After the promulgation of the law establishing universal suffrage in 1925, many villages revised their codes to ensure that their representatives would be chosen by election (Kamiya 1976). This was followed by the rural corrective movement in the early Shōwa Period. During this period, most villages became impoverished and saw the emergence of new types of landlords that they had never experienced before. In a large number of villages, this caused significant changes in long-standing control systems that had been in place since the Edo Period (1603–1867).

The lifestyles in these villages were characterized by the unity of production, living and religion and the cyclic structure of not only time but also resources. However, there were unlimited variations in management method. This was because the various elements involved, including relatives, landlord–tenant relationships, business styles, productivity and distribution, created an unlimited number of combinations.

What, then, is the logic supporting the idea that a village is the parent of the creation and maintenance of one culture? Eitarō Suzuki finds in villages 'the existence of a spirit that runs through individuals in each time' (1968 [1940]: 126). Suzuki defines it as 'a systematic principle of behavior covering all aspects of life' and calls it the 'spirit of village' (1968 [1940]: 126). Suzuki argues that the spirit is 'one expanding code which controls individuals and the present time and binds them to the entirety and to the past and future.' He asserts that the 'spirit of village' is what makes a village a village and what lies behind the accumulation of various ways and means of living there. According to Torigoe, the 'consciousness of life' proposed by Kizaemon Aruga is similar to the 'spirit of village' in nature. However, Torigoe states that while Suzuki focuses on the 'expansibility' in his argument of the spirit of village, Aruga focused on 'creativity' (Torigoe 1982).

Specifically, while its form may depend on the conditions, the 'spirit of village' or the 'consciousness of life' exists in a village as long as it is maintained. While the spirit or consciousness helps villagers develop their creativity, villagers' activities are inevitably restricted by such spirit.

In this chapter, I have described a village as a whole, or as a single body, and as an ideal type. A village, however, was not an entity that cannot be divided further. A village consisted of households. Let us focus on the mutual relationship between households and their village from the viewpoint of changes in village life. The various organizations that supported village life did not consist of individuals. The memberships of these organizations consisted of household representatives.

Most of the various activities in a village were conducted as village affairs—from the management of various organizations and agricultural affairs to affairs related to births and deaths. Rice planting and rice-planting breaks[2] were scheduled on a village-wide basis. In a certain village, a newborn was recognized as a child of the village and declared one-year old (according to traditional Japanese reckoning) only when its birth was notified to the village seniors. Even aging was not personal but a village affair. This is closely related to the unity of agricultural, religious and administrative affairs. Agricultural affairs and childbirths were both closely related to religious and administrative affairs (Sekizawa 1988).

Then, with the loosening of the unity of agricultural, religious and village affairs, village affairs were gradually replaced by household affairs. Most affairs are now conducted as household affairs and not village affairs. Further, a major shift from household to personal affairs occurred, as typified by birthday celebrations. This shift to affairs that are not even on a household level became a major trend in Japanese rural villages during the latter half of the twentieth century.

Even so, we need to pay attention to the following point when we analyze villages: Japanese village culture was created and maintained through village affairs, not through personal or household affairs. Even if some affairs may seem to be conducted by individual households or persons now, we must attempt to understand the underlying meanings of those affairs as village affairs.[3]

In early-modern times, villages were territories of feudal domains and controlled by these domains. Upon the establishment of the Meiji government (1868), villages were placed under centralized control by the national government. The Meiji government achieved direct control of villages through the Land Tax Reform and reforms of the local government systems. This national government control over villages has been studied from many perspectives: the consolidation of shrines, the integration of forestlands owned by village communities, and reforms of agricultural techniques brought about by the local community improvement movement; and top-down systematization through industrial associations during the period of the rural corrective movement. Only a very small number of studies have, however, dealt with villages and the state during World War II or during the period from immediately after the defeat to immediately before the post-war rapid economic growth. The relationship between villages and the state during this period, when the most significant changes after the Meiji Period occurred to villages, is probably one of the most important research topics at the present time, when the framework of a nation-state is undergoing significant changes and attempts are being made to reorganize communities in the waves of globalization.

In the following sections, I refer to descriptions recorded in the Diary (literally: 'Records') of Chinai Village during the 1930s and the 1940s. The Diary is a semi-official, semi-private document of the village and has been kept continuously including during the war. I intend to analyze the following points: How did Chinai Village experience the periods during and after the war? How did the state appear in the village's experiences? If a rift occurred between the state and the village, how was it experienced by the village? And what arose from the rift?

The Diary is a record of Chinai Village which has been kept by secretaries of the village for over 260 years. Chinai Village is located on the shore of Lake Biwa, in the northern part of Shiga Prefecture. The village has a total of something over 130 households. In the period discussed below, Chinai Village had already been consolidated with other villages and, in administrative terms, constituted one of the districts of larger Momose Village. Nonetheless, I use the designation of Chinai Village in this chapter for the sake of convenience. The village was entirely a farming community, where most of the households lived on agricultural production. Roughly thirty households lived on fishing, but most engaged in farming as well.

## Village and war experience

According to the Diary, it was in 1887 when the village sent out its first draftees in response to the establishment of the national draft system. The Diary relates that all of the village officials went to the harbor in the next town to see them off. Twelve years later, the village was designated as the battalion headquarters of an army division which conducted military exercises in nearby mountains. A total of 238 soldiers stayed in the village. The Diary contains detailed records of meal menus for different classes and of income and expenditure. The village thus unexpectedly accumulated experience in 'rear services' (i.e., 'behind the lines' support activities). Finally in 1905, Chinai Village suffered the first deaths of soldiers from the village in the Russo-Japanese War. The village performed an official funeral service for the dead. Many of the articles in the Diary written around this period are records of drafted soldiers, but let us skip these articles and turn our focus to the periods of the Sino-Japanese War and the Pacific War.

On 4 February 1932, a summons went out to supply soldiers to the Manchurian Incident. Chinai Village awarded five yen to each of the five draftees from the village. Surprised by the enrollment of five villagers at one time, the village held a general meeting on the night of 11 February. The following resolutions were made: '1. Provide workforce to the families of the men in the services; 2. Comfort the soldiers' families that do not live in but have their houses in the village with approximately one half of the award; and 3. Helpers to the families must not be treated with meals whatsoever' (the Diary, 4 February 1932). The article for 29 March 1932 relates without attachment the first deaths of soldiers from the village in the Sino-Japanese War and that an official funeral service was performed by the village at the primary schoolyard. This clearly shows that military service was not a matter of individual households but had to be dealt with by the village as its own affairs.

After the North China Incident in 1937, the war expanded further. Soldiers in the reserves and veterans were called for service one after another. Many of the articles for this period describe send-offs for soldiers going to war at Chinai Pier. Villagers discussed assistance to the families of these active soldiers. They decided to provide the families with a gift of money and 'household aid equivalent to five persons per household' (the Diary, 5 October 1937).

While the village took these internal measures, it also responded to directions from the outside. The Diary describes military exercises such as air-raid drills and restrictions on lighting instructed by the military authorities. There are also descriptions of a party in celebration of the fall of Nanking, which was held at the request of the national government. Since the Taisho Period (1912–1926), the village had the custom of general worship service on 1 January each year. The general worship service for 1938 was, unlike previous services, dominated by war.

> 1 January: At the start of the year in the ceremony hall of the general worship service, the following vow was read aloud at the request of the

authorities, in order to present congratulations to the Emperor for his longevity and, in accordance with mobilization of the national spirit in light of the seriousness of the current situation, to overcome the present hardship by patience and endurance through renewing the sense of unity of the whole nation and of national service, to wish good luck to the Emperor and to be further prepared to increase national prestige in and outside Japan. (the Diary, 1938)

Thus, at the 'request of the authorities,' all villagers vowed aloud to congratulate the Emperor for his longevity and to overcome the situation by patience and endurance. This general worship service was followed by a significant increase of articles on drafted soldiers, soldiers killed in action and village funeral services. At the same time, many articles detail how the entire village provided obligatory supplies of all kinds of goods and materials to the government. While send-offs of soldiers going to war are events within the bounds of Chinai Village, funeral services for soldiers killed in action were performed as official events of the greater, consolidated village beyond the bounds of Chinai village. The general worship service for 1939 was performed under the National Mobilization Law proclaimed in 1938 and is described as follows:

1 January: All of the district residents participated in the general worship service. Faced with the prolonged war to establish peace in the Orient, all read aloud the following vow and renewed their pledge, in order to send their New Year greetings and to seek perfection of their home-front defense under the national mobilization program. (the Diary, 1939)

February saw the celebration of the 2600th year of the Imperial reign and an Imperial edict was read aloud.

11 February: At the 2600th year of the Imperial reign, His Majesty the Emperor granted the following gracious Imperial edict to his 100 million people (the Diary, 1939).

With the enactment of the National Mobilization Law as a turning point, these requests from the national government for the maintenance of the state under imperial rule changed from spiritual to spiritual *and* material demands. In addition to patriotic delivery of rice, the village experienced repeated collections of goods and materials, including:

approx. sixty-five kilograms of pickled plums for military use; approx. 5.6 kilograms of *perilla* (Japanese basil); 106 blocks (2,385 kilograms) of hay; three straw bags of barley; eighty bundles (approx. 10.1 kilograms [*sic*]) of straw; approx. 13.6 kilograms of mosquito net rings; 13.5 straw bags of patriotic rice delivery; vegetables; temple bells; contribution of antique coins; special collections of metals; floor cushions for use in the production of gunpowder; cotton; pine oil for fuel and; ninety-seven straw bags of potatoes for consumption and twelve straw bags of those for seed. The village was further forced to supply cash, through the allotment of government bonds, and a workforce including women and junior high school students, and many more. The national mobilization program seems to have deprived the village of all its people, goods, money and manpower.

The Diary contains an article for 23 July on the obligatory delivery of ninety-seven straw bags of potatoes for consumption and twelve straw bags of those for seed, an article for 30 July on draftees, and an article for 14 August on the repairs of breaches in the embankment along the Momose River. These articles are followed by an article for 14 August, whose date is wrong by one day for some reason, announcing the end of the war: 'An order of cease-fire and peace was issued. An Imperial mandate was given' (the Diary, 1945). This is followed by articles describing the village's daily life which was quite the same as before the war.

> 17 August: Collection of the first harvest of barley for seventy-four yen forty-one sen. The crop was delivered to the shrine guardian after reserving some for seed.
>
> 18 August: Dredging of the ditches.
>
> 19 August: Mobilization for repairs of breaches along the Momose River.
>
> 19 August: Dredging of the riverbed (the Mae River).
>
> 20 August: Restrictions on lighting lifted.
>
> (the Diary, 17–20 August, 1945)

However, the article for 6 September 1945 describes a village funeral service for soldiers killed in action announced in an official gazette after the war. The article says, 'At the official funeral service for the late Mr N, Mr T and Mr F, who were killed in service in the Central Pacific, this *Aza* offered a pair of flower arrangements and a *tamagushi* fee [a cash offering in Shintoism] of ten yen per dead soldier.' Then, an article written in December 1945 describes the US occupation as follows:

> An occupation force is stationed at Fukudaya Hotel in Imazu. According to the occupation authorities' orders, an order was issued to forcibly confiscate firearms, swords, spears and other types of weapon. This *Aza* made obligatory delivery of seventy-two swords and seventy-two spears.

According to the Diary, Chinai Village, which had a total of about 130 households, provided a total of 139 drafted soldiers and suffered a total of twenty-eight deaths of soldiers.

What we can read from the above articles describes a lower branch of the government of the state under imperial rule—a branch that presents congratulations to the Emperor for his longevity and supports the war by eagerly providing all of its goods, money and workforce under the national mobilization program. This reflects the unwavering belief in the village that public peace in Japan will inevitably lead to the well-being of the village. This seems to be a typical state for a village which has been portrayed as a hotbed of grassroots fascism. The state of a village thus portrayed is a monolith: the smallest unit of administrative organizations linked to the national government.

What, then, was daily life like within the village? Did the hotbed of fascism run further through individual households and individual persons in the village? In the following section, I use the same historical material used above. I refer to descriptions on daily living activities in the village that are not directly related to the war in an attempt to analyze the trends within the village during the same period.

## Daily village life and the state

The Diary contains 674 articles written during the period from the Manchurian Incident in 1931 to the Japanese defeat in 1945. Many of these articles deal directly with the war or report activities for the maintenance of the village's infrastructure, including river improvement and dredging. There are also many articles concerning the village's administration, such as general and consultative meetings.

Particularly noticeable of these articles are those reporting resignations of village officers written after 1939. This is because for the 190 years since 1745, there had never been a single case where a person elected as an officer refused to take, or resigned from his post, unless the person was disqualified according to the criteria approved by the village, such as the death of a member of his family or relatives.

The administrative posts of Chinai Village comprised the community representative (*sōdai*) and his deputy (*dairisha*), both of whom were chosen by election, and three managers called *nengyōji* (literally: 'annual events manager'). Apart from these, the village had a council, which was a publicly elected assembly. The community representative and his deputy also chair the council. The Chinai Village Bylaws (established in 1924) effective during the period covered by this paper provide that the community representative shall also serve as the head of the district (*kuchō*). This means that '*kuchō*' is the title of the head of Chinai as a district of the greater village, whereas '*sōdai*' is the title of the head of Chinai as a village before the consolidation. As described below, the community representative had enormous duties.[4]

After the Meiji Period, village administration had a double nature. Put simply, a village had to be administered both as a self-governing body and as a lower branch of the national government. The community representative played a pivotal role in this double nature. He was both the head of the village and the agent of a lower branch of the government under imperial rule. As the agent of a lower branch, the community representative played a pivotal role in ensuring that the principles of control ran through all households in the village under his jurisdiction. Resigning from the post of community representative meant abandoning his role to be played in the context of the principles under imperial rule, even more than abandoning his responsibility as the head of the village.

In the Diary, the first article on refusal to take the post of community representative appeared in March 1934.

> 11 March 1934: Regular election of the community representative and his deputy. N.I. was elected as the community representative and T.S. was elected as the deputy. However, T.S. firmly refused to take the post without reason. A council meeting and a general meeting were held but he still firmly declined. Finally, at the general meeting held on March 23, it was resolved that T.S. would be prohibited from participating in any public meetings for three years.

The village was puzzled by the experience that it had never had before. At the council meeting and the general meeting, they urged Mr T.S., who had firmly refused to take the post, to think twice. Faced with his continued refusal, the village took the decision to impose strong sanctions against him—prohibition from attending any public village meetings for three years.

As a matter of fact, Mr T.S.'s family had been a major landowner for many generations and had provided many prominent persons and office-holders to the village. Mr T.S. himself had served as village officer for many decades. His refusal to take the post was a serious incident that had to be dealt with by imposing such heavy sanctions on him, previously a prominent village figure.

However, in 1938, when Mr T.M. resigned from the post of deputy for family reasons, no sanctions were imposed on him, unlike in the incident of Mr T.S. four years earlier. Four days after the resignation of Mr T.M., an election was held to elect a successor deputy.

> Deputy Mr T.M. wished to resign from the post for family reasons. The matter was referred to at the general meeting. The matter was approved and Mr T.M. was allowed to resign. (the Diary, 6 May 1938)

Finally, in 1939, the village had no choice but to insert provisions in its bylaws that would allow a deputy to resign 'if the deputy submits his resignation after more than one year of taking the post' (the Diary, 29 March 1939). Let me briefly describe the situation by summarizing the article for 21 March concerning this matter. The amendment of the bylaws came about under the following circumstances.

On 26 September, 1938, Mr N.T., the deputy at that time, submitted his resignation for family reasons. After unsuccessful attempts to dissuade him, it was decided at a general meeting that he would remain in the post on condition that 'some revisions...be made to the bylaws as to the duties of the deputy' (the Diary, 21 March 1939). However, even December that year failed to see new bylaws. This further resulted in the submission of a resignation by the community representative, Mr N.U. A council meeting was held at short notice, where the following draft amendment was formulated.

1. When the deputy is excessively busy, he may hire some hands to help him with his performance of village affairs.
2. The village shall give some consideration to the remuneration.

3. For the time being, the term of the deputy under the bylaws shall be one year. (the Diary, 21 March 1939)

Still, the deputy did not change his mind to resign. The community representative also remained determined to resign unless his successor was appointed. Another council meeting was held immediately, where a resolution was passed that the community representative's resignation would not be accepted. They managed to wriggle their way out of the situation by presenting the following conditions to the community representative and his deputy.

1. With respect to the issue of deputy, it was assured by the general meeting and understood [by the community representative and his deputy] that all possible measures would be taken by the general meeting no later than the end of March.
2. With respect to the issue of bylaw revisions, how to make such revisions will be left to the absolute discretion of the community representative. (the Diary, 21 March 1939)

However, that March 'failed to see any final revisions to the bylaws' (the Diary, 21 March 1939). The situation was so serious that the community representative Mr N.U. left his seat halfway through the general meeting held on 17 March. Let me quote the whole series of articles written immediately after this incident, as they show how the administration of the village changed significantly.

A general meeting was convened in the early morning of the following day, the 18$^{th}$. After discussion from morning till night, no solution was found. The general meeting chose six representatives who, in turn, requested three former officers of the village, including elders who were former community representatives, to seek an amicable solution to the issue. However, their best possible request was flatly refused by Mr N.U. Another meeting was held on 19 March, at which they had no choice but to accept Mr N.U.'s resignation. A vote was taken to determine whether the reason for his resignation was considered justifiable. It was found that a majority considered it unjustifiable. A resolution was thus passed to impose a penalty on N.U. that would be equivalent to three times a councilor's contribution, in accordance with Article Seven of the Chinai Village Bylaws. The results of the meeting were notified to N.U. On 21 March, N.U. replied that he rejected the resolutions passed by the general meeting. His reply was referred to the general meeting held that night. The participants agreed that they had no choice but to urge him to reconsider the matter from a moral point of view, and gave the following notice to N.U.

21 March 1939/Chinai Village (seal)/To: Mr N.U./Notice of Request to Comply with General Meeting's Resolutions/This is to notify you that you must unconditionally comply with the resolutions passed at the general meeting held on 19 March 1939, which have been notified to you earlier today.

Upon issuance of notice, N.U. turned it down and gave the following answer in writing.

21 March 1939/N.U. (seal)/To: Deputy Community Representative, Chinai Village/Answer to General Meeting's Resolutions Dated 19 March/With reference to your request to unconditionally comply with the matters above, as I have already notified you, I absolutely object to and cannot comply with the resolutions. This is my answer.

Thus, another notice was given, which was as follows.

21 March 1939/Chinai Village/To: Mr N.U./Second Notice to Comply with General Meeting's Resolutions/This is to notify you that you must absolutely comply with the general meeting's resolutions dated 19 March 1939, which have already been informed to you, and that whatever objections you may submit would never be accepted.
    The above results have come about to safeguard the Chinai Village Bylaws. (the Diary, 21 March 1939)

The Diary tells us that the village had often seen disputes before this one. However, this kind of dispute over the posts of village officers had, at least, never been recorded in the Diary. According to the article for 29 March 1939, the following internal rules were adopted at the meeting in response to the results of the previous exchanges.

1. If the deputy submits his resignation after more than one year of taking the post, such resignation shall be accepted for the time being.
2. When the deputy is excessively busy, he may hire some hands. (the Diary, 21 March 1939)

Thus, the bylaws were modified to suit the reality. A year later, on 11 March 1940, a regular election was held. Both of the men who were elected as community representative and deputy declined to take the posts for family reasons. The village council immediately sent its two representatives to the men's respective houses. The representatives earnestly requested the two men to take the posts but failed to obtain their ready consent. Three representatives of the general meeting also begged the two men to withdraw their refusals, only to face the same outcome. Finally, the representatives of the general meeting visited relatives of the man who had been refusing to take the post of community representative and begged them to take appropriate measures. At last, the relatives proposed the following conditions: '1. The post can be taken only for the time being; 2. Any resignation submitted at any time during the term must be accepted' (the Diary, 11 March 1940). Meanwhile, relatives of the man who was elected as deputy replied, 'The post can be taken only for the time-being' (the Diary, 11 March 1940). These conditions were referred to the general meeting and were approved unanimously. The men thus took the posts on these conditions.

However, only two months later, on 7 May, the still-fresh community representative submitted his resignation for family reasons. Again, the council and the general meeting sent their representatives to his house and begged him to remain in the post. Yet the community representative insisted on resigning on the strength of the conditions approved by the general assembly upon his taking the post. They had no choice but to accept his resignation.

On 14 May, an election was held to fill the vacancy. The man elected as community representative refused to take the post. So did the other men who were elected in the series of elections that followed. By 14 July, the village had held a total of four elections to fill the vacant post. The man who finally agreed to take the post did so on the following conditions, just like his predecessor did: '1. The post can be taken only for the time being; 2. Any resignation submitted at any time during the term must be accepted' (the Diary, 16 July 1940). Six months later, on 17 January, the community representative visited a senior councilor and expressed his intention to resign. Again, like his predecessor, he was firmly resolved to resign and the others had to accept his resignation.

This time, requests were made to establish an advisory panel to discuss this series of refusals and to propose a drastic reform plan. On 25 January, a proposal from the panel was approved by the general meeting. While the proposal contained many provisions that confirmed the methods of election that were becoming perfunctory, its main point was to double the amount of remuneration for the community representative and his deputy. It was proposed that the remuneration for the community representative and his deputy be raised to 180 yen and 130 yen, respectively. The proposal was approved by both the council and the general meeting.

In the period that followed, when the war situation turned towards Japan's defeat, the village was busy sending soldiers and dealing with those who were killed in action and their families. Under the circumstances, refusals to take, and resignations from, the administrative posts were not seen as often as before. Still, several refusals and resignations and revisions of the bylaws did occur. Through these revisions, refusals and resignations for family reasons gradually became more easily accepted. At the same time, the heavy duties of the community representatives were gradually divided between other posts.

Taking administrative posts was, as seen in the numerous letters of thanks recorded in the Diary, an honor and an obligation of village seniors. It is an obligation under the Japanese Civil Code and stipulated as such in the Chinai Village Bylaws. The bylaws were established by the village under the double influence of the state under imperial rule and the self-government of the village. A breach of the bylaws would constitute both an act of treachery towards the village, and a deviation from the control of the state under imperial rule. The villagers' notion of the significance of this breach took the form of fiery argument that was unthinkable considering the close personal relations in the small village. These considerations were put into words in the last line of the Diary, 'The above results have come about to safeguard the Chinai Village Bylaws' (the Diary, 21 March 1939).

The village they were attempting to protect in the above situation was not a village playing the role of a lower branch of the state government under imperial rule. It was a village that had maintained its order, as well as its norms, in the hope of survival. As described above, demands from the central government became limitless after the Manchurian Incident in 1931, particularly following the enactment of the National Mobilization Law in 1938. The village was impoverished after being deprived of its people as soldiers and of large amounts of goods and resources and money as obligatory supplies as well as providing a labor-force. By the time the above series of events occurred in March 1939, the village had sent a total of thirty-nine soldiers to the front and suffered thirteen deaths (by the end of the war, a total of 139 soldiers were sent to the front and twenty-eight were killed). The village had reached its first peak of exhaustion. Under these circumstances, the village was struggling to maintain its connection with the central government and the village's traditional norms.

However, at that time the situation had already started to undergo a significant change, no matter how hard the village may have tried to stay the same. In this lower branch of the imperial control, the village's ruling class, which provided a basis to this control, had already started to deviate from the norm. The village's exhaustion with its everyday life must have reached a level at which its bylaws as an absolute norm had to be denied by the head of the village himself.

## Conclusion

In this paper, I have described how Japanese villages experienced World War II during the period from the Manchurian Incident in 1931 to the Japanese defeat in 1945. During the period, Chinai Village did not directly experience air raids, much less was it turned into a battlefield. It seems to have remained a typical village that provided home-front support.

I described several factors that changed the previous relationship between a village and the state during the fifteen-year war. In discussing the experience of the village during the war, I focused solely on descriptions on communications between the national government and the village. By doing so, we can see that the village, as a typical home-front village that played the role of a lower branch of the government under imperial rule, supplied labor and goods to the state waging the war. This is the image of a village which has been portrayed as a hotbed of grassroots fascism.

I next followed a series of events that occurred inside the village based on records made during exactly the same period. These events comprised a series of refusals to take, and resignations from, the post of community representative of the village. They were unprecedented events in that no similar events can be found in the articles contained in the village's Diary before then. The post of community representative is stipulated as follows in the village bylaws, which were established with the enactment of the Meiji Civil Code: 'The community representative shall supervise and represent the Village' (Article Thirty-one of the Chinai Village Bylaws). By holding additional posts concurrently, the community representative was to play a role as the center of the centralized authority controlling the village's religious, agricultural and administrative affairs. In addition, the community representative was to represent the village to the outside world. Under the provisions of the bylaws, he was supposed to serve as head of the district and, as such, to play a pivotal role in the lower branches of the national administration. In other words, the community representative was placed in a pivotal position to perfect the state control system from the Emperor down to the village and to individual households. These were exactly why the first resignation from the post of community representative, in 1931, was severely punished with a prohibition from participating in any public meetings for three years. The series of refusals to take and resignations from the post of community representative that started in 1939 and the series of amendments to the bylaws in a manner that would accept the refusals and resignations, show the loosening of the village's norms as well as the beginning of the breakdown of imperial state control.

The above can be analyzed as follows. The village was impoverished by the war. In particular, it underwent experiences that were beyond its imagination—the drafting of soldiers, which siphoned off the village's vitality, and the return of many soldiers killed in action. These experiences weakened the previous view of well-being—the concept that the village should share the well-being of the whole state as a community. The unit of well-being that had been built up since the Meiji Period under the principle of imperial rule was the state, which was regarded as equal to villages and households. In this view, the security of the Japanese nation, with the Emperor at the top, leads directly to the well-being of households and villages. In other words, if the state is happy the village should be happy, and if the village is happy its households should be happy. This unit of well-being was beginning to break down as early as the period of our analysis. The bylaws' confirmation of the refusals to take and resignations from the post of community representative resulted in a change in the nature of the post from an absolute norm to an optional one. In addition, the reason for the refusals and resignations—'family reasons'—clearly indicates the process of individualization through which the unit of well-being shifted from the state to villages and then to households.

Space does not permit discussion of the post-war period, but let me add that this reduction of the unit of well-being finally resulted, under the influence of the post-war democratization policy, in the idea that the well-being of the state is totally separate and different from that of households or individuals. However, this reduction of the unit of well-being or, to put it in extreme terms, the individualization of well-being, did not lead to the breakdown of villages. Instead, post-war Japanese villages were to become bases for the reorganization of the reduced unit of well-being.

# 11
# Materialism, Pragmatism and the Pursuit of Happiness in Singapore

*Chee Kiong Tong*

## Introduction

This paper addresses the issue of materialism, pragmatism and the pursuit of happiness in Singapore. It has a rather simple problematic. Singapore, a small island nation-state with about four million people, has an extremely high Gross Domestic Product per capita by purchasing power parity of US$28,600. This ranks it very highly, 29th in the world, and only behind Brunei and Japan in Asia. Singaporeans enjoy a very high quality of life. Singapore has an excellent health care system, with one of the lowest infant mortality rates in the world, and a very high life expectancy rate of 81.71, ranking it fourth in the world. The incidence of crime in Singapore is very low. Similarly, Singaporeans enjoy a high standard of living. Ninety percent of Singaporeans own the houses or apartments that they live in. It is ranked as one of the best cities in the world to live, just behind Toronto and London, and ahead of Paris and Hong Kong. It is also rated by *Fortune Magazine* as one of the best business cities in Asia.

Anyone who visits Singapore will be impressed by the city. It is clean, green, orderly, efficient and very safe. It can be regarded, and some have characterized it as, a paradise or utopia.[1] Yet, if one examines the World Index on Happiness (WIP), Singapore does not score very well. For example, the WIP rated Singapore at 7.62 on the Happiness index, putting her in the twenty-nine to thirty-three rank band. Singapore's rank for satisfaction with life (7.12) and life as a whole (6.81) is also at the twenty-nine to thirty-three rank band. These scores are behind many developed and even developing countries. In fact, in one survey, Singapore was ranked the 'unhappiest' country in Asia, and graded a dismal 131st out of 178 nations surveyed.[2] The obvious question is why is this so? How do we account for the generally very high standard of living, and quality of life, but the relatively lower score on the Happiness index? Before I proceed to answer these questions, a brief background of Singapore is provided.

## Singapore: An introduction

Singapore is a small nation state situated at the southern tip of the Malay Peninsula. Straddling the trade routes from Europe and India to China and Japan, and bestowed with a deep natural harbor, Stamford Raffles set up a trading post in Singapore for the British East India Company in 1819 and later purchased the entire island in 1824. To lure traders to the port of Singapore, the British established Singapore as a free port, which accelerated its development into a major entrepot by the late nineteenth century. European, Arab, Indian, Chinese and other traders were attracted to Singapore, and the steady increase of immigration, particularly of the Chinese and Indians, soon led to the immigrants—especially the Chinese—overtaking the Malays to form the majority of the population.

Singapore became a Crown Colony in 1946 and acquired internal self government in 1959. In 1963, Singapore joined the Federation of Malaysia as an independent state, but was expelled after two years, having independence thrust upon her unilaterally in 1965, and ending over 150 years of colonial rule by the British. The government, under the People's Action Party, won the 1965 elections and has dominated Parliament until today.

Since 1965, the PAP government has adopted a pragmatic policy to industrialize the country. Singapore's economic growth has been regarded by many as an economic miracle. For example, from 1966 to 1973, Singapore achieved double digit real GDP growth. Even with the unfavorable international world economic conditions of the 1970s and 1980s, Singapore's economy grew between four to ten percent from 1974 to 1985. Through various pragmatic policies, the Singapore economy continued to grow in the 1990s and 2000s. For example, in 2006, the Singapore economy grew by 10.7%.

The economic growth has led to attendant improvement in the standard of living of Singaporeans. Since the 1960s, Singapore has experienced a dramatic reduction in unemployment. In 1966, the unemployment rate was 8.9% of the population. By 1971, it was only 4.8%, and by 1984, only 2.7%. Statistically, Singapore in the 1990s and 2000s has full employment, requiring the importation of foreign labor to supplement the labor force. Similarly, the wages of Singaporeans grew in all sectors. From 1972 to 1983, real wages grew at an annual rate of 9%. In the 1980s, with the policy of encouraging high technology industries to Singapore, real wages grew even faster, at a rate of more than 10% annually.

What all these statistics suggest is that over the last forty years Singaporeans have had, and continue to enjoy, an increasingly better standard of living and quality of life. This, however, begs the question as to why the improved quality of life has not resulted in even higher levels of happiness among Singaporeans. I am not suggesting that Singaporeans are terribly unhappy. However, given its high standard of living, and the fact that it is ranked among the world's best in so many categories, it is interesting to analyze why Singaporeans are not happier.[3]

## Sociology of happiness

What is happiness? From the outset it is important to note that happiness, as a construct, is notoriously difficult to measure and a comparative study of national happiness is fraught with even more difficulties. Moreover, different disciplines have differing views on what constitutes happiness. Psychologists, for example, see it as a matter of personality, emotions and cognition. Biologists perceive it to be the result of chemical processes. Philosophers view it mostly in a moral context. Socrates, for example, said that an evil man cannot be a happy man (see Glatzer 2000). Some have even tried to define happiness as a mathematical equation. Rothwell and Cohen (2003), for example, after interviewing one thousand people concluded that happiness can be exactly calculated using the equation $H = P + 5E + 3H$, where P stands for personal characteristics such as outlook on life, adaptability and resilience; E stands for existence (health, friendships and financial stability); and H represents higher order (self-esteem, expectations and ambitions.) They continue by arguing that men and women found happiness in different ways. Sunny weather, being with family and losing weight were more of an influence on women's happiness, while romance, sex, hobbies, and victories by their favorite sports teams were more important for men.

Sociologists tend to view happiness as a social condition rather than a moral or individual condition. For many disciplines, especially psychology, happiness is defined in purely individualistic or psychological terms. Sociologists, however, argue that the individual's state of happiness is socially grounded. It is interesting that when Auguste Comte coined the term 'sociology,' he related it to the concept of happiness. He felt that sociology as a discipline leads to the development of systematic knowledge that in turn leads to understanding the laws of human existence. Happiness, for Comte, requires systematic knowledge about the world we live in, particularly about the things we can change. Comte also argues that freedom will raise the level of happiness. Thus, the future positivistic age of society will be an age of happiness. For Simmel, happiness is commensurate with individuality. Simmel developed the modern idea of individuality and located it as the central characteristic of modernity, and happiness is connected to individuality.

Sociologists have attempted to measure happiness in a variety of ways. As with the definition of happiness, a measurement of happiness is notoriously difficult to operationalize.[4] One mode is to simply ask respondents whether they are happy; here, the focus is based on subjective perceptions. Over time, the scales have been improved to measure both short- and long-term happiness. One indicator that happiness research is possible is the fact that longitudinal studies have shown measurements of happiness to be relatively stable, even those that measure happiness of nations over time.

More recently, sociologists have attempted to measure happiness empirically through concepts such as quality of life or subjective well-being. For example, subjective well-being is defined as the presence and frequency of positive emotions, the absence of negative emotions. Cognitive beliefs about one's overall level of life satisfaction are also an important element in defining subjective well being. However, equating happiness with subjective well-being, conceptually, can be problematic. As Glatzer (2000) noted, 'in a narrow sense, happiness is regarded as a component of subjective well-being, that is, the overall appreciation of life as a whole.' There is a positive differentiation of positive aspects of well-being in specific satisfactions and pleasures. Subjective well-being is ambivalent in the sense that for many individuals positive and negative aspects of happiness are present at the same time. Some individuals can be satisfied despite the fact that they are exposed to a lot of misery (Glatzer 2000).

This is in fact the position taken by many philosophers, who harbor deep skepticism about happiness. For example, Schopenhaur felt that happiness was the absence of misery, and that suffering is inevitable in human life; we can only taste happiness in short moments of delusional ecstasy. This is true, in my view, to the degree that happiness is a state of mind; that evanescent feeling as well as the stable appreciation of life. Conceptually, for sociologists, happiness is the degree to which a person positively evaluates the overall quality of his present life.

## Materialism, pragmatism and happiness

In the study of happiness, sociologists have tried to examine the relationship between materialism, sometimes operationalized as income, and happiness. At the theoretical level, wealth should predict higher levels of happiness or subjective well-being because greater resources allow people a greater ability to achieve some of their goals, and also because higher income confers higher status. However, studies have shown that the relationship between wealth and happiness is not a simple one. Some have argued that income is not a strong predictor of individual well-being (Diener et al. 1993). Veenhoven (1991), in his comparative study of nations' happiness, found that while there is a correlation between wealth and happiness—that citizens of wealthier nations are relatively happier than those in poor nations—increasing wealth may have a diminishing effect on happiness. He suggests that differences in wealth have very little influence in the higher level income bracket, because wealth contributes to subjective well-being primarily in terms of meeting basic physical needs. Easterlin (1974) argues that people compare their income to those around them, and therefore differences between nations in income do not produce differences in subjective well-being.

Singapore is generally regarded as a very materialistic country. In fact, one way in which Singaporeans define their social position is known as the Five Cs: car, condominium, credit card, country club and children. Except for children, all these factors are materialistic concerns. In a sense, the national culture in Singapore is driven by a desire to accumulate material wealth. These findings are important when related to the level of happiness in Singapore; that is, although Singapore is a relatively rich country, the weak correlation between income and happiness suggest that Singaporeans need not necessarily be happy because they are rich.

In fact, the desire to pursue wealth may have a negative effect on happiness, as this leaves little time for other social activities. For example, in a study of quality of life in Singapore, Foo (2000) found that leisure, an aspect which is often highly rated in terms of importance in developed countries (Andrew and Withey 1976, Campbell et. al. 1976), is very poorly rated in Singapore. He concluded that this finding lends weight to the notion that Singapore is a very competitive society and its residents are generally people who find little time or interest in leisurely pursuits.

Materialism, of course, in and of itself, is not a bad thing. Studies (Veenhoven 1991) show that citizens in developed countries are generally happier than those living in poor countries. Economic affluence provides the opportunity to make choices, and it allows individuals to pursue and fulfill their basic needs. However, materially oriented people may be continually dissatisfied with their lives, as material goods constantly outpace their expectations. Moreover, the persistence of unfulfilled needs causes unhappiness, and materialistic people tend to let dissatisfaction in material domains spill over into life in general. As argued earlier, it is not simply the possession of material goods, but rather, the notion of relative deprivation that affects the level and perception of happiness.

Singapore has an extremely high GINI co-efficient (the measure of inequality of income distribution in a country) between the haves and the have-nots. Singapore's GINI co-efficient has risen rapidly over the last five years, from 0.490 to 0.522, compared to the GINI co-efficient of the United States, at 0.469, and Japan, at only 0.24. With such stark inequality between the haves and have-nots, the sense of relative deprivation among Singaporeans, it can be argued, will be very great.

Singaporeans are also a very pragmatic people. In fact, it can be argued that the national ideology of Singapore is based on pragmatism and meritocracy. For example, government policies are based on the efficient use of resources, worked out according to rational cost benefit analysis. Chan (1976) calls this the 'non-ideology of pragmatism.' This idea of pragmatism pervades all aspects of Singaporean society. Lian (2007), for instance, argues that social policy in Singapore is driven less by ideological underpinnings than by pragmatic considerations. There is a rational-calculative focus in governance, and Singapore is a utilitarian state. Understanding why the state pursues a pragmatic stance in its governance is relatively easy. When Singapore became independent in 1965, the government inherited massive social and economic problems; high unemployment rates, a largely poor and uneducated population, a large national debt, poor housing and slums, and so forth. In the process of trying to solve these problems and develop the nation, the focus was on raising the economic standard of the nation through measures such as the creation of jobs, the eradication of slums, countering poverty and disease, education reforms, and housing initiatives.

The economic policies have largely been successful, as witnessed by the rapid economic growth in Singapore. However, in solving these problems, the state has privileged economic and fiscal policies in order to advance the well-being of its citizens. These policies are about the maintenance of economic and social stability, not about measures of equity or equality. Also, given the massive problems, the state has sought to solve the physiological and safety needs of its citizens, and has paid less attention to higher order needs, such as the need for self-actualization and self-esteem. In fact it is only in recent years, with Singapore achieving a relatively high degree of affluence, that state policies have begun to address these higher order needs.

## Communitarianism versus individualism

In economic planning and industrialization, the state deploys a high degree of social engineering. It intervenes in all aspects of social life, both in terms of public issues and matters which would be considered private in other countries. Indeed, Singapore has been described as a 'patriarchal' state (Chan 2000). Leong (1989) notes that '...in Singapore, the presence of the state is everywhere felt...every institutional sphere of social life is in one way or another under the vigil of the state.' For example, to deal with the low marriage rate among graduate women, the state set up the Social Development Unit—in a sense, a national dating agency—which aims to promote marriage among single women. Here, the rationale was that the national interest is more important than personal interests. Singapore has a very low birth rate, about 1.24 in 2005, way below the replacement rate of 2.1. Thus, encouraging women to marry does not necessarily have to do with their happiness, but is rather aimed at the reproduction of children so that they can contribute to the economic growth of the country. This reflects the national ideology of Singapore society—communitarianism over individualism, prioritizing national interests over group interests and group interests over individual interests.

The preeminence of community over the individual is clearly reflected in the national ideology of the state. Known as the Shared Values, these principles include: nation before community and society above self; family as the basic unit of society; community support and respect for the individual; consensus, not conflict; and racial and religious harmony. Adopted in 1993, the objective of the Shared Values was to sculpt and promote a Singaporean identity based on the country's cultural heritage as well as attitudes and values that had served it well in the past. These values, at the same time, promote communitarianism over individualism. In fact, it can be argued that individualism as a social value is not highly promoted in Singapore. Rather, there is a social contract between the state and its citizens. The state ensures that the people are comfortably housed, well educated, and have a good standard of living and in exchange, citizens give up certain personal rights. There is nothing in the social contract that says the state must provide happiness for its people, at least not in the sense of personal happiness. Rather, the state seeks to ensure the economic well-being and security of the people, and to ensure the stability and viability of the state.

Studies, however, have shown that individualism and personal freedom are correlated with happiness. For example, Simmel suggests that happiness is incommensurable individuality (see Glatzer 2000). Gupta et al. (1994) noted that nations differ markedly in the liberties they afford their citizens. In some there are few civil and political rights, while in others there are extensive civil rights and freedoms. Diener et al. (1995) found that nations with greater rights would have higher subjective well-being. They argue that this has to do with the fact that nations with a higher degree of personal liberties have citizens who feel that they have more control over their destinies.

Similarly, Kasser (2000) found that people in individualistic countries tend, on average, to be happier than people living in collectivist countries. He suggests that this has to do with intrinsic and extrinsic goals. Intrinsic goals have to do with personal growth, while extrinsic goals have to do with acquiring wealth or an attractive physique aimed at increasing one's esteem in the eyes of others. Kasser's research shows that people who put more emphasis on intrinsic goals, such as having rich social relationships, and less on extrinsic goals of financial gains, tend to have higher levels of subjective well-being. Moreover, people who live in developed (direct) democracies tend to score higher on the happiness index (Frey and Stutzer 2000).

Finally, Veenhoven (1996) demonstrates that nations which are individualistic societies have higher levels of happiness. Measuring individualistic societies as the moral appreciation of individualism, the opportunity to choose, and the capacity to choose, Veenhoven concluded 'Although life in individualistic societies is not without problems, the costs of individualism are clearly outbalanced by its benefits' (1996: 180). Also, studies on the individual level within nations show clearly that happy people tend to be more autonomous and well directed than unhappy people (Veenhoven 1989; Diener et al. 2000). However, it is important to point out that the correlation between freedom and happiness is higher in wealthy nations whose citizens are well educated. The correlation between freedom and happiness is not strong in poverty-stricken nations.

In Singapore's recent history, the state has emphasized the community over the individual and the preeminence of economic considerations over personal interests. In fact, the very idea of the state is sometimes couched in economic terms, such as 'Singapore Inc.,' or 'Singapore Unlimited.' All aspects of social planning are connected in some way to economic development. For example, Singapore has recently completed a massive cultural development blueprint, including the construction of a multi-million dollar state of the art performing arts center and a number of new museums. While it is true that Singaporeans will, through these developments, have access to greater enjoyment of the arts and benefit from these cultural activities, the cultural policy blueprint, conceptually coined as making Singapore a 'Renaissance City,' has more to do with attracting tourists and drawing in foreign talent for economic reasons.

The rationale underpinning these endeavors is that Singapore has to become a vibrant city in order to attract foreign talent to migrate and remain in Singapore. It has to be a nice place to live and work. As one government minister speaking on the 'Renaissance City' concept noted, 'Developing Singapore into a world class city is vital. A better and more exciting Singapore will keep and attract foreign talent. Talent is highly mobile. Good talent will go where economic opportunities abound and where life is comfortable and enjoyable.'

## Vulnerability and the nation-state

Singapore had nationhood thrust upon it. It was a reluctant nation. In fact, on the eve of the declaration of independence in 1965, the then Prime Minister, Lee Kuan Yew, remarked that Singapore was a 'political joke.' Since its founding, Singapore has had to deal with the dangers posed by communism and communalism, followed by separation from Malaysia and the concomitant threat to its economic and political survival as a state, and more recently, the increasing economic competitiveness of its neighbors and the threats posed by international terrorism. Singh (2004) for example, noted that

Singapore is a small state and size has always been a key determinant of how the state develops its social policies and international relations. Savage (2004: 197) writes, 'The smallness of Singapore, its lack of natural resources and of a vast untapped hinterland give it very little margin for error,' and in a way, has always been the 'credo of the political leadership's politics of survival.' In addition to the problem of size, Singapore also has to manage the problems and difficulties of a multi-ethnic, multi-lingual and multi-religious population. Ban (2004: 9) notes that, in the early days of nationhood, when Singapore's survival was frequently in doubt, the 'poisoned shrimp' scenario was very much in vogue. To be a poisoned shrimp, he argues, 'imagistically warned would be aggressors that the nation was prepared to engage in all out war. It acknowledged that Singapore could not beat off a determined attack for long but warned that she might very well poison a would be predator.'

Since those early days of nationhood, Singapore has made remarkable progress in the economic, political and social spheres. As noted in the introduction, Singapore has achieved a high standard of living. In addition, it has developed an extremely capable armed force to act as a deterrent against would be aggressors. Through its economic and social policies, the threat of communism and communalism, although still capable of causing instability in Singapore, has largely been resolved. It also has an extremely well educated and well trained work force to ensure its economic survival. Although some of these vulnerabilities do surface from time to time, such as during the Asian Financial Crisis in the late 1990s, and the Sars Epidemic in 2002, Singapore has developed from a 'Third World' country to a 'First World' nation through excellent economic planning and careful management of social and cultural issues within Singaporean society. Singapore now has one of the highest standards of living in Asia, and is a generally peaceful and harmonious social environment.

The idea that Singapore remains a vulnerable state and society, however, still pervades the national psyche. Singaporeans are constantly being reminded by the state that they must be vigilant to face up to the challenges of the modern globalized world. Citizens are constantly told that despite their achievements, they have to continue to strive and work hard, and not to relax and become complacent. In a sense, this is creating a sense of perpetual anxiety. As Hill (2000) noted, it is important to take into account the powerful 'myths,' in the sociological sense of the word, promulgated by the state. First is the perceived threat that there are persistent underlying communal tensions in Singapore that are a source of ethnic conflict. Second is the idea that there is an ever present conspiracy by communist elements to subvert the state. These two threats, from the state's perspective, have the potential to undermine social cohesion in Singapore. Singapore is projected as a vulnerable society and the state emphasizes the 'crisis' and 'survival' motifs in justifying its social policies.

The state constantly reminds its citizens that the alternative to its firm control over their lives is a reversion to what is portrayed as the anarchy and violence of its early days. Hill (2000) further argues that there is a process of constant 'crisis construction' in Singapore that involves highlighting the potential for serious social disorder and hence justifying the use of legislation specifically targeted at pre-empting this possibility. The strategy of 'nipping in the bud' any perceived threat to stability is a central feature of public policy in Singapore.

There is an 'achievement complex' in Singapore. To stay ahead of the competition, Singapore must be 'number one.' Singapore has one of the best airports in the world and one of the best airlines (SIA), is one of the busiest ports in the world, has the best workers in the world, is one of the most competitive economies and is one of the most globalized nations. This constant reminder of and emphasis on not being satisfied with present conditions, good as they may be, undoubtedly result in a relatively high degree of stress among Singaporeans, whether in the educational system or in the workplace. A survey of Singaporeans who migrated or intend to migrate noted that among the reasons for their move stress, particularly in terms of the education of children, was one of the important factors influencing their decision. In fact, according to Seah (2006), Singapore has an outflow rate of 26.11 migrants per one thousand people, one of the highest in the world.

The push to constantly upscale has undoubtedly caused a great deal of stress among many Singaporeans, as the emphasis on excellence conveys the message that 'You're not ok because you're merely average' (Yeo 1985: 75–7). In Singapore the anxiety associated with the need for high achievement is a major source of mental health problems for both children and adults (Macner-Licht 1991: 181). The highly competitive education system is blamed for problems among children and teenagers. Lee (1991: 106) noted that among the different problems felt by youth, stress topped the list. There is also intense anxiety among parents to ensure that their children do well academically. This results in a great deal of tutoring and enrichment classes for children. Youth who do not obtain good school results also suffer from loss of self-confidence, self-esteem, as well as a sense of guilt for disappointing their families. For adults, jobs are stressful because competition and constant pressure to be productive are combined with overwork and a fear of losing out. Stress among school children and working adults is mainly due to the notion that one's personal worth is often measured by performance. This can generate a feeling of inferiority in Singapore where high fliers are singled out for mention and achievement is the hallmark of a successful life (Yeo 1985: 75).

The stress engendered by the 'achievement complex' among many Singaporeans is exacerbated by the concern for 'face.' The desire for a good reputation and the fear of disgrace makes even relatively confident people susceptible to being controlled by the fear of shame. Competitive school and work situations create environments which encourage the attitude expressed by the term *kiasu* (literally meaning 'afraid to lose'). It is a mentality where failure is perceived to be a disgrace (i.e. a loss of face) which would bring embarrassment to the individual and family. Therefore, it is generally accepted that failure is to be avoided at all costs (Tamney 1996: 107).

The success (or failure) of an individual is closely connected with the ideology of meritocracy which has been consistently imprinted on the social body in Singapore. Meritocracy argues that one's advancement should be based solely on one's ability or achievement and this has the tendency to individualize success and failure (Chua 1999: 216). In its desire to extract excellence from every individual Singaporean, the government has consistently promoted meritocracy, stressing the individual's responsibility to strive for his or her own betterment. The Singapore government adopts the meritocratic system because it has brought about social mobility and improvements since people were motivated by rewards and do their best to achieve what they want (*Straits Times*, 19 January 1992).

However, at both the societal and individual levels, meritocracy serves to legitimize income stratification which the state views as the natural outcome of individual effort or the lack thereof (Chua 1989: 1019). It also encourages people to raise their expectations and to demand just returns for their efforts.

In his National Day Rally speech in 2002, then Prime Minister Goh lamented that:

> This is a predicament for Singapore. The more the Government provides for Singaporeans, the higher their expectations of what the Government should do.

During a Parliamentary debate in 1992, an opposition Member of Parliament claimed that Singapore was worse off than in the 1970s. In rebuttal, then Deputy Prime Minister Lee Hsien Loong cited wealth statistics to show that Singaporeans had a better quality of life than the previous generation. He cited statistics to show the increased level of home ownership and savings, as well as higher incomes and better educational achievements among Singaporeans (*Straits Times*, 16 January 1992). However, this led Member of Parliament Dr Wang Kai Yuen to comment that while the wealth statistics used by Deputy Prime Minister Lee were not incorrect, many Singaporeans did not consider themselves better off due to differences in expectation. With better education and employment opportunities, people's aspirations of leading a more comfortable life had also changed (*Straits Times*, 17 January 1992). Therefore, in striving to scale greater heights, the individual ironically felt less fulfilled because the expectation of reward for effort had also risen.

The focus on economic imperatives has worked well for many years, but things are gradually changing; as the new generation of younger Singaporeans are more educated, better traveled, better informed, and did not live through the difficult years of independence, they have different aspirations than previous generations. Thus, over the last few years, there has been a shift in policy from merely focusing on economic aspects to also meeting the higher order needs of Singaporeans. This has been termed the 'heartware' of Singaporean society. For example, in 1997, a committee known as S21 was established, seeking to open up Singapore society and get Singaporeans to practice active citizenship and involve them in shaping the kind of Singapore they want to live in. The idea is to provide Singaporeans with a greater say and more freedom, as the campaign slogan evinces, 'Together, We make the Difference.' As one government minister commented,

> It misleads us into thinking that life is measured in terms of wealth and relationships defined only in terms of contracts. But life is more than this. Our quality of life can never be measured by how much we have, nor can peace and stability be assured by how many guns we can buy. Camaraderie, solidarity, trust, happiness and fulfillment are qualities that hold the people together. And unless we can hold the people together no new economy can bring wealth and prosperity... We need to increase our social capital to cope with the new economy, to strengthen the social glue that makes us not just a diverse collection of immigrants and their descendants, but a nation.

The changes we are seeing in Singapore are gradual and incremental. For example, over the past few years the government has allowed bungee jumping in Singapore, previously banned because it was thought to be too dangerous. Recently, the ban on 'bar-top' dancing was lifted. It had been banned, according to the authorities, because it was dangerous and may lead to accidents or fights among the clients in the bars. And after twenty-five years, the authorities finally allowed the publication of the magazine, *Cosmopolitan*. It had been banned because it supposedly contained risqué material unsuitable for Singaporean consumption.

## Singapore: A 'fun' city

The need to be one step in front of the competition has also been a significant driving force behind the nation's recent campaign to reinvent itself as a fun and exciting global city. The government has been keen to transform Singapore into a culturally vibrant city as other global cities such as New York, Paris and London have been reinventing and successfully marketing themselves as 'hip' capitals of arts and culture; exciting places to work and live. Cities in the region, such as Shanghai, Hong Kong, and Kuala Lumpur, have also been beefing up their infrastructure and drawing more tourist and convention traffic (PM Lee Hsien Loong, Ministerial Statement, 18 April 2005).

While Singapore has often been lauded for its economic success and its safety, it is often perceived as a restrictive city. However, in his National Day rally speech in 2001, Prime Minister Goh Chok Tong envisioned Singapore as a 'Renaissance City,' by which he meant a fun city with creative people, artistic events and a culturally vibrant environment:

> New Singapore will be one of the world's finest, most livable cities. Arts, theatres, museums, music and sports will flourish. Singapore will be a lively and exciting place, with plenty to do and experience. Our city will not only have depth, but also the richness of diversity.

The desire for cultural vibrancy and economic accomplishment is not a divergent goal, as PM Goh Chok Tong pointed out that studies in the US have shown that entrepreneurship is closely correlated with the level of cultural vibrancy. Cultural vibrancy has the added advantage of making Singapore a magnet for tourists and foreign talent—a pool of labor which is perceived as crucial to support Singapore's economic progress.

> Furthermore, a culturally vibrant city attracts global creative talent. Creative people are highly mobile. They do not slavishly go to where the jobs are. They choose where they want to work based on their lifestyle interests, and the jobs and prosperity follow them. They want an authentic street and neighborhood environment, a thriving music and arts scene, openness and diversity. (PM Goh Chok Tong, National Day Rally speech, 2002)

Although Singapore's vision of becoming an arts and cultural hub stems from global and economic reasons, it is deemed to be a strategy to fulfill local socio-cultural objectives. While the economic goal of attracting foreign talent and encouraging tourists is important, arts and cultural events could offer locals a higher quality of life and perhaps retain Singaporeans who might otherwise prefer to emigrate to less restrictive cities (*International Herald Tribune*, 23 August 2005). The government also believes that art and culture can impart a 'softer' image of Singapore and can temper Singaporeans' 'materialistic' attitude. Equally important is the notion that locals can cultivate an arts heritage and culture which can strengthen an emotional attachment to Singapore (Chang 2000: 823).

The city state's plans to develop a vibrant arts, cultural and night-life scene are indeed a bold attempt to re-invent itself. In order to project an image of vitality and openness, Singapore has relaxed several regulations which were deemed too restrictive. In October 1998, the police announced a new set of relaxed regulations for pop concerts. For example, previously entertainers could not step off the stage or mingle with the crowd, and members of the audience were not allowed to go on stage or dance during the concerts. With the new regulations, performers can now mingle with members of the audience and concert-goers can dance in designated areas (*Straits Times*, 5 October 1998).

The authorities also showed some flexibility on the issue of bar-top dancing. Previously under the Public Entertainment Act, bar-top dancing was not permitted and in 2002, a nightclub was fined $500 for allowing two men to dance on its bar-top. However, in an attempt to soften its stance, in August 2003, the authorities allowed bar-top dancing by patrons in any club with a public entertainment license. A separate license was needed if dancers were hired. At the peak of its popularity in 2004, bar-top dancing was a key attraction in at least five nightclubs (*Straits Times*, 27 April 2007). On a micro-level, the revision of rules seemed only to affect concert-goers and those who party at pubs and nightclubs. However, on a larger scale, it was a reflection of the inevitable changes that the government was willing to undertake to show that it was serious in its desire to inject fun and a greater sense of freedom in Singapore. After all, metropolitan cities such as London, New York and Paris have long had a liberal cultural and entertainment scene.

> Now, when I allowed bungee jumping and bar-top dancing, it is not because I encourage these activities...What I had done was to signal a shift in our mindset to being more relaxed and open-minded, and less strait-laced and Victorian. (PM Goh Chok Tong, National Day Rally Speech, 2003)

Currently, however, no prominent club or bar uses bar-top dancing as a main attraction. Despite much lobbying by operators in the entertainment industry and debate among local Singaporeans, bar-top dancing now seems to have been just a passing fad. However, Andrew Ing, chief executive officer at local nightclub St James Power Station noted: 'It was more significant as a move that sparked off the changes in the industry' (*Straits Times*, 27 April 2007).

The other changes include allowing nightclubs to remain open twenty-four hours in non-residential areas and the introduction of The Crazy Horse, a popular Paris attraction which featured erotic choreography and artistic lighting to showcase its topless female dancers. Opening to great fanfare, the show was supposed to be a significant milestone in the adult entertainment scene but it closed after fifteen months because it could not attract enough big spending visitors to fill the 450 capacity venue for thirteen shows a week (*Bloomberg News*, 29 March 2007).

However, this has not proven to be a deterrent to other plans to enhance Singapore's reputation as an attractive tourist destination. After a forty-year ban on gambling, the government legalized gambling in 2005 and made a deal with major gaming companies to develop two integrated resorts (IR) that incorporate casinos. Earlier proposals to develop gaming facilities had been rejected on the basis that gambling would have a negative social impact on the population. However, the government decided on the integrated resorts because Singapore's share in tourism was declining, with tourists spending less time in the country because Singapore was perceived as unexciting (PM Lee Hsien Loong, Ministerial Statement, 18 April 2005).

The IR developed by American casino operator Las Vegas Sands will be one of the attractions of the New Downtown area at Marina Bay. It will comprise hotel rooms, convention spaces, theatres, an ice skating rink, shops and restaurants. The Marina Bay area will also boast the Singapore Flyer—a giant Ferris wheel—and a 100 hectare botanical garden. To add even more buzz to the city, Singapore also secured a deal to become a stop on the Formula One World Grand Prix circuit in 2008, with hopes that the Singapore leg of the circuit would be unique as it may host the first ever night race on its downtown streets (*Times International Asia Edition*, 4 June 2007). Another IR featuring a casino, theme parks, resort hotels, restaurants and shops will be developed by Malaysia's Genting International on the island of Sentosa, complementing the luxury waterfront housing development that specifically targeted wealthy locals and foreigners.

In his Chinese New Year speech, Minister Mentor Lee Kuan Yew reiterated Singapore's aspirations to be a 'tropical version' of New York, London and Paris with the development of the Marina Bay area becoming like world famous St Mark's Piazza in Venice (*Times International Asia Edition*, 4 June 2007). The desire to keep up with the best that other cities have to offer is a trademark of Singapore. As Singapore attempts to transform itself into a vibrant global arts city, the government shows that it is still very conscious of the important economics behind the business of being 'fun':

> We cannot stand still. The whole region is on the move. If we do not change, where will we be in twenty years' time? Losing our appeal to tourists is the lesser problem. But if we become a backwater, just one of many ordinary cities in Asia, instead of being a cosmopolitan hub of the region, then many good jobs will be lost, and all Singaporeans will suffer. We cannot afford that. We need to do many things to become a global city. (Ministerial Statement by PM Lee Hsien Loong, 18 April 2005)

## Conclusion

Singapore is clean, green, efficient, well-planned and orderly. It was also regarded by critics, including international publications such as *Time Magazine*, as artificial, boring, docile, controlled and sterile. In the short history of Singapore, given its historical and environmental circumstances, the state has placed greater emphasis on economic development and the collective interest than on personal interests. Social psychologists suggest that human beings have a hierarchy of needs (see Maslow 1954). At the base level are physiological needs, such as the need for food and nutrients. When physiological needs are largely met, human beings will be interested in meeting their safety and security needs. When these are met, humans will seek to satisfy their love and belonging needs, such as the need for friends, affectionate relationships, even a sense of community. Then, they will seek to satisfy their self-esteem needs, for respect, status, fame and recognition. Finally, there is the need for self-actualization.

Singapore is a victim of its own success. The state's economic and social policies have meant that the more basic needs—physiological, safety and security needs—have been met. In such an environment, people will seek to satisfy their higher order needs, such as autonomy, personal satisfaction, freedom, creativity and human relationships. As noted earlier, the then Prime Minister, Goh Chok Tong, in his National Day Rally Address in 2001, urged Singaporeans to have fun, 'Singapore should be a fun place to live. People laugh at us for promoting fun so seriously. But having fun is important. If Singapore is a dull, boring place, not only will talent not want to come here, but even Singaporeans will begin to feel restless... (W)e have every intention of making Singapore a fun place.' Singapore must be one of the few countries, if not the only one, where the government has initiated a national campaign for its citizens to learn how to have fun. However, the fact that there has to be a 'fun' campaign speaks volumes about the level of happiness of Singaporeans.

# 12
# The Happy Family in Contemporary Rural Vietnam

*Do Thien Kinh*

## Introduction

This research is based upon data from 'The Interdisciplinary Research Project on Rural Families in Transitional Viet Nam (2004–2007).' The aim of the project is to understand the changes in the rural Vietnamese family during the period of Economic Renovation (called Doi Moi in Vietnamese). The research sample for the project consists of 900 households selected from three communes, with 300 households selected in each commune. The three communes are located in three areas representing the three regions of Vietnam: the northern region (Yen Bai), the central region (Thua Thien Hue) and the southern region (Tien Giang). Data collection methods used in the project consisted of questionnaires, in-depth interviews and focus group discussions. Data collection took place in three periods: 2004 (Yen Bai), 2005 (Tien Giang) and 2006 (Thua Thien Hue).

The questionnaire does not pose any question to measure perceptions of family happiness directly. Nevertheless, results of the qualitative investigation carried out in this project have revealed widely held views about family happiness, as indicated in Figure 12.1.

The 'happy family' in this research only encompasses families with both husband and wife. The 'happy family' is determined on the basis of the question: 'On the whole, do you consider your family a "harmonious and happy family" or not, and to what extent?' There

## Figure 12.1: *Representative ideas about the concept of 'happy family'*

> First of all, the happy family is where everyone in the family lives in harmony, respecting those who are older and making sacrifices for those younger. The family economy is stable, the children are healthy and study is going reasonably well. This is an unchanging concept. In the past it was and now it remains the same...Together with this is the issue of the material and economic life of the family. If there is not enough finacially the family will end up fighting and arguing with each other.
> (In-depth interview, 2006. Male, sixty-five years old, Thua Thien Hue Province)

> Question: According to you, to have a happy family one must have money, or to have a happy family the husband and wife must be in harmony, or to have a happy family means the children must achieve successfully and be well behaved?
> Response: We think that a harmonious family is a family of happiness. If there are all three [money, harmony and successful children], then all the better.
> Question: If there were all three, then it would be better. If not, then what would you pick as the most important factor of all?
> Response: When there is harmony all other matters [money and successful children] can be worked out.
> (Focus group discussion, 2005. Women's group, forty-five–fifty years of age, Tien Giang Province)

are five responses to choose from: (a) my family is very happy and harmonious; (b) my family is relatively harmonious and happy; (c) my family is not a harmonious and happy family; (d) difficult to respond; (e) don't know. The determination of what a happy family is actually like is completely up to the respondent's perception. Several statistics from this question (for all three provinces) are presented in Table 12.1.

Broadly understood, Table 12.1 has up to 97.4% happy families (consisting of 48.1% households 'very happy' and 49.3% households 'relatively happy'), with just 1.9% families 'not happy.' The number of households examined in the 'not happy' group of families is too small (fifteen) to make meaningful comparisons with the happy families. Due to this, in order to clarify the comparison between families who are genuinely happy and the other remaining groups, happy families

*Table 12.1: Family happiness statistics*

| Level of happiness | Households % | (N) | Average number of children | Type of family — Nuclear family | Type of family — Non-nuclear family | Total % |
|---|---|---|---|---|---|---|
| Very happy | 48.1 | (375) | 2.2 | 65.9 | 34.1 | 100.0 |
| Relatively happy | 49.3 | (384) | 2.2 | 68.0 | 32.0 | 100.0 |
| Not happy | 1.9 | (15) | 2.5 | 73.3 | 26.7 | 100.0 |
| Don't know | 0.6 | (5) | 1.6 | 60.0 | 40.0 | 100.0 |
| Total | 100.0 | (779) | 2.2 | (522) | (257) | |

Note: ( ) = number of observations.

as defined in this research consists of only the 375 'very happy' households. The remaining families that identified as 'relatively happy,' 'not happy' and 'don't know' are described as other families. Determining that the category 'very happy' is the only happy family category implies certainty in the assertion that a particular family is genuinely happy. As for the remaining families, happiness for them is not really stable.

# Profile of happy families in rural Vietnam

## Characteristics of individuals

Table 12.2 reveals clear general trends. For male respondents, the proportion of happy families is greater than that of other families (51.7% > 48.3%). On the contrary, for female respondents the proportion of happy families is less than the proportion of other families (44.1% < 55.9%). As such, more male than female respondents usually feel that their families are happy (51.7% > 44.1%). This may be because the husband in the family has more power than the wife. Perhaps it is this that makes him feel happier?

In the groups forty-nine years and younger, the proportion of happy families is less than that of other families (44.4% < 55.6%; 48.9% < 51.2% and 49.1% < 50.9%). During this period of life children have yet to reach adulthood and are still living with their parents. Father and mother must strive to care for the children and to consolidate the economic life of the family. Perhaps due to this, the family happiness is not great. On the contrary, in the groups of fifty years of age and older the proportion of happy families is greater than the proportion

*Table 12.2: Characteristics of individuals*

| Individual characteristics of the respondent (usually the head of household) | Very happy family | Other family | Total % | (N) |
|---|---|---|---|---|
| *Sex* | | | | |
| Male | 51.7 | 48.3 | 100.0 | (414) |
| Female | 44.1 | 55.9 | 100.0 | (365) |
| *Age* | | | | |
| Under 40 | 44.4 | 55.6 | 100.0 | (302) |
| 40–44 | 48.9 | 51.2 | 100.0 | (131) |
| 45–49 | 49.1 | 50.9 | 100.0 | (116) |
| 50–54 | 52.5 | 47.5 | 100.0 | (80) |
| 55–59 | 54.4 | 45.6 | 100.0 | (57) |
| 60 or over | 50.5 | 49.5 | 100.0 | (93) |
| *Education level* | | | | |
| Illiterate | 41.7 | 58.3 | 100.0 | (48) |
| Primary school | 45.4 | 54.6 | 100.0 | (280) |
| Years 6 to 9 | 49.4 | 50.6 | 100.0 | (336) |
| Upper secondary & higher | 53.9 | 46.1 | 100.0 | (115) |
| *Ethnicity* | | | | |
| Lowland[a] | 52.8 | 47.2 | 100.0 | (608) |
| Minority ethnic group | 31.6 | 68.4 | 100.0 | (171) |
| *Religion* | | | | |
| No religion | 45.2 | 54.9 | 100.0 | (474) |
| Buddhism | 59.8 | 40.2 | 100.0 | (204) |
| Other religion | 38.0 | 62.0 | 100.0 | (100) |
| *Occupation* | | | | |
| Non-agricultural | 57.6 | 42.5 | 100.0 | (245) |
| Agricultural | 43.8 | 56.3 | 100.0 | (528) |

a = The Lowland (Kinh) group is the majority ethnic group in Vietnam.

of other families (52.5% > 47.5%; 54.4% > 45.6% and 50.5% > 49.5%). At this stage of life children have grown up, mother and father have more leisure time and the family's standard of living is better. Perhaps due to this, families feel more happiness. The general trend is that the older the age of the respondent the greater the feeling of family happiness: 44.4% → 48.9% → 49.1% → 52.5% → 54.4%.

Among groups with low levels of education (Year Nine or below) the rate of happy families is less than that for other families (41.7%

< 58.3%; 45.4% < 54.6% and 49.4% < 50.6%). On the contrary, in the cohort with high education levels (upper secondary and higher) the proportion of happy families is greater than that of other families (53.9% > 46.1%). The general trend is that the higher the level of education achieved by the respondent, the greater the proportion of happy families. Specifically, as the level of education increases there is a corresponding increase in happy families: 41.7% → 45.4% → 49.4% → 53.9%. This may be because the highly educated person will nurture family life better and the family will be happier.

In relation to the remaining characteristics of respondents: the cohorts of lowland (Kinh) ethnicity, followers of Buddhism and non-agricultural occupations have higher proportions of happy families than those of other families: 52.8% > 47.2%; 59.8% > 40.2% and 57.6% > 42.5%. With other responses the proportion of happy families is less than that of other families: 31.6% < 68.4%; 45.2% < 54.9%; 38.0% < 62.0% and 43.8% < 56.3%.

*First observation*: respondents who are male, older aged with a high level of education, those of lowland (Kinh) ethnicity, followers of Buddhism and those working in non-agricultural occupations all experience living in a happy family more than respondents with characteristics of being female, young, having a low level of education, belonging to minority ethnic groups, not following Buddhism and working in agricultural production. Accordingly, examination of the correlation between these characteristics and happy families will probably find them to be the dynamic factors related to happiness of the family. This point will be made using statistical regression modeling in the following section.

**Concerning material welfare**

In Table 12.3, for families who have a moderately wealthy standard of living and where the husband makes the largest contribution to regular family spending, the proportion of happy families is greater than that among other families: 60.4% > 39.6% and 57.0% > 43.0%. This illustrates the pivotal role the husband plays in family economics. In relation to the remaining responses, the proportion of happy families is smaller than that of other families: 49.2% < 50.8%; 38.1% < 61.9% and 46.2% < 53.9%; 46.2% < 53.8%; 49.3% < 50.7%.

*Second observation*: examining the correlation between the moderately high standard of living and the husband contributing most to daily expenditure in terms of identifying as a 'happy family' reveals

*Table 12.3: Concerning material welfare*

|  | Very happy family | Other family | Total % | (N) |
|---|---|---|---|---|
| *Family household standard of living* | | | | |
| Moderately wealthy | 60.4 | 39.6 | 100.0 | (144) |
| Average | 49.2 | 50.8 | 100.0 | (417) |
| Poor | 38.1 | 61.9 | 100.0 | (218) |
| *Who contributes to regular family spending?* | | | | |
| Husband mainly | 57.0 | 43.0 | 100.0 | (100) |
| Wife mainly | 46.2 | 53.9 | 100.0 | (39) |
| Husband & wife equally | 46.2 | 53.8 | 100.0 | (500) |
| Other | 49.3 | 50.7 | 100.0 | (136) |

that these are factors impacting upon family happiness. This will be shown by statistical regression modeling in the following section.

## Concerning married life

In Table 12.4, regardless of who decided to have the marriage, the proportion of happy families is always smaller than that of other families. However, if the couple (husband and wife) themselves decided to marry, then the proportion of happy families will be greater

*Table 12.4: Concerning married life*

| Married life | Very happy family | Other family | Total % | (N) |
|---|---|---|---|---|
| *Who decided you should marry?* | | | | |
| Parents (mainly) | 46.8 | 53.2 | 100.0 | (201) |
| We did | 48.7 | 51.3 | 100.0 | (571) |
| Other | 42.9 | 57.1 | 100.0 | (7) |
| *Are you satisfied with married life?* | | | | |
| Satisfied | 50.0 | 50.0 | 100.0 | (744) |
| Not satisfied | 9.1 | 90.9 | 100.0 | (33) |
| *Did you argue during the past year?* | | | | |
| Frequently | 9.5 | 90.5 | 100.0 | (21) |
| Sometimes | 33.3 | 66.7 | 100.0 | (267) |
| Rarely | 49.3 | 50.7 | 100.0 | (229) |
| Never | 65.4 | 34.6 | 100.0 | (260) |

(48.7% > 46.8% > 42.9%). This may be because when it is the couple deciding to marry they will have a more harmonious married life. Simultaneously when husband and wife are satisfied with married life and never argue, then the proportion of happy families will be greater (50.0% > 9.1%; and 65.4% > 49.3% > 33.3% > 9.5%). Particularly when a husband and wife never argue, the proportion of happy families to other families is far greater than the proportion for other families (65.4% > 34.6%).

*Third observation*: when the husband and wife assume responsibility for deciding to marry, are satisfied with married life and never argue with each other, then the proportion of happy families will be greater. It is very likely that these are also factors impacting on family happiness. This point will be shown in statistical regression modeling in the following section.

## Allocation of housework

In Table 12.5 the absolute numbers (N) indicate that the wife is the main person in charge of expenditure (606 cases), cooking (570 cases), washing the dishes (546 cases) and washing clothes (596 cases). From another perspective, the relative numbers (percentages) also demonstrate that when the wife is primarily responsible for cooking, washing dishes and clothes, then the proportion of happy families is also greater compared with that of other responses (50.0% compared with (35.9%, 46.2%, 43.6%); 49.1% compared with (42.9%, 47.4%, 45.7%); 48.7% compared with (47.4%, 42.3%, 47.8%)). These are tasks compatible with women. The husband would have other more appropriate work. When there is reasonable sharing out of the work between the husband and wife, then the life of the family will be happier. This is the *fourth observation*. It may be that these are also factors impacting upon the happiness of the family. This point will be made by statistical regression modeling in the following section.

## Distribution of productive work and social activity

In Table 12.6, in relation to productive work, purchasing expensive goods and the relationships in the family and among relatives, it is only when both husband and wife make decisions together that the proportion of happy families is greater compared to cases where the wife (or husband) alone is primarily responsible for decision-making. Specifically, the corresponding comparative proportions

*Table 12.5: Allocation of housework*

| Sharing domestic tasks | Very happy family | Other family | Total % | (N) |
|---|---|---|---|---|
| *Who looks after spending money?* | | | | |
| Husband mainly | 46.5 | 53.5 | 100.0 | (71) |
| Wife mainly | 48.2 | 51.8 | 100.0 | (606) |
| Husband & wife equally | 52.0 | 48.0 | 100.0 | (75) |
| Someone else | 40.7 | 59.3 | 100.0 | (27) |
| *Who cooks?* | | | | |
| Husband mainly | 35.9 | 64.1 | 100.0 | (39) |
| Wife mainly | 50.0 | 50.0 | 100.0 | (570) |
| Husband & wife equally | 46.2 | 53.9 | 100.0 | (52) |
| Someone else | 43.6 | 56.4 | 100.0 | (117) |
| *Who washes the dishes?* | | | | |
| Husband mainly | 42.9 | 57.1 | 100.0 | (21) |
| Wife mainly | 49.1 | 50.9 | 100.0 | (546) |
| Husband & wife equally | 47.4 | 52.6 | 100.0 | (38) |
| Someone else | 45.7 | 54.3 | 100.0 | (173) |
| *Who washes the clothes?* | | | | |
| Husband mainly | 47.4 | 52.6 | 100.0 | (19) |
| Wife mainly | 48.7 | 51.3 | 100.0 | (596) |
| Husband & wife equally | 42.3 | 57.7 | 100.0 | (52) |
| Someone else | 47.8 | 52.3 | 100.0 | (111) |

are: (54.0% compared with (39.2%, 46.4%); 52.9% compared with (42.0%, 45.5%); and 49.7% compared with (40.2%, 48.0%)). In relation to social activities together as husband and wife, when the husband makes decisions about these activities then the proportion of happy families is greater than that when only the wife (or both husband and wife) are mainly responsible (50.8% compared with (36.3%, 48.1%)). Furthermore, when the husband makes decisions about social activities, the proportion of happy families is greater than the proportion of other families (50.8% > 49.2%). Possibly these activities are factors impacting on the happiness of the family. This point will be made by statistical regression modeling in the following section.

## Family well-being determinants model

Even though we examined the mutual relationships between factors in Tables 12.2 to 12.6 for happy families, these tables are likely to have

*Table 12.6: Distribution of productive work and social activity*

|  | Very happy family | Other family | Total % | (N) |
|---|---|---|---|---|
| *Who makes decisions about the family's productive work?* | | | | |
| Husband mainly | 46.4 | 53.6 | 100.0 | (375) |
| Wife mainly | 39.2 | 60.8 | 100.0 | (125) |
| Husband & wife equally | 54.0 | 46.0 | 100.0 | (250) |
| Someone else | 56.5 | 43.5 | 100.0 | (23) |
| *Who decides to buy expensive goods for the house?* | | | | |
| Husband mainly | 45.5 | 54.6 | 100.0 | (286) |
| Wife mainly | 42.0 | 58.0 | 100.0 | (119) |
| Husband & wife equally | 52.9 | 47.1 | 100.0 | (350) |
| Someone else | 45.5 | 54.6 | 100.0 | (22) |
| *Who attends to relationships in the family and among relatives?* | | | | |
| Husband mainly | 48.0 | 52.0 | 100.0 | (298) |
| Wife mainly | 40.2 | 59.8 | 100.0 | (87) |
| Husband & wife equally | 49.7 | 50.3 | 100.0 | (376) |
| Someone else | 60.0 | 40.0 | 100.0 | (15) |
| *Who decides what social activities you do together?* | | | | |
| Husband mainly | 50.8 | 49.2 | 100.0 | (317) |
| Wife mainly | 36.3 | 63.8 | 100.0 | (80) |
| Husband & wife equally | 48.1 | 51.9 | 100.0 | (368) |
| Someone else | 60.0 | 40.0 | 100.0 | (10) |

overestimated the effect of each factor upon the family's happiness. For example, when respondents have a high level of education then their families' living standards are also high. Moreover, happy families which have high living standards also have household heads with high levels of education. So, are happy families the result of good living standards? Or is it because of a high level of education? This issue can be resolved by using independent variables concurrently in the same regression model. This model allows the measurement of the direct effect of each individual variable, provided that the effects of the other variables remain unchanged. After an assessment selection process from amongst a number of models, the best fit logistic regression model for happy families was selected.

In Table 12.7, the dependent variable is the happy family of the respondent. This dependent variable is a binary variable with two values 0 or 1. This variable is 1, if the respondent's answer is a happy family, and is 0 if otherwise. The independent variables of the model are mostly kept unchanged as described in Tables 12.2 to 12.6. The independent variables are dummy variables with two values 0 or 1 (except the age variable which is a continuous variable). With statistically significant variables (P-values ≤10%, or coefficients are marked + or ++), a negative coefficient shows that the independent variable has a reverse effect on the dependent variable; a positive coefficient shows a favorable effect. In other words, if there is a negative coefficient, the change in the dependent variable will be a decrease; or if the coefficient is positive, the change in the dependent variable will be an increase. Only statistically significant variables are analyzed. When observing the direct effect of each independent variable upon the dependent variable there is a limiting condition that other independent variables remain unchanged. To gain specific understanding of the coefficients' values, the clear illustration of percentages in the last column in Table 12.7 could be considered. These figures are the results of calculations based upon the coefficient of independent variables. Remember, all of the families have the initial probability of 48% of being a happy family because the rate of happy family in the sample is 48% (Table 12.1). The analysis of variables in Table 12.7 is as follows:

1. There are ten statistically significant variables in Table 12.7, including two variables that make family well-being decrease. These are the variables 'occupation' and 'the wife decides on social activities for the couple.' If the occupation of the respondent is in the agricultural sector, the probability of being in a happy family drops from 48.0% to 35.3% compared with similar households in which the respondent's occupation is in a non-agricultural sector. Working in a non-agricultural sector will provide a life with more material things and a happier family. If the wife decides what social activities the couple will engage in, the probability of having a happy family drops from 48.0% to 34.0% compared with similar households where the husband (or someone else) decides on social activities. In a family, the husband tends to hold more power than the wife. This is one of the significant factors in the formation of a family at the time of marrying and afterwards when maintaining a growing family. In the case where the wife holds more power than the husband, the family well-being is reduced.
2. In regard to variables which increase family well-being, there are clear examples such as those above. Specifically, the probability of having a happy family increases gradually from 48.0% up to

## Table 12.7: Estimation of the best fit logistic regression model for very happy families

| | Coefficients | | P-values[a] | Estimated probability of having a happy family[b] |
|---|---|---|---|---|
| *Dependent variable* | | | | |
| Is the family very happy? (Yes = 1) | | | | |
| *Independent variables* | | | | |
| 1. Nuclear family (Yes = 1) | 0.026 | | 0.883 | - |
| *Respondent profile* | | | | |
| 2. Gender (Male = 1) | 0.154 | | 0.381 | - |
| 3. Age | 0.009 | | 0.235 | - |
| 4. Education level (Upper secondary and higher = 1) | 0.230 | | 0.327 | - |
| 5. Ethnicity (Lowland Vietnamese = 1) | 0.741 | ++ | 0.001 | 65.9 |
| 6. Religion (Buddhist = 1) | 0.646 | ++ | 0.001 | 63.8 |
| 7. Occupation (Agriculture = 1) | -0.527 | ++ | 0.003 | 35.3 |
| *Family living standard* | | | | |
| 8. Living standard (Moderately rich = 1) | 0.391 | + | 0.067 | 57.7 |
| 9. Husband contributing to most of expenses (Yes=1) | 0.401 | + | 0.100 | 58.0 |
| 10. Wife contributing to most expenses (Yes = 1) | 0.334 | | 0.399 | - |
| *Married life* | | | | |
| 11. Both husband & wife make decisions in their marriage (Yes = 1) | 0.167 | | 0.385 | - |
| 12. Husband & wife are happy with their married life (Yes = 1) | 2.521 | ++ | 0.000 | 92.0 |
| 13. The couple never argue with each other (Yes = 1) | 1.247 | ++ | 0.000 | 76.3 |
| *Distribution of home duties and social activities* | | | | |
| 14. Husband & wife have equal share of money for expenses (Yes = 1) | 0.007 | | 0.981 | - |
| 15. Wife does most of the cooking in the home (Yes = 1) | 0.360 | + | 0.060 | 57.0 |
| 16. Husband & wife decide on expensive household item purchases together (Yes = 1) | 0.472 | ++ | 0.004 | 59.7 |
| 17. Wife decides on social activities for the couple (Yes = 1) | -0.584 | ++ | 0.043 | 34.0 |
| Constant | -4.558 | | 0.000 | |
| Observance | 766 | | | |
| $R^2$ | 0.14 | | | |

a = all: P-values > 10% (or not statistically significant), except:
   ++ = P-values ≤ 5%.   + = 5% < P-values ≤ 10%.

b = provided that one independent variable changes by one unit, the remaining variables are unchanged, and the initial probability is 48.0%

65.9% for the lowland (Kinh) Vietnamese (compared with the ethnic minorities), up to 63.8% for Buddhists (compared with non-Buddhists), up to 57.7% for the moderately rich (compared with households with average incomes or less), up to 58.0% when the husband contributes the most to expenses (compared with the wife or someone else contributing most to expenses), up to 92.0% when both husband and wife are happy with the marriage (compared with unhappy couples), up to 76.3% when the couples never argue with each other (compared with couples who argue with each other often or sometimes), up to 57.0% when the wife is the main person who does the cooking in the home (compared to cases where the husband or someone else cooks).

3. Looking into the examples of the probabilities to have a happy family, the underlying meaning behind the numbers can be seen. Specifically, the lowland (Kinh) Vietnamese and followers of Buddhism have a relatively higher probability of having happy families. This may be due to the philosophy of Buddhism which teaches people to lead a more honest lifestyle. The moderately high living standard of a family is also an important contributing factor to enhance family well-being. Where the husband is the one contributing most to the expenses, this is also a contributing factor in enhancing the family well-being (compared with the wife contributing most to the expenses). This shows the husband's pivotal economic role determined as being the key role in enhancing and maintaining his family's well-being. Particularly when couples are happy in their marriage and never argue with one another, the probability of having a happy family is very high. This proves that marital factors and husband and wife compatibility play a key role in maintaining family well-being. This factor is far more important than moderate material wealth in the family. This corroborates the qualitative research findings shown in Figure 12.1.

4. Finally, the wife being the main person who does the cooking in the home is indicative of the domestic role of the wife in nurturing and maintaining family well-being. This task is compatible with women. This has been a traditional and stable way of sharing home duties between the wife and the husband in rural areas in Vietnam from ancient times until the present day. In this way, the family is happy.

Through the above exposition and analysis, it is possible to summarize the description of the happy family in rural Vietnam as follows:
1. Type of family: The nuclear family is becoming dominant. In excess of half (65.9%) of all happy families are nuclear families. The proportion of nuclear families in the very happy families is smaller than the proportion of nuclear families in other families (Table 12.1).
2. The average number of children in the very happy family is 2.2 children. This rate is lower than (or the same as) that of other families (Table 12.1).
3. Employment and allocation of house work between the husband and wife: Processed data from this project has given the research results that most husbands and wives in the research sample have employment generating income, but the proportion of husbands with work is greater than the proportion of wives working. At the same time, the predominant occupation of husband and wife is work in the agricultural sector, but the proportion of wives with agricultural jobs is higher than that of husbands. Besides this, the proportion of husbands with other supporting jobs is higher than that of wives. The wife is predominantly the person who does the housework in the family. From this it may be concluded that the employment model of rural Vietnamese husbands and wives at the present time is that the husband is always in a more advantageous situation than the wife in terms of main occupation, secondary and other supporting jobs and household work. This point means that the economic contribution of the husband in the family is more than the wife's. That is, the husband is the main economic pillar; the wife is the smaller support (Do Thien Kinh 2007). The employment situation of the husband and wife in the very happy family is also similar to the general employment model above. However, in the group of very happy families, the husband's advantageous situation is more prominent than in other families. The husband has more power than the wife (Table 12.7).
4. Household standard of living: The happy family is better off with a moderately prosperous standard of living compared with other families; or it could be said that households with moderately prosperous living standards have a greater proportion of happy families than that of other families (Figure 12.1, Table 12.3 and Table 12.7).

5. Harmony in the family: The husband and wife are satisfied with their married life and everybody in the family lives together in harmony (Figure 12.1, Table 12.4 and Table 12.7).
6. Position of the children within the family: Mother and father care about children, desiring that they are healthy, obedient, and studious and successfully achieve in their lives (Figure 12.1 and Table 12.7).

Data in this research does not refer to urban families in Vietnam. However, the author's understanding is that urban families can be observed to be different from rural families in four aspects: (1) the main sector of employment for urban families is non-agricultural, whereas in rural areas it is agricultural; (b) the standard of living for urban families is higher than the standard in rural areas; (c) urban families are concerned with the education and life achievements of their children more than rural families; and (d) rural families do not hire people to assist with housekeeping work, while there appear to be a number of urban families who hire people to help in the home. From this perspective, the family in urban Vietnam has many features that resemble the model of the European modern family.

## The happy family: Rural Vietnam and Europe

According to Ochiai Emiko, the modern family in Europe made its appearance in the middle of the eighteenth century and at the start of the nineteenth century among the middle class. These families had domestic servants, the husband and wife were bound together by love and obedient children. This was one among several types of family that co-existed in society. At that time families belonging to the working class presented a completely different profile. Of particular note was the family in poorer classes: the children were addicted to alcohol and the husband and wife argued with each other (Ochiai 1997: 79–81). Although the modern family was more prevalent than other types of family, it did not attain pre-eminence throughout society. Every person during the nineteenth century still chose different types of family living. The modern family only became widespread during the twentieth century in Europe. In these families there were two or three well-behaved lovable children with the wife usually taking responsibility for the housework. This is indicated by the declining proportion of women participating in the workforce and declining birth rates (Ochiai 1997: 81).

Besides the common features and functions of the family in general, some other important features of the twentieth century modern family (compiled from Ochiai 1977: 76-8) are as follows:
1. The modern family is a nuclear family with two or three children.
2. Allocation of work is based on gender: household work in the home is usually done by the wife and the husband is the economic pillar of the family.
3. The husband and wife are bonded together by love; or the marriage is for love, not an arranged marriage.
4. The children are the focus of attention and receive care and concern from the family.
5. The individuality of family members is valued and respected.
6. From feature (4) the basic function of the family is the socialization of the young children.
7. From features (3) and (5), the central function of the modern family is to increase the happiness of all family members. In other words, the value of the modern family is the pleasure and happiness of the family.

Examining the two types of families, the 'happy family' in rural Vietnam and the modern family of twentieth century Europe, it is seen that they have several basic features in common. In essence, these two family styles belong to the same type but are labeled differently. The one called 'happy family' in rural Vietnam is named from the perspective of psychology with the aim of demonstrating the value of the strong emotional relationships among family members. The name aims to signify the central function and value of the family. At the same time, the name 'modern family' aims to mention the one type of family in the modern age. Therefore, the analysis using the 'happy family' in this research refers to the modern family. Besides a number of similar fundamental features shared by the happy family in rural Vietnam and the European modern family, there are a number of distinct characteristics and issues posed by the happy family in rural Vietnam:

1. The number of families having a wife devoting all of her time to domestic duties is very small. Most husbands and wives have jobs to generate income. Besides this, the wife must do additional housework in the family. At the same time, happy families in rural Vietnam do not yet hire domestic workers to help look after the house, and the majority of these families have a moderately

wealthy (comfortable) standard of living. Meanwhile, it has been observed that middle class Vietnamese urban families do hire people to assist with work in the home. Examination of the characteristic of hiring house workers by middle class families reveals that this characteristic of urban Vietnamese families is analogous to the European modern family at the beginning of the nineteenth century and the Japanese modern family during the Taisho period (1912–1926). Is it therefore likely that rural happy families will be transformed like urban families? That is, will the rural happy family have domestic servants? This was the trend with modern European families in the middle of the eighteenth century.
2. Generally, the husband is the main financial pillar for the family. More specifically, the husband is the large pillar with support from his wife as the smaller pillar. This is because both husband and wife have jobs providing income and together they contribute relatively equally to expenditure in the household. Meanwhile, in the modern family of twentieth century Europe the husband was the economic pillar with the wife responsible for a lot of housework within the home. This was evident by the reduced proportion of women participating in the workforce.
3. Factors relating to married life and the harmony of the couple play a major role in increasing happiness in the family (Table 12.7). This proves that in order to perform the central function of the modern family in Vietnam (to increase the happiness for family members), it is most important to maintain the romantic love between spouses and contentment with their marriage. It is also important to maintain harmony and contentment of family members generally.

The points above concerning the happy family in rural Vietnam have been viewed in the context of the European modern family model. At the same time, it has been seen that there are a number of distinct features and several problems posed for the happy family in Vietnam. These points also indicate ways to increase family happiness for the Vietnamese people.

# Postscript

# 13
# The Conditions Essential to Alternative Sociology
*Kenji Kosaka*

## Introduction

At Kwansei Gakuin University, Japan, a number of Sociology and Social Work faculty members have been engaged in an ambitious and grand program for the past five years, in pursuit of social research that can best serve the enhancement and implementation of human well-being in this 'desert of the real' that is the contemporary world (Žižek 2002). We have continually revised the strategic points we wish to pursue in order to achieve this goal, as the past five years has been a process of trials and errors involving hundreds of scholars, both domestic and international. The goal is not as yet realized in its fullest sense, due to the dialectical process involved in scientific advances. We are nevertheless determined to report our initial conclusions to the academic community at this time. These findings have been reached after a chain of arguments, disputes, proposals and deconstructions among the participants in the program. We now wish to report these conclusions to colleagues who share our interest in upgrading the scientific status of sociology. A decade, at least, might be needed for any program, if it is to be an ambitious and grand one, to deserve to be called an 'intellectual Odysseus' or an 'academic Argonaut.' Yet, even at this intermediate stage of research we have managed to achieve some notable results. Our present concern is to make explicit the conditions essential to alternative sociology by reflecting on and referring to the past activities related

*Figure 13.1: Triadic paradigm of the enquiry*

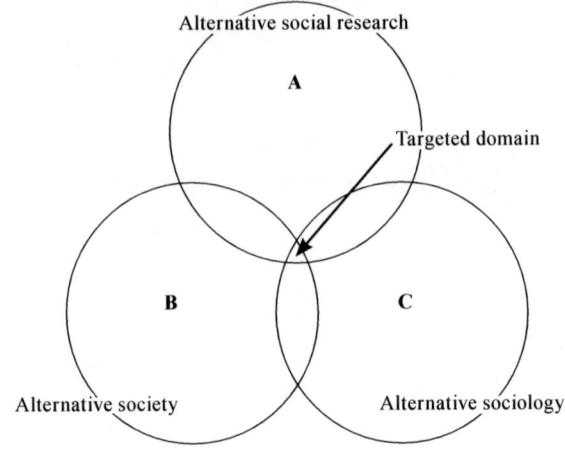

to our program. In short, we ultimately want to propose what we call the intersected domain as our academic target and pursuit, consisting of three sub-domains named (1) alternative social research, (2) alternative society and (3) alternative sociology. The targeted domain is shown in Figure 13.1.

In the following, we first depict the paths lying ahead that will allow us to explore each sub-domain primarily in connection with the aforementioned program.

## Ways to explore alternative social research

There are several ways, from the technical to the philosophical, to explore alternative social research. Through a variety of workshops and publications, we have emphasized basic methodological orientations, rather than purely technical methods as such, or difficulties we might face during the course of fieldwork, which are seldom questioned once we are engaged in social research. Our own research orientations may well be summarized as follows (Furukawa 2007).

### Beyond the dualism of researcher and subject

Whether in quantitative research, qualitative research, or experimental research, a sharp demarcation between researcher and subject is assumed, which naturally reflects the division of labor or differentiated social roles in implementing social research. The researcher is expected to 'take the attitude of a disinterested observer' (Schutz 1996: 143), while subjects are interested enough to express themselves by responding to questions asked in the form of YES or NO (quantitative research) or in discursive form (qualitative research). However, the researcher is not able to dissociate himself or herself from being a member of those ordinary actors living within a social world, or from a socio-cultural background. One solitary social scientist can best cover only limited aspects of social reality; hence, it is difficult to describe realities objectively (Clifford and Marcus 1986). Therefore, a sharp distinction between researcher and subject turns out to be problematic once it leads us to the conviction or belief that there are some objective realities on the researcher's side which are hard for a subject to access. In actuality, as we often experience it, there are any number of influential processes underlying the researcher-subject relationship even before the formal research activities begin. As a result, there are feedback processes between these relationships. In some cases, research schemes are revised, concepts used are changed, and subjects supply more information to the researcher than is expected. A sharp distinction between the researcher and subject relates to the image that the researcher is experienced, while subjects are laymen with poor investigative skills. We are now convinced that this is not the case: ordinary citizens are sometimes well-equipped to go deeper into the investigative process if properly directed (Miyauchi 2007).

## Beyond a quantitative/qualitative dichotomy

The dichotomy of quantitative and qualitative research has haunted many disciplines including sociology and social research for a very long time. Most textbooks in social research only mention vantage points of both types of methods. Some textbooks suggest an 'overlap' or 'fusion' of both traditions with such approaches in mind as grounded theory, ethnomethodology, conversational analysis and content analysis (Payne and Payne 2004), although this assertion is very rarely made explicit. The dichotomy of the two traditions seems indispensable. Hence, the possibility of building a bridge across different traditions and methods of social research is all the more difficult because each social scientist is ordinarily trained only in one or the other methodology. Barthe's suggestion, cited by Clifford and Marcus (1986), argues that a truly interdisciplinary approach is to find and formulate a 'subject' to be examined, which has never belonged to any discipline before. In line with this reasoning, we want to formulate a 'subject' to be examined by both quantitative and qualitative methods, thus integrating the two traditions. Seiyama (2007) suggests that we should create an explanatory 'story' as a part of sociological explanation even in quantitative oriented studies. Our experience in the program makes us feel that day-to-day dialogue among those who are oriented in diverse methodologies is needed, in addition to our individual sociological imagination, in order to create such a 'story.'

**To overcome the preponderance of text oriented literacy**

At a very early stage in our program, we were determined to use methods which were unexplored methodologically, hoping that these unexplored methods would elucidate the aspects of phenomena that would not be clarified otherwise. The principle of the drunkard's search can be modified to the methodological situation we face. This well-cited principle tells a story of a drunkard who is looking for his lost house-key under a street lamp, when he had actually dropped his key some distance away. Being asked why he did not look for the key where he thought he had lost it, he replied, 'It's lighter here!' Kaplan (1964) used this epigrammatic story to illustrate the use of logic in methodology, but the story can also be used to describe the situation where a drunkard is liable to use whatever methodological tools he already has at hand. Consequently, we attempted, by evading the foolery of the drunkard, to use non-verbal communication in contrast to verbal communication, and visual methods in contrast to the conduct of writing, as a method of information gathering, both primary and secondary. From this methodological orientation, we came up with two remarkable outputs. The first is a brief animation concerning the bullying problem among young children in contemporary Japanese society which was made by one of the program's participants, Masahiro Ogino. It was his hope that this animation would depict the landscape of social settings where bullying incidents are likely to occur. The animated sketch is not subject to scientific testing in its rigorous sense, but seems to be used as a methodological tool to explore the derivative and secondary information from among those who have seen the film. After having seen the film, participants start talking about their own images and perceptions regarding bullying activities, and about their own experiences of being involved in bullying, if any, as well as their collective memories (Ogino and Yukimura 2006).

The second outcome in this line of methodological orientation is linked to a series of studies of sign languages (Kamei 2007). Sign language is regarded as both a subject and a set of tools. Who has ever dared to use sign language to size up opinion among the deaf? The idea is closely linked to the recommendation of 'sketch' as a methodological tool to describe the subject in social research, which is also an attempt to extend our understanding 'beyond text oriented literacy.'

Another program faculty participant, Kōkichirō Miura, proposes the use of an epistolary style which is also far beyond text oriented literacy, as long as 'text' implies something written in an academic style. By allowing a letter or correspondence style, Miura (2007) himself succeeded in conveying the subtle messages implied between lines and covert comments he has made but never previously published in an academic journal. Letters are used not as materials for analysis but as articles in themselves.

## In recognition of cultural and linguistic diversity within universals

Overcoming text oriented literacy is strongly related to the orientation towards the recognition of cultural and linguistic diversity. Using a native tongue as a tool for collecting information has been a task that anthropologists have faced since the nineteenth century in various corners of the globe. This is not a simple problem of using a native language or performing an equivalent translation. The success of collecting information depends on forming a research team that is fully equipped to conduct investigations in diverse socio-cultural settings. Nepal was the setting where Furukawa, another faculty participant, has been dedicated to the task of seeking out the perspective of happiness among the indigenous people living there. He successfully formed a research team with the help of Nepal Environment and Culture Research Institute (NECRI), a research-oriented NGO, and some staff members of the Tribuvan University who are all engaged in a painstaking but intellectually pleasing inquiry through the use of four languages (Nepalese, Newar, English and Japanese) and fully reciprocal translation among them. Their efforts are bearing fruit in the form of editing a thesaurus from transcribing the oral history records. Kurosaka (2005) illustrates problems involved in interviewing and transforming depicted text (from translated, to edited and finally to described text) to show how, for instance, in the Newar language 'jaat' (roughly meaning caste) is to be interpreted depending on the context. We encounter similar problems again and again when we interview people whose native languages are different from those of the researcher in the Philippines, Vietnam, Cambodia, China, and France. From our own experience we know that equivalence of transcriptions described in different languages depends on the quality of a research team in terms of language skill, cultural sensitivity, respect for the heterogeneous, recognition and integrity, and academic capability. In the Newar study, interviews were done in Newar which is the native language for both interviewer and interviewee. Recorded tapes were transcribed in Japanese by those interviewers whose native language is Newar, and whose language proficiency in Japanese is good enough for them to translate the texts into Japanese. Editing and final description were completed with some additional comments by Kurosaka, a Japanese living in Nepal, who is married to a Nepalese male. She also suggests that finding a 'sharer' who can communicate with both an interviewer and an interviewee is necessary for quality interviewing. Still, because of the limited array of castes among NECRI members, the researchers failed to find a suitable 'sharer' for the interview with anyone from the Pode caste (people who traditionally work as sweepers).

Recognition of cultural diversity is one way of conceiving, defining or practicing the alternative social research. We think that methodological consideration for the recognition of cultural diversity is not sufficient or adequate for the comparison of societies unless there is some universal analytical framework formulated within which we could compare the societies. Structural communality or a formal notion of structural equivalence has to be elaborated for further study.

## Significance of de-elaboration

In survey analysis, the logic, the notion of elaboration in particular, is one of the most important strategies in social research (Rosenberg 1968). Given a cross-tabulation of two variables, we automatically think of the third possible variable involved in the original tabulation. Admitting this importance, we still want to emphasize the importance of 'de-elaboration' as it were from the standpoint of long-range scientific advancement.

For instance, a hypothesis was demonstrated by Matsuura concerning the incidence of festivals and higher birthrate (Matsuura

2005). A decline in the birthrate to less than 1.3 children per woman is now regarded as a 'social problem,' since this decrease in the number of newly-born children transforms the population structure of a society as a whole. The birthrate in Tokyo is now 1.29, while in Okinawa it is 1.72. Matsuura goes so far as to closely examine the variation within a province, Hyogo Prefecture in this case, by indicating that the birthrate in Kobe (an urban area) is 1.23 while that in Tajima (a rural area) is 1.84. To be more specific, he found a significant relationship in Hyogo Prefecture between the number of shrines and the birthrate. He inferred that the existence of many shrines is a sign of active religious rites, and is an indicator of strong community power, which might lead people to hold various festivals. He then concluded that the incidence of active festivals and a higher birthrate is strongly correlated. Here the 'incidence of active festivals' itself is an interpreted intervening variable. Allowing for that, we are still puzzled by the possible relationship between the incidence of active festivals and a higher birthrate. Perhaps, a sociologist would adopt a strategy of elaboration as a conventional step to clarify the causal relationships between the two variables by introducing a third variable such as, say, social cohesiveness, which encourages local residents to produce children with minimal inconvenience, either financial or social. However, our many research experiences suggest that such an elaboration could, even if we managed to gain access to the relevant data under examination, raise only a small coefficient of determination, which indicates that the entire causal configuration sometimes remains undetermined despite the strategy of elaboration employed. Note that we do not deny the relevance of the strategy as such. We rather wish to emphasize the originally designated relationship between the two variables as a baseline model before the strategy of elaboration is taken, using our imagination and more abundant possibilities for any future elaboration. We call the strategy of NOT-introducing the third variable, remaining at the initial constellation of variables, the 'de-elaboration' strategy.

Ogino adopts this 'de-elaboration' strategy in his paper in this volume, suggesting a strong relationship between old arms-facility bases and incidences of suicide of people suffering from *ijime* (bullying). An ordinary sociologist would go so far as to search for intervening variables such as degree of suburbanization, a heterogeneous and isolated migrant population, lack of sense of community or belonging, weak ties among residents, or high rates of social mobility, etc. Perhaps partly because of the absence of relevant data, Ogino remained at the initial baseline and would not go further. This allows him to successfully convey the untested but powerful hypothesis. The reader, whether scientist or not, might recall the incidence related to the initial hypothesis or give counter examples, then contribute to the task of elaboration in the future. If an elaboration strategy were taken immediately, the reader would not be given a chance to ponder over the rudimentary hypothesis, and would hasten to make an evaluation by introducing the third variable.

## Ways to explore an alternative society

As is the case with alternative social research, there are many ways to explore an alternative society at various levels of analysis, more diverse than in the case of social research. Historically, there was a time when proposals as to an alternative society consisted of the choice between a socialist society or not, an approach that continues to this day in the form of neo-Marxism (Wright 2006). Since even under the socialist system, we believe, human well-being would not be fully realized, we chose the enhancement of human well-being as our global goal instead. The tasks of achieving well-being are then broken down to the following.

### Which is 'better'?

Popper (1984) once published a collection of papers under the title *Auf der Suche nach einer besseren Welt* (In search of a better world). Popper seems to believe that western democracy was already a better world than any other preceding or contemporary societies because it had succeeded in forming a social order that allows people to reform the system from within. Among the necessary reforms he identified were, in particular, eliminating penury, and the reform of the criminal laws to extirpate crimes. Whether or not we share Popper's view of reforms and the evaluation of reforms, we can follow his lead as we continue asking which is better.

Unless we manage to determine which social states are better, we cannot interrogate the alternatives. Although our use of the term 'alternative' might recall some particular historical movement or incident in the late sixties and seventies which occurred in diverse advanced societies around the world, we do not want to be tied to our history or to the history of thought as such. Rather, we want to confine ourselves to discussing the problem in a more general way, while recognizing that it is sometimes difficult to demarcate between the historical problem and the general problem.

We have established human well-being as the supreme value to be pursued. Certainly, human well-being deserves to be set as the supreme value. But this focus or concern as our goal remains a tautological statement until the notion of human well-being can be specified so that we can tell which social states are better than others by inventing some way to measure them. The task is all the more difficult since people have different outlooks or perspectives of well-being and happiness, even among students of happiness studies (Veenhoven 2000).

## Decreasing ill-being rather than increasing well-being

No matter how much we strive to increase well-being, as Ichii (1971) points out, there is always someone who suffers from ill-being after the reforms are 'completed'. Ichii proposes to decrease the unreasonable unhappiness that characterizes contemporary society. In an earlier paper (Kosaka 2006: 5–11), in line with this proposal, we summarized the three elements of the ill-being of humanity as (1) Many, (2) Casualties, and (3) Innocent. 'Many' implies that an incident or condition involves 'a large number of people' or is not an 'accidental occurrence' according to 'the dialectic leitmotif conversation of quantity to quality' (Adorno 1966). 'Casualties' refers symbolically to ill-being as a whole, that is, as the 'deprivation of life opportunities.' Indeed, 'In many cases, people are not happy even when things in general seem to be satisfactory' (Comte-Sponville 2000). This may well be particularly the case with so-called advanced industrialized societies where high levels of affluence have been achieved but misery remains rife. 'Casualties' as 'worst conditions,' however, are still part of daily life even in such societies. By 'Innocent' we mean to imply that those involved in an incident are not responsible for its occurrence, although this becomes problematic as in the case of the 'responsibility' of the Japanese Showa Emperor for the occurrence of World War II.

Roemer (1996) attempts to quantitatively estimate the degree of responsibility of someone (or, some social group) by contriving to divide the society under concern into factions of equivalent classes according to environmental factors in order to more clearly see the magnitude or degree of personal responsibility. Hamada (2006) daringly takes an axiomatic approach to the disadvantage index, producing a sustained mathematical grounding for the level of ill-being. In both of these cases, the breakdown of ill-being into three elements is the first attempt to allow us to talk of an 'increase' or 'decrease' of ill-being.

## Conflicting values and human well-being

If we accept that the goal of realizing human well-being is best achieved through efforts to decrease ill-being, numerous problematics remain. Among other things, we have a number of competitive values and norms such as justice, equality, liberty, fraternity, hospitality, recognition, common goods, economic growth, sustainability, and so on. These values are competing against each other in determining which principle should come first. Depending on the particular ordering of multiple normative principles, we would have different orderings of societies.

For example, the so-called Human Development Index (HDI) of the UNDP project ranks all nation-states on the basis of three indices: the life expectancy index, education index, and the GDP index, which are operationally defined respectively (UNDP 2005). The 2003 HDI ranked Norway the highest and Niger the lowest with every nation state ranked hierarchically in between. Obviously, a different set of indices would result in a different ranking of nations. We would be interested in the resultant order when, for example, a Gross National Happiness index—a measure coined by the Kingdom of Bhutan—was introduced into the system. Almost all disputes in the social sciences and political philosophy, of which the libertarian / communitarian dispute is one, are concerned with preferences of leading normative principles.

The task of forming a ranked order among competing normative principles is not the endpoint. There is a possibility that competing principles are not only competitive but also contradictory. For example, two distinctive normative principles—say, equality on the one hand, and the Pareto optimum on the other—may not work simultaneously. Suppose that the fixed amount of resources, say, 100 units is distributed among two players in such a way that one player gets one unit and the other gets ninety-nine units. This state of distribution meets the Pareto optimum since no other way of distribution of resources would satisfy both players simultaneously in terms of betterment of payoff newly obtained. It obviously does not, however, meet the principles of equality.

In the end, we are not yet fully prepared to ask for an alternative society, except for setting human well-being as the ultimate value, since we have not yet reached any agreement about possible hierarchies of normative principles and the incompatibilities between these principles. We are at present satisfied, though, no matter how imperfect our thinking may be, with that which we are entitled to discuss. It is sufficient at this time that we are endowed with a public space where we are allowed to discuss what we want to discuss.

## Levels of society

In the quest for an alternative society, levels of society have to be specified in terms of, firstly, the level that is responsible for threatening well-being and/or producing ultimate ill-being typical of the times. Secondly, we need to specify the level of society at which reformative actions, private or public, for the alternative are to be taken. Three levels are to be distinguished: the level of globalization, of micro everyday life processes, and of organizations within a society. These levels correspond roughly to nation-states, individuals within families, and intermediate groups. Since these levels are substantively intertwined, distinctions are a matter of convenience to some extent.

### The nightmare of globalization

Within a given nation-state, alternatives could be realized by choosing a new political leader, voting for an oppositional political party, forming a new constitution, and so on, which obviously affect the level of well-being and ill-being. However, our main concern here is with the well-being and ill-being of humanity, not of people of a given nation-state or country. Neither individual people nor whole societies can be happy without well-being at the global level.

Hubert Sauper's film *Darwin's Nightmare* (2005) tells a tale about humans between the North and the South, about globalization, and about fish. As functionalism and a Parsonian social systems theory once disclosed, everything is related to everything else at the global level, producing a disparity of wealth, hence poverty as human ill-being, and lack of recognition and respect for heterogeneity and minorities, invisible or visible.

Everyday life processes leading to war: In his collection of essays titled 'Senso toiu Shigoto (Job of War),' Japanese philosopher Uchiyama (2006), points out that many people in contemporary society are deeply involved in the activities of war, trying to protect themselves by making a living. Contemporary societies produce masses of people who are motivated mainly by their own daily interests, and a constellation of nations, with the super-state of the USA as a leading nation, attempts to sustain stability by expanding its economic and political order to form a system which allows wars and strife here and there, no matter how local. A non-fiction writer, Shimamoto (2006), describes how wars have provided people with job opportunities. This implies that the deterioration of economic opportunities could eventually lead people, even though the effort of overcoming economic difficulties could produce 'small happiness' temporarily, to irreparable disaster and the human ill-being of war. A possible causal relationship between everyday life processes and war as an end-result remains hypothetical, sometimes intractably hypothetical, but deserves to be examined closely. This is particularly the case where corporate warriors prevail, and the rise of the privatized military industry is flourishing at a global level (Singer 2003).

## Organizational accidents and miseries

In *Life and Death at Work*, Dwyer (1991) examines the hypothesis that social relations at labor settings which are determined by rationalization and modernization processes produce serious industrial accidents, drawing upon case studies of medical error and educational fiasco in Brazilian society. He points out that images supporting this hypothesis contribute to providing a cognitive map by which we can transform a stagnant society. Reason (1997), an engineer, discusses various organizational accidents in detail, asking what produces or causes the miserable results. Organizational accidents are depicted as accidents that have ramifications beyond the individual level, impacting upon those who are not initially connected with the accidents, ultimately destroying environments and assets. Such accidents are brought about by those working within organizations and are caused by a variety of factors. Organizational accidents are potentially involved in all sorts of things involving human activities such as atomic power, aircraft, railways, financial trade, mass behavior in sports arenas, human error in maintenance, medical management and maltreatment including dosage error.

Organizational accidents, we believe, have to be examined closely not only in terms of engineering and the natural sciences but also sociologically, incorporating human factors, decision-making processes, power and authority relations among those working in organizations, in addition to ethical issues. Sociological examinations of accidents by way of social research prepare the way for preventive prescriptions, thereby leading us to an innovation in sociology itself. Ironically, the experience of the Great Hanshin Earthquake, which occurred in Kobe and surrounding areas in Japan, brought us remarkable advances in the sociology of disaster.

## Ways to explore alternative sociology

In the late sixties and early seventies, a movement within the discipline of sociology began to flourish and move toward a radical and alternative sociology. This new movement was sparked by the idea of a crisis looming in Western sociology (Gouldner 1970), a crisis that reflected the anti-systems movements and counter-culture of the time. We do not wish to be involved in any evaluation of these forms of sociology. Instead, we ask, what are the required conditions for a discipline to be called 'alternative'? We claim that a discipline deserves to be called 'alternative' in its narrower sense when, firstly, those in the discipline manage to pose problems, both theoretical and empirical, which have seldom been regarded as problems in previous investigations. Secondly, 'alternative' sociology as a discipline is valid when some new methodological or paradigmatic frameworks are shown. Thirdly, sociologists themselves must fulfill new roles if an alternative sociology is to be substantiated. In the following section we want to indicate explicitly in what sense our program has been a sustained effort to pursue 'alternative sociology.'

### Academic absence and discursive absence

As mentioned earlier, our program has been primarily concerned with human well-being. The topic of happiness has been an investigatory focus and repeatedly discussed with academic interest since the time of classical Greek philosophy (Nussbaum 1993). The collected works of the utilitarian philosophers could be positioned as studies of human happiness. Spencer, one of the first generation of sociologists in the nineteenth century, wrote a book concerning the essential conditions of human happiness. However, the subsequent history of sociology shows that the issue of human happiness was put aside, the result being that the problem of social order has mainly been highlighted instead. This twisted history will provide an interesting issue to be investigated in detail in the future. Succinctly, the problem of happiness has been ignored until quite recently in sociology. In economics also, very few studies have been relevant before the recent work by Frey and Stutzer (2002). In this respect, the investigation of human happiness itself is already an alternative, in that the issue or importance of human happiness has rarely been questioned for the last two centuries.

We have been engaged, under the umbrella of the program, in a series of workshops and symposia under the title of 'S'interroger l'implicite' (Interrogating and eliciting the implicit) and have published a collection of papers in relation to the controversial problems and new directions of minority group studies. All these workshops and symposia were attempts to pose problems which have been scarcely interrogated and problem-solving lines of investigation which have been scarcely employed before. For example, Corbin (2006), in his lecture on advanced social research, emphasized the importance of bringing back the senses of hearing, smelling and touching which construct landscape as social surroundings. The history of landscape has thus far been occupied by students of the arts but, Corbin claims, should or needs also to be occupied by students of historical anthropology. We additionally want to claim that the history of landscape should be of deep concern to students of sociology, in ways that other disciplines would not explore or investigate.

Problems hardly questioned range between the theoretical and empirical: Pande in this volume poses the problem of commercialized surrogate motherhood in India in the present age of globalization, which is an empirical question, perhaps never posed before. Questions of that which has previously remained unquestioned, highlighting shaded aspects of a society, and indicating the least indicated questions itself is part of a sustained effort for seeking an alternative sociology. We call such problems 'academic absence.' This stance is a reflection of 'a philosophy of negation,' which attempts to 'call the place of the investigator into question where the existing researchers and scholars are located and where they are not' (Spivac 1988).

There is another type of absence which we might call 'discursive absence' (Kavalski and Zolkos 2006), which attempts to highlight hidden messages or messages never referred to. Indeed illiterate societies do not have means to record their own histories in written form. It is well known among historians, however, that some social groups such as those who lack education, the oppressed, the discriminated, and minorities have not been successful in recording their miseries as well as they have been in recording positive experiences they have encountered. Furthermore, people intentionally suppress certain information and beliefs when they voice something. A sustained analysis of a series of what has been suppressed, we believe, will elucidate intellectual findings that would otherwise remain undisclosed.

## A sociology of missed opportunity

Karl Marx pointed out in his Eleventh Thesis on Feuerbach that philosophy has only been active in interpreting the world; what is more necessary is to change the world. Despite all the effort that has been made, this critical comment seems to be applicable to the current status of sociology. This is particularly the case when we characterize sociology's *raison d'être* as contributing to the increase of well-being or the decrease of ill-being. The alternative sociology, in this line of thought, is to be pursued so as to provide action/policy proposals which would increase happiness and lessen unhappiness. This quest may well be achieved in many ways but, here, we want to propose a sociology of missed opportunity as at least one of the promising means of seeking the alternatives.

A sociology of missed opportunity is defined by Kosaka (2006) as a sustained effort to find out what opportunities have been missed, opportunities which could have helped avoid human miseries and ill-being, and how these opportunities were missed. For example, the Vietnam War is obviously a disastrous episode in the world of contemporary history, a conflict where the huge death toll did not result in any increase in happiness or life chances for anyone, but was instead a disaster for many. In a conference organized by Robert McNamara and others, including former-North Vietnamese generals, to assess the causes of the war's escalation, it was observed that the Pleik Incident, an attack by North Vietnamese forces in February, 1965, drastically escalated the war. Their discussion/analysis revealed that a terrible misunderstanding about centralization and decentralization regarding communication systems was involved in the incident (McNamara 1999: 204). This was clearly one of the missed opportunities of the Vietnam War.

In response to General W. Y. Smith's question regarding whether there was some point in the 1963–64 period when the North Vietnamese orders were changed to grant greater authority to local commanders, Nguyen Co Thach (then-Officer of the Foreign Ministry, North Vietnam) replied:

> You must keep in mind that our economy is an agricultural economy, not an industrial economy, nor did it develop like the US economy... With an agricultural economy there is always decentralization, because communication is so difficult. But industrialization leads to urbanization and centralization. So you see: You were very centralized in your decisions and commands, and we were very decentralized in ours.

We are not so optimistic as to believe that the Vietnam War would have ended earlier, or might not even have occurred to begin with, if it were not for this misplaced knowledge held by the authorities. We admit that any historical and current incident is an accumulation of the end-results of a series of minor actions among ordinary people and the authorities in particular who are in a better position to make substantial decisions in the political processes within and outside a nation state. Furthermore, we could and should locate every possible opportunity which might have led to a state of misery, and search for the one(s) which we should not have missed for the sake of human well-being as a whole. Recognizing that decision-makers' knowledge and perspectives—whether right or wrong, biased or unbiased—is deeply implicated in decision-making processes of both individuals and collectivities, it appears that sociology—the sociology of knowledge in particular—is well positioned to reveal ex post facto how knowledge and perspecitves were formed among the people who are responsible for the incidents leading us to human ill-being or misery.

Sociology thus far has rarely succeeded in proposing specified solutions to solve social problems, partly because these problems were not successfully formulated in an explicit way. The first thing to do is to formulate the problems we want to be answered. In our program, we have been mainly interested in how to lessen human ill-being. Therefore, all problems are to be formulated in tune with this task. Some problems may be fuzzy and/or too general, no matter how deep they may be in philosophical terms, such as overcoming the *Dialektik der Aufklärung* (Dialectic of Enlightenment), the task set by Adorno and Horkheimer. Other problems may be very specific, such as how the nuclear power plant accident at Three Mile Island or the Piper Alpha Disaster could have been avoided (Reason 1997). No matter which level of specification the problem may be, we should specify the problem in such a way as to allow us to find a solution or solutions to the problem.

The notion and practice of alternative sociology thus signifies a type of sociology which contributes to concrete solutions, no matter how hypothetical they may be, to the problems for lessoning human ill-being. Should we be satisfied with hypothetical solutions? Sometimes yes, because problems to be solved arise in succession over time. 'Economic growth or environmental conservation?' is a commonplace type of question we repeatedly experience in our daily life situations almost everywhere in the world. A decision in daily political processes needs to be made sometimes even before any robust solution based on a solid basis is found. To equip sociology with the theoretical apparatus necessary to meet these conditions, we propose three perspectives as follows.

First, systems theory has to be revisited. A rise and decline of systems theory in the social sciences needs to be examined in the sociology of knowledge, although we cannot yet discuss this in detail. As suggested by Kosaka (2000), the notion of 'system' is closely linked with the perceptual framework to identify the actual problem to be solved. For example, if we assume that the parents' child-rearing practices are responsible for their child's misbehavior, we then define, implicitly or otherwise, the system of concern to include both the child's behavior and his or her parents' child-rearing practices, as well as perhaps changes in the broader social system. If we assume that the misbehavior of the child is ascribed to the behavior or response (or non-response) of school teachers, we then define a system under study as school teachers' behavior and the behavioral change(s) over time in addition to the above. In sum, we are led to define the system to be examined in as specific a way as possible. No matter how vague or unclear the problem itself may be, the definition of a system must be specific.

Secondly, as mentioned above, we may well end up with some or many solutions which remain hypothetical in nature. How can we evaluate plural hypothetical solutions? Here we cannot avoid some value-laden and ethical judgments, without which evaluations of solutions may not be achieved since they are all in the same hypothetical status. In the modern history of the social sciences—and sociology in particular—perhaps due to the overwhelming influence of Max Weber, we sociologists have become ascetic and timid in investigations which might involve value-judgments. However, we believe that it is time to liberate ourselves from this excessively ascetic attitude. Otherwise we become cynical and agnostic in the face of a situation where we are required to order the hypothetical solutions in terms of, say, the principle of lessening human ill-being. If we attempt to be too scientific, hypothetical solutions do not permit us to take actions to solve problems since they may be too premature to determine what the ultimate cause of the problem is and who is or who is not responsible for the problem and to what extent. However, when we manage to confirm the hypothetical nature of the proposed solutions, it may be too late to prevent misery and ill-being, as was illustrated in the case of Minamata disease (caused by organic mercury poisoning in the waste water discharged by a fertilizer plant). A type of scientism encapsulated in the claim that 'As a scientist, I refrain from making statements unless I am sure of the facts' led to a failure to grasp available opportunities to avoid the deterioration of the situation caused by that disease (Kosaka 2006).

Thirdly, we need a theoretical apparatus which is subject to the way solutions are realized during the interaction processes. Control systems theory, in particular, seems to be capable of being reformulated so that it can capture and picture the realization process of designated solutions. According to Powers, behavior is the control of perception which produces a negative feedback system (1973: 61). Reference signals come from memory, drives, operative ideals, interests, senses of value, pleasure and pain, pride and resentment, sense and sensitivity, that which haunts us, and from prejudice, as well as the amount and types of knowledge held. However, Powers' scheme is limited in that it reflects an organism model which cannot account for multiple actors in a system. Even a simple interaction system between a child and his or her parents is more complex than a single actor system. Control systems theory that allows multiple-agents is needed because alternative sociology should picture the processes of transformation from the existing society to the alternative, processes that involve many diverse actors in the political process.

## Roles of sociologists in alternative sociology

An alternative sociology will not be substantiated or realized unless it is 'used' by the public or other agents, even if it provides us with a new perspective and possible solutions toward the enhancement of human well-being. Sociological knowledge, we believe, may well not be 'used' directly as it is without mediators. We need people called 'middlemen' (Lazarsfeld et al. 1967) or 'facilitators' in PLA (Participatory Learning and Action) research (Takeda 2005), who are basically social scientists, or sociologists in particular, and who are able to apply the findings or hypothetical—but promising—solutions to concrete situations for the betterment of a society and its people.

A middleman is a scholar who has a tremendous amount of flair in praxis by way of understanding the nature of the problem, demands of clients and a sustained motive to improve the social settings for the better with a well-equipped disciplinary knowledge and a normative orientation. A middleman as defined by Lazarsfeld et al. (1967) faces the tasks of choosing a general strategy, opening communication channels with targeted subjects and specifying general concepts. A middleman, located between clients and the social sciences—sociology in this case—is expected to act as an intermediary with clients by translating practical problems into sociological problems on the one hand, and translating sociological findings into practical policy-orientated actions on the other hand.

## Concluding remarks

We have proposed the strategic points for alternative social research, the alternative society, and alternative sociology respectively, each of which can be pursued independently of the other. This means that endeavors based on either one of the three sub-domains can be undertaken without paying much attention to the other two. To take only one example from recent publications, Wright (2006) explores a way 'Towards a Socialist Alternative,' which seems to focus more on an alternative socialist society allowing social empowerment and on alternative social science which he calls 'emancipatory,' rather than on alternative social research as such. Consequently, there are eight types of sociological investigation depending on which sub-domain is focused on. Wright's effort toward a socialist alternative can be characterized as the fifth type.

We want to emphasize as mentioned at the beginning of this chapter that our final goal lies in the intersection of the three sub-domains, represented as Type 1 in Table 13.1, no matter how difficult it may be to fulfill this goal. Conditions essential to alternative sociology are, in the final analysis, necessary conditions of the three sub-domains within which we have specified some possible strategic

*Table 13.1: Eight types of investigations toward the alternative*

| Types | Alt social research | Alternative society | Alt sociology |
|---|---|---|---|
| 1st | 1 | 1 | 1 |
| 2nd | 1 | 1 | 0 |
| 3rd | 1 | 0 | 1 |
| 4th | 1 | 0 | 0 |
| 5th | 0 | 1 | 1 |
| 6th | 0 | 1 | 0 |
| 7th | 0 | 0 | 1 |
| 8th | 0 | 0 | 0 |

Note: '1' means 'focus,' while '0' means 'out of focus.'

points. This means that we need to focus on the three sub-domains simultaneously.

Even though we attempt to focus on the three sub-domains at the same time, different combinations of strategic points can be used to fulfill the purpose. Among these possibilities, combinations of the following—which I personally have prioritized and have been pursuing with colleagues—seem to be most pressing and promising:

1. Cross-cultural analysis of views of happiness: Views of well-being and happiness are varied. We have differentiated these perspectives into four types: active/passive and inclusive/expansionistic (Kosaka 2007) to cross-tabulate partly from ethnographic studies and partly from Sen's argument for and against human security and HDI, respectively. Sen (2003: 8) points out that 'HDI is focusing on progress and augmentation in its basic idea and is extremely expansionist in nature. HDI aims to cultivate and achieve new areas in order to improve human life. It has to be complemented by the notion of human security.' If we pursue happiness in its expansionistic terms, we would leave an even greater amount of human ill-being behind us, which we do not want.

2. Sociology of missed opportunities: This is one of the most promising fields of study for alternative sociology—since it allows for any number of connections and linkages—with the quest for alternative society and alternative social research. Indeed, history repeats itself. But the history of human misery might be blocked from repeating itself through historical examination of the number and type of missed opportunities,

along with a determined commitment to take action for the fulfillment of lessening human ill-being. One remark deserves special mention: the lessons to be learnt from missed opportunities and examining these in the following historical course of action are not sufficient conditions for the goal of lessening human ill-being. The removal of the main cause for phenomenon X may easily be replaced by another cause or causes which also might lead us to phenomenon X. Note that our society is full of 'equifinality,' implying that different causes produce the same result by way of a different process or processes.

3. How to increase human well-being and decrease ill-being given limited resources: Any society dreams of economic development, particularly sustainable development designed to expand resources, economic and otherwise. However, we argue that the mere expansion of resources and the expansionistic development of resources are two different things. Thus, our concern here is how we can increase the aggregated level of life satisfaction, hence of happiness or subjective well-being, by redistributing the given total amount of resources without thinking of enlarging the pie. This analysis is now called 'Virtual Re-distributional Analysis (VRA)' by Ishida, Hamada and myself (in preparation) at the global level as well as at the domestic level. A large body of literature has been interested in finding the determinants of human subjective well-being through a rather conventional statistical method of analysis, using a given data set. We have attempted to discern the pattern of variables which influences the level of subjective well-being using the Boolean approach based on the dataset the World Value Survey and Human Development Report (Ishida, Kosaka and Hamada 2006). However, our ultimate goal lies in detecting the specific ways through VRA to achieve the goal of either the increase of well-being or the decrease of ill-being, which surely reflects a certain principle of distributive justice.

The current age is full of a sense of the pursuit of human well-being, not only among academic scholars but also among ordinary literate people (*News Week*, May 2007) who exist all over the world (*Journal of Happiness Studies*, Bhutan's idea of General National Happiness and Thailand's Green and Happiness Index, to name just a few examples). This shows us that the pursuit of human well-being is prevalent in both Western and Non-Western societies. Although the views, academic or otherwise, of non-Western societies seem to have been under-represented even in the quest for alternative sociology, it is now high time to go beyond Western versus Non-Western perspectives.

# Notes

## Chapter 1

1 No official statistics exist on *ijime* suicide cases. We collected information from newspaper articles, identified *ijime* suicide cases in which junior high school students killed themselves, and used data regarding the number of such cases. We identified 142 *ijime* suicide cases (eighty-nine boys, forty-nine girls and unknown for four cases). The total number was broken down by prefecture. The resulting numbers for different prefectures were compared with the frequency distribution of the average number of *ijime* cases per 1000 students for each prefecture over five years. The comparison revealed that a higher frequency of *ijime* cases does not indicate higher likelihood of *ijime* suicide cases occurring.
2 In the Shimoyama incident, Sadanori Shimoyama, the president of the Japanese National Railways, went missing on his way to work and was, fifteen hours later, found dead beside train tracks. Some suspect that Shimoyama's death was instigated by the GHQ.
3 In spaces without hybrid landscapes, such as a large city, people are less likely to face a situation where they fail to draw a line between life and death due to the abstraction of death. This is because shrines, Buddhist temples and churches function more effectively in large cities (as seen in the large numbers of visitors they attract, including tourists), which helps residents draw a clear line between skyscrapers and religious facilities in terms of space and prevents individuals from being completely wrapped up in the variety of spatial components, unlike the case with hybrid landscapes.

## Chapter 2

1 The Hirabayashi lawsuit was brought on the grounds that both the imposition of a night time curfew and the 'evacuation' orders violated the US Constitution and were an aggression against civil rights. The Korematsu lawsuit, similarly, was also fought with reference to the 'evacuation' orders and the incarceration. The term 'evacuation' is an euphemism the federal government used to refer to the forced removal of the Japanese and Japanese Americans on the West Coast.

2 *Adarand Constructors v. Pena*, 515 US 200 (1995), 215–16, 236.
3 Act of March 26, 1790, 1 Stat. 103 (1790); Act of July 14, 1870, 16 Stat. 250 (1870).
4 163 US 537 (1896).
5 347 US 483 (1954).
6 Single men who had travelled to the US sent their own photographs home to their parents and received photographs of prospective brides from their parents. If both parties agreed, then the wedding ceremony was held without the bridegroom being present and once the bride had gone through the process of being entered on the family register, she applied for a passport. Women who came to the US in this manner are referred to as 'picture brides.' In the eyes of white people in the US this practice was seen as odd and the Japanese government stopped issuing passports on the grounds that this practice was encouraging the Japanese exclusion movement.
7 An outstanding example of this is the ignoring of the Munson Report that rejected suspicions such as that of spying by Japanese and Japanese Americans (Commission on Wartime Relocation and Internment of Civilians 1982: 52–53).
8 Japanese American National Museum Website: http://www.janm.org/jpn/ general/ history.html; and http://www.janm.org/jpn/general/mission.html: Accessed: May 20, 2007.
9 We thank Mr. Shino for kindly sending us the transcript of his lecture.

# Chapter 3

1 For a critical analysis of neo-liberalism, see Harvey 2005a, 2005b.
2 The notion of 'civil society' has been situated as a vital element in the discourse of the liberal-versus-communitarian debate. However, the opposing camps in the debate have not adequately addressed the fact that the violence of globalization has become so intense that the very feasibility of 'civil society' is being radically reappraised. See Delanty (2003) for an exploration of the vicissitudes of the way 'community' has been discussed in connection with the state, society and the individual. See Rasmussen (1995) for a discussion of the liberal-versus-communitarian debate from the perspective of intellectual history or philosophy.
3 For a more recent attempt to outline a 'middle path' from the communitarian standpoint, see Etzioni (2001).
4 The results of a survey on security awareness show a tendency for affirmative opinions of 'installation of surveillance cameras' to increase with age. This can be understood to show, albeit indirectly, a division between the generations, with adults as the actors in 'watching,' and young people as the objects being 'watched.' Source: *http://www.toppan.co.jp/ news/newsrelease455.html#top* (Toppan 2006).

# Chapter 5

1 IVF is simply the uniting of egg and sperm in vitro (in the lab). The embryos are subsequently transferred into the uterus through the cervix.

2 This surrogate was an exceptional case, much more educated than the rest, with higher than the average family income. She did not belong to that area and had traveled from East India just to be a surrogate.
3 See Debra Satz (1992) for more on the thesis that there ought to be an asymmetry between our treatment of reproductive labor and our treatment of other forms of labor.

# Chapter 9

1 This estimation was given by former UN Secretary General, Kofi Annan during the 19th commemoration of the accident. This is roughly equivalent to the total number of people living in the three former states of Belarus, Ukraine and Russia, which were then all parts of the USSR and which have received direct radioactive fallout from the accident. This general estimation however, does not take into consideration all possible stigmas/manifestations of rare sicknesses that have appeared since then and that could have been induced by the accident.
2 Numerous controversies surround the expected consequences of the explosion so it is hard to give a definite number. Depending on the methodology one uses, numbers can be drastically different, as illustrated by reports written in 2006 giving an estimation of the number of deaths due to radioactivity-induced cancers from a minimum of 4000 to a maximum of 400,000!
3 Some Websites published pictures of Belarussian children with tremendous malformations, without any details about their origins.
4 Cesium 135 and strontium 90 would take approximately 300 years to disintegrate. For the areas contaminated with plutonium 239, this will take thousands of years as its 'half life' (time period required for half of the radioactive material to disappear) is approximately 24,000 years.
5 This district's South border is about fifteen kilometres away from the Chernobyl nuclear plant.
6 Thyroid cancer is the most common form of cancer initiated by radiation in the region. It is the result of large absorption by young children (through milk) of iodine 131 in the week following the accident. Its quick appearance, development and strength surprised all scientists.
7 A 710 kilometre-long river which flows along the Narovlia District and the thirty kilometre 'forbidden zone's' circle around the Chernobyl nuclear plant.
8 A radioactive sample is characterised by its activity, the number of disintegrations of radioactive nodes. The Curie (Ci) is the old unit of radioactivity measurement, equivalent to the activity of one gram of radium, the naturally radioactive element found in the ground with uranium. The new measurement unit is the Becquerel (Bq), equivalent to the number of disintegrations per second. The Becquerel, as a very small unit of measure, helps measure very small activity: one Curie is equal to thirty-seven billion Becquerel. As a reminder, the human body's natural radioactivity is 114 Becquerel per kilograms. A seventy kilogram-man has an approximate body radioactivity of 8000 Becquerel.
9 This medical watch has now disappeared in the visited area. Since 2001, the electronic surveillance equipment has been out of order. Numerous

demands for its replacement made by local doctors have never been met and the equipment had not been replaced when we last visited the area (October 2003).
10. Official statement by the Chernobyl Committee of the Republic of Belarus on Important Issues Concerning Nuclear Accident at Chernobyl, Minsk, 2001.
11. One private institution, the Belrad Institute, headed by Professor Nesterenko, was refused by the Health Ministry the right to assure measures of radionuclide incorporation using a Human Radiation Spectrometer (SRH), under the pretext he was not a health doctor.
12. Since then Belarus has improved its economy (6.8% GDP increase in 2003). The national economy however remains heavily in debt with a very high inflation rate and is very sensitive to variations in energy prices.
13. Relapse: repeat of a behavior dangerous for one's health.
14. Alexander Grigorevitch Loukachenko (fifty-three years old), a former sovkhoze (state-owned farm) manager and member of the Belorussian Communist Party, was elected to the Supreme Soviet of the Belorussian Republic in 1990. Opposed to the collapse of the Soviet Federation (1991), he came under the spotlight in 1993 as head of a parliamentary commission in charge of fighting corruption. This is the same platform he adopted when he contested the election and was elected President in 1994 with more than eighty percent of expressed votes. Missing the Soviet system, he is in favor of creating a new union with Russia to set the stage for future reunification. This foreign policy initiative has been pilloried by the opposition, which saw Loukachenko, in 1996, pass several laws to reinforce his presidential power. These reforms were put to a popular referendum where he received seventy percent support. Numerous frauds and irregularities were reported however. Boosted by such strong support, the President decided to reduce the power of any opposition forces, whether political, in the media or among trade unions. This made him very unpopular among the international community. He was, however, re-elected in 2000 (with 75.6% of the vote), again following a vote full of irregularities and fraud. In 2004, he submitted to referendum a constitutional reform that would allow him to run for a third mandate, and was successfully re-elected in March 2006 in, again, dubious conditions. The international community rejected the election result and the European Community issued a travel ban on him and several other dignitaries of the regime.

Alexander Loukachenko has not ruled out running again in 2011 and can expect popular support, mostly in rural areas, while the younger generation as well as the city-based new middle class support goes more to the opposition party. On the foreign affairs front, following the energy-related struggle with Russia, the President started a process of closer ties with Venezuela's Hugo Chavez and Mahmoud Ahmadinejad's Iran. Finally, to deal with Chernobyl and its consequences, Alexander Loukachenko launched a so-called 'rehabilitation policy' towards contaminated territories while easing repopulation.
15. During its twenty-seven month-long occupation, the German army demolished nineteen villages and partially demolished a further fourteen,

while damaging most public buildings. Six-hundred inhabitants were executed.
16 As early as 1951, Narovlia was back to its pre-war level of economic development. Belarus, which had suffered terrible losses during the war (1.3 million victims, 209 ruined cities as well as 9200 villages, 616 of them having been burned and their inhabitants executed), had a growing economy between 1945 and 1955. Minsk, ninety percent of which had been demolished, was rebuilt, agricultural lands were rehabilitated and large building projects as well as mechanical industrialization plans were launched. The general standard of living was one of the highest in the USSR.
17 There used to be a boat service going from the city, along the Pripyat and Dniepr River, to the Black Sea.
18 The park which includes an old manor (that has been entirely plundered) and an arboretorium, are due to undergo renovation sometime soon.
19 Birth rates are also on the rise, but one would probably credit that to the material advantages granted to mothers living in the contaminated area.
20 The land is still owned collectively, and the products are still sold at a price decided by the state.
21 The Soviet planning of towns followed very rigorous criteria: local infrastructure was created proportionally to the number of *expected* inhabitants.
22 Young patients with thyroid cancer are being treated at the Gomel hospital located more than 200 kilometres away from Narovlia which makes separation even harder for split families.
23 Radiophobia, the irrational fear of anything related to atoms, is a theory that was very early proposed by Soviet authorities to try to explain the sudden increase in some pathologies. As this had never been observed before, pathologies were quickly recorded as psychosomatic. This concept was also acknowledged by international scientists.
24 A law was passed, adding to the March 2005 checks, requiring authorisation for any student wanting to study abroad.
25 There are two types of universities: one can attend a free university after succeeding in a competitive entry examination, or one can attend fee-paying universities, with tuition fees varying from US$500 to US$3500 on average.
26 To the noticeable exception of *Armillaria mellea* and *Armillaria ostoyae*, two types of mushrooms that grow on old trees. Compared to most other mushrooms, these are not contaminated since radio elements cannot penetrate the tree. Contamination can occur from the soil to the tree or flower, thanks to the water it absorbs, but in that case, old trees are less contaminated as their roots reach layers of soil that are deeper than the radioactive contamination.
27 During such a meal in Narovlia, our hosts had a food contest, each family member cooking mushrooms according to his/her own recipes.
28 Mushrooms as well as some rare fruits are part of a profitable underground economy: one day of mushroom-picking can be as profitable as a full months wage for a kolkhoz worker. Sold as 'cash in hand' to dealers ar-

riving from distant towns with their trucks, they end up being sold on road sides, as is, for example, dried fish.
29 Compared to its Finnish counterpart (dried heat), the Russian Spa is made of steam—heated rocks on which one pours cold water.
30 The *isba* is the traditional country house, the *datcha* being more of a holiday home in the country for people usually living in cities.
31 A sparkling and slightly alcoholic drink, made of rooted bread fermented into water.
32 All *isbas* do not have their own *banya*, which remain extremely rare in small villages. In cities there are public paying baths that some companies or administrations can also use.
33 Established by Lenin as early as 1921 and extended to all of Eastern Europe from 1946, it was adopted by several countries thanks to United Nations action in 1977.
34 The official armistice and actual surrender was signed by Germany on 9 May 1945—this new humiliation being put on Germany by Moscow. This was the second one as Germany had already signed an armistice without condition the day before with France in Berlin.
35 Edgar Morin (2001) in his complex vision of the Human condition suggested the concept of numerous *anthropos* mixing some contradictory but complementary aspects. He therefore suggested the existence of an *Homo complexus*, both *sapiens* and *demens* (rational and irrational), *faber* and *ludens* (hard-worker and player), *empiricus* and *imaginarius* (empirical and imagined), *economicus* and *consumans* (money-saver and money-spender), *prosaïc* and *poeticus* (pragmatic and poet). He then adds: 'Leisure, whether games, parties or celebrations are not just simply relaxing activities before starting regular life or work again...: they are roots that go in the anthropological depth of human nature itself' (2001: 29–30).
36 'More than any other event, the Chernobyl disaster opened the way to a freedom of expression such that the system we then knew could not last forever,' Mikhaïl Gorbachev, analysis submitted to the Project Syndicate Agency during the twentieth commemoration of the accident (24 April 2006).
37 The so-called 'Restoration' policy applied to those territories is managed by the central administration, without any active involvement by local populations. The exception is an experiment initiated by some French scientists and backed by the UN's Cooperation for Rehabilitation Program (CORE) which is taking place in four districts. Narovlia was excluded.

# Chapter 10

1 This section is a modification of part of a paper published earlier by the author (Furukawa 2007).
2 A break of 1 to 2 days taken at the same time by everyone of the village to celebrate that the rice planting was completed with no problems for/from the rice-paddy-god, normally followed by a ritual.
3 This is also a task to take a reading of various cultures among wanderers, people who were discriminated against, and others who were excluded from village affairs and lived in the periphery of the village's culture.

4 The Chinai Village Bylaws (as amended in February 1924):
Affairs for which the community representative shall be responsible include the following:
   1. To submit agenda items on matters to be resolved by the council or the general meeting and to take votes on these matters.
   2. Affairs relating to festivals and rituals at the shrine and devotional services at the temples and events related thereto.
   3. To manage assets and public works; provided that if the community representative specifically appoints a manager, he shall supervise the manager.
   4. Affairs relating to revenue and expenditure and accounting.
   5. Affairs relating to budget formation and settlement reports.
   6. Affairs relating to wages and tenant farming.
   7. Affairs relating to collection and full payment of rice paid as rent and joint sale of rice paid as land tax.
   8. Affairs relating to industry, traffic, river improvement and waterways.
   9. Affairs relating to rescue work and poor relief and poverty prevention.
   10. To exercise caution by supervising the embankment protection committee members and *nengyōji* (annual events manager) in the event of a flood and, if necessary, to impose compulsory service on villagers or to give an alarm signal.
   11. To take measures suited to the occasion in the event of emergency or a disaster.
   12. Any other affairs required according to custom.
The community representative shall hold the following posts concurrently:
   1. Head of the district and his deputy
   2. Ujiko Sōdai (the representative of shrine parishioners)
   3. Representative of the Ōmi Kome Kyōdō Kumiai (Ōmi Rice Trade Association)
   4. Health union president and vice president
   5. Director of the village's agricultural society
   6. Director of the Momose Mura Shin'yō Hanbai Kōbai Kumiai (Momose Village Credit Sales and Purchase Association)
   7. Director of the Nōji Shōrei Kai (Agricultural Promotion Society)
   8. Chairman and vice-chairman of the Kosaku Shōrei Kai (Tenants Promotion Society)
   9. Manager of the cemetery
   10. Chairman and vice-chairman of the neighborhood association

# Chapter 11

1 As Ashish Nandy, the noted Indian political scientist noted, 'You can be unhappy in Utopia' (personal communication, 2005).
2 This ranking is known as the Happy Planet Index, conducted by the New Economics Foundation based in Great Britain. It actually ranked Vanuatu as the happiest place on earth. In reality, this ranking was not about happiness, but rather, as the website noted, it is based on the 'relative efficiency with which nations convert the planet's natural resources into long and happy lives for their citizens.' Even so, the fact that so many Singaporeans,

including many blogging sites in Singapore, used this ranking to justify their point that Singaporeans are an unhappy lot, tells us a great deal about the state of happiness or unhappiness in Singapore.
3 For example, Singapore is often ranked as having the best airport in the world, the world's busiest container port, and the best and most productive workers in the world, among the best in the world in terms of competitiveness and the world's most global city.
4 In studying and measuring happiness, a word of caution is necessary. In this paper, there is a positivistic assumption that concepts such as happiness, subjective well-being, freedom and individualism can in fact be measured and that there is a degree of reliability and validity in these measurements. For example, some studies have argued that there is actually little correlation for the same individual on the happiness index over time or even over a short period of time, so measuring individual happiness is not very reliable. Clearly, these concepts are very difficult to define and measure and we have to be very careful in using them. In addition, there is the issue of cross-cultural applicability. Most of the scales to measure happiness were developed in the West, and we have to evaluate their usefulness in different societies. We seem to assume that everybody wants to be happy, at least in the sense of personal happiness. It can be argued that in some societies, this may not be true. For example, it can be suggested that in Asian societies, there is less concern with personal happiness with greater emphasis placed on the idea of harmony and social obligations.

# Bibliography

Abe, Kiyoshi (2004), 'Everyday Policing in Japan: Surveillance, Media, and Government and Public Opinion,' *International Sociology*, 19(2): 215–31.

—— (2006), 'Kōkyō kūkan no kaiteki: kiritsu kara kanri e (The pleasantness of public space: away from discipline and towards control),' in Kiyoshi Abe and Hiroshi Narumi (eds), *Kūkan kanri shakai: kanshi to jiyū no paradokkusu* (Space-management society: the paradox of surveillance and liberty), Tokyo: Shin-yo-sha, pp. 18–56.

Adams, Robert (2003), *Social Work and Empowerment* (3rd ed.), Hampshire: Palgrave.

Adorno, Theodor W. (1966), *Negative Dialektik*, Frankfurt am Main: Suhrkamp Verlag.

Alkire, Sabina (2002), *Valuing Freedoms: Sen's Capability Approach and Poverty Reduction*, Oxford: Oxford University Press.

Altpeter, Mary, Janice H. Schopler, Maeda J. Galinsky, and Joan Pennell (1999), 'Participatory research as social work practice: When is it viable?' *Journal of Progressive Human Services*, 10(2): 31–53.

Alvarez, Ann R. and Lorraine M. Gutierrez (2001), 'Choosing to do participatory research: An example and issues of fit to consider,' *Journal of Community Practice*, 9(1): 1–20.

Amato, Paul R. and Alan Booth (1997), *A Generation at Risk: Growing up in an era of family upheaval*, Cambridge: Harvard University Press.

Ami-machi Shi Hensan Iinkai (Ami Town History Editorial Committee) (1983), *Ami-machi shi*, Ami: Ami-machi.

Anderson, Elizabeth (1990), 'Is Women's Labor a Commodity?' *Philosophy and Public Affairs*, 19: 71–92.

Andrews, Frank M. and Stephen Withey (1976), *Social Indicators of Well-Being: American Perceptions of Life-Quality*, New York: Plenum Press.

Andrews, Lori B. (1987), 'The Aftermath of Baby M: Proposed State Laws on Surrogate Motherhood,' *Hastings Center Report*, 17(5): 31–40, October/November.

*Asahi Shimbun*, the evening edition, 5 December 1994.

ATLAS.ti GmbH Company (2004), ATLAS.ti 5.0. [Computer software]. Berlin, Germany: ATLAS.ti GmbH Company.

Baker, Brenda M. (1996), 'A Case for Permitting Altruistic Surrogacy,' *Hypatia*, Spring, Bloomington: Indiana University Press, pp. 34–48.

Ban, Kah Choon (2004), 'Narrating imagination,' in Ban Kah Choon, Anne

Pakir and Chee Kiong Tong (eds), *Imagining Singapore*, Singapore: Marshall Cavendish, pp. 1–15.
Batis Center for Women (1995), *Filipino Women's Diaspora: Causes, Costs and Challenges*, Manila: Batis Center for Women.
Bauman, Zygmunt (1989), *Modernity and the Holocaust*, Ithaca, NY: Cornell University Press.
⸻ (2001), *Community: Seeking Safety in an Insecure World*, Cambridge: Polity Press.
Bhargav, Padma (2006), "Gujarat becomes the preferred medical tourism destination," Canada Free Press, http://www.canadafreepress.com/2006/india120706.htm, as seen on 6 April 2007.
*Bloomberg News* (2007), 'Singapore can't doff its strait-laced ways,' 29 March.
Bourdieu, Pierre (1983), 'Ökonomisches Kapital, kulturelles Kapital, soziales Kapital (Economic, cultural and social capital),' in Reinhard Kreckel (ed.), *Soziale Ungleichheiten* (Social Inequality), Göttingen: Otto Schwartz, pp. 183–98.
⸻ (1999 [1993]), *The Weight of the World: Social Suffering in Contemporary Society* (translated by Priscilla Pankhurst Ferguson), Stanford: Stanford University Press.
Bundesregierung Deutschland (2005), *Lebenslagen in Deutschland. Der 2. Armuts- und Reichtumsbericht der Bundesregierung* (Life Situations in Germany. 2nd Report of the Federal Government on Poverty and Wealth), Berlin: Bundesregierung.
Burton, Jeffrey F., Mary M. Farrell, Florence B. Lord and Richard W. Lord (2000), *Confinement and Ethnicity*, Seattle and London: University of Washington Press.
Campbell, Angus, Philip E. Coverse and Willard L. Rodgers (1976), *The Quality of American Life: Perceptions, Evaluations and Satisfaction*, New York: Russell.
*CBC News* online, "Medical tourism: Need surgery, will travel," http://www.cbc.ca/news/background/healthcare/medicaltourism.html, as viewed on 21 August 2006.
Chambers, Robert (1997), *Whose Reality Counts?* London: ITDG Publishing.
Chan, Heng Chee (1976), *The Dynamics of One Party Dominance: The PAP and the Grass-roots*, Singapore: Singapore University Press.
Chan, Jasmine (2000), 'The status of women in a patriarchal state: The case of Singapore,' in Louise Edwards and Mina Roces (eds), *Women in Asia: Tradition, Modernity and Globalization*, London: Allen and Unwin, pp. 39–58.
Chang, Tou Chuang (2000), 'Renaissance revisited: Singapore as a "global city for the arts",' *International Journal of Urban and Regional Research*, 24 (4): 818–31.
Chua, Beng Huat (1989), 'The business of living in Singapore' in Kernial Singh Sandhu and Paul Wheatley (eds), *Management of Success: The Moulding of Modern Singapore*, Singapore: Institute of Southeast Asia Studies.
⸻ (1999), 'The attendant consumer society of a developed Singapore,' in Linda Low (ed.), *Singapore: Towards a Developed Status*, Oxford: Oxford University Press, pp. 210–25.
Clifford, James and George E. Marcus (1986), *Writing Culture: the Poetics and Politics of Ethnography*, Berkeley: University of California Press.

Cohen, Lawrence (1999), 'Where It Hurts: Indian Material for an Ethics of Organ Transplantation', *Daedalus* 128(4): 135–65.
Commission on Wartime Relocation and Internment of Civilians (1982), *Personal Justice Denied: Report of the Commission on Wartime Relocation and Internment of Civilians*, Washington, DC: GPO.
Comte-Sponville, André (2000), *Le bonheur desésperément* (Happiness pursued desperately), Nantes: Éditions Pleins Feux.
Corbin, Alain (2006), 'Le corps et la construction du paysage (The body and the construction of landscape),' *Advanced Social Research* 4: 408–31.
Correa, Gena (1986), *The Mother Machine: Reproductive Technologies from Artificial Insemination to Artificial Wombs*, New York: Harper Collins.
Dahrendorf, Ralf (1979), *Life Chances: Approaches to Social and Political Theory*, London: Weidenfeld and Nicolson.
Dannefer, Dale and Peter Uhlenberg (1999), 'Path of the life course: A typology,' in Vern L. Bengtson and Klaus W. Schaie (eds), *Handbook of Theories of Aging*, New York: Springer, pp. 306–26.
de Wind, E. (1966), 'Directe en late gevolgen van extreme belastingssituaties—het concentratiekamp" (Immediate and Late Consequences of Situations of Extreme Stress—the Concentration Camp), *Maandblad Geestelijke gezondheid (MGv)* (Monthly on Public Mental Health), vol.21, pp. 287–300.
Delanty, Gerald (2003), *Community*, London and New York: Routledge.
Derrida, Jacques (2003), 'Autoimmunity: Real and Symbolic Suicides—A Dialogue with Jacques Derrida,' in G. Borradori, *Philosophy in a Time of Terror: Dialogues with Jürgen Habermas and Jacques Derrida*, Chicago and London: The University of Chicago Press, pp. 85–136.
Diener, E., E. M. Suh, R. E. Lucas and H. L. Smith (2000), 'Subjective well-being: Three decades of progress,' *Psychological Bulletin*, 125: 276–302.
Diener, E., E. Sandvik, L. Seidlitz and M. Diener (1993), 'The relationship between income and subjective well-being: Relative or absolute,' *Social Indicators Research*, 28: 133–58.
Do, Thien Kinh (2007), 'The employment pattern of husbands and wives in Vietnamese rural families,' *Sociological Review* (in Vietnamese), 3(99): 37–46.
Döring, D., W. Hanesch, and E.-U. Huster (1990), 'Armut als Lebenslage. Ein Konzept für Armutsberichterstattung und Armutspolitik (Poverty as a life situation. A concept for poverty reports and politics),' in D. Döring, W. Hanesch, and E.-U. Huster (eds), *Armut im Wohlstand* (Poverty in Wealth), Frankfurt a.M.: Suhrkamp, pp. 7–30.
Drèze, Jean, and Amartya Sen (1989), *Hunger and Public Action*, Oxford: Oxford University Press.
Drilling, Matthias (2004), *Young Urban Poor: Abstiegsprozesse in den Zentren der Sozialstaaten* (Young Urban Poor. Collective Descents in the Center of the Welfare States), Wiesbaden: VS Verlag.
Dworkin, Andrea (1978), *Right Wing Women*, New York: Perigree Books.
Dwyer, Tom (1991), *Life and Death at Work: Industrial Accidents as a Case of Socially Produced Error*, New York: Plenum.
Easterlin, R. A. (1974), 'Does economic growth improve the human lot? Some empirical evidence,' in Paul A. David and W. R. Levin (eds), *Nations and Households in Economic Growth*, Palo Alto: Stanford University Press, pp. 189–215.

Elder, Glen H. (2007), 'Life course,' in George Ritzer (ed.), *Blackwell Encyclopedia of Sociology*, Malden: Blackwell, pp. 109–131.

Etzioni, Amitai (2001), *Next: The Road to the Good Society*, New York: Basic Books.

Firestone, Shulamith (1970), *The Dialectics of Sex: The Case for Feminist Revolution*, New York: Bantam.

Flynn, Beverly C., Dixie W. Ray, and Melinda S. Rider (1994), 'Empowering communities: Action research through healthy cities,' *Health Education Quarterly*, 21(3): 395–405.

Foo, Tuan Seik (2000), 'Subjective assessment of urban quality of life in Singapore (1997–1998),' *Habitat International*, 24: 31–49.

Freud, Sigmund (1989 [1930]), *Civilization and Its Discontents*, (translated from German, *Das Unbehagen in der Kultur*, Vienna), Paris: PUF.

Frey, Bruno S. and Alois Stutzer (2000), 'Happiness prospers in democracy,' *Journal of Happiness Studies*, 1: 79–102.

—— (2002), *Happiness and Economics*, Princeton: Princeton University Press.

Fujita, Shōzō (1996), *Shinpan: Tennō sei kokka no shihai genri* (The principles of imperial state control, new edition), Tokyo: Kage Shobō.

Furukawa, Akira (2004), *Mura no seikatsu kankyōshi* (Village life in modern Japan), Kyoto: Sekai Shisōsha.

—— (ed.) (2007), *Frontiers of Social Research: Japan and Beyond*, Melbourne: Trans Pacific Press.

Gamburd, Michele R. (2000), *The Kitchen Spoon's Handle,* Ithaca: Cornell.

Gensuibaku Kinshi Nihon Kyōgikai Senmon Iinkai (1961), *Gensuibaku higai hakusho: Kakusareta shinjitsu* (White paper on the casualties of atomic and hydrogen bombs: Hidden realities), Tokyo: Nippon Hyoron Shinsya.

George, Susan (2000), '"Dirty Nurses" and "Men who Play,"' in Michael Burawoy (ed.), *Global Ethnography: Forces, Connections and Imaginations in a Postmodern World*, Berkeley: University of California Press, pp. 144–74.

—— (2004), *Another World is Possible if...*, London: Verso.

Giddens, Anthony (1985), *The Nation-State and Violence*, Cambridge: Polity Press.

Glassner, Barry (1999), *The Culture of Fear: Why Americans are Afraid of the Wrong Things*, New York: Basic Books.

Glatzer, Wolfgang (2000), 'Happiness: Classic Theory in the Light of Current Research,' *Journal of Happiness Studies*, 1: 501–11.

Glenn, Evelyn N. (1992), 'From servitude to service work: Historical continuities in the racial division of paid reproduction labor,' *Signs*, 18: 1–43.

Gouldner, Alvin (1970), *The Coming Crisis of Western Sociology*, New York: Basic Books.

Grodzin, Morton (1974), *Americans Betrayed: Politics and the Japanese Evacuation* (1949; reprint), Chicago University Press.

Guerin-Gonzales, Camile (1996), *Mexican Workers & American Dreams: Immigration, Repatriation, and California Farm Labor, 1900–1939*, New Brunswick, NJ: Rutgers University Press.

Gupta, Dipak K., Albert J. Jongman and Alex P. Schmid (1994), 'Assessing country performance in the field of human rights,' Paper presented at the *XIII ISA Congress*, Bielefeld, Germany.

Gutierrez, Lorraine (2003), 'Participatory and Stakeholder Research,' in Encyclopedia Supplement Committee (eds), *Encyclopedia of Social Work*, 19th Edition 2003 Supplement, Washington DC: NASW Press, pp. 115–23.

Gutierrez, Lorraine and Edith A. Lewis (eds) (1999), *Empowering Women of Color*, New York: Columbia University Press.

Hall, Budd L. (1979), 'Knowledge as a commodity and participatory research,' *Prospects*, 9(4): 393–408.

—— (1981), 'Participatory research, popular knowledge and power,' *Convergence*, 14(3): 6–19.

—— (1994), 'Participatory research,' in Torsten Husen and T. Neville Postlethwaite (eds), *The International Encyclopedia of Education* (2nd ed.), Oxford: Pergmon.

Hall, Kermit L. (ed.) (1999), *The Oxford Guide to United States Supreme Court Decisions*, New York: Oxford University Press.

Hamada, Hiroshi (2006), 'An axiomatic approach to the disadvantage index,' In Kenji Kosaka (ed.), *A Sociology of Happiness: Japanese Perspectives*, Melbourne: Trans Pacific Press, pp. 40–60.

Harvey, David (2005a), *A Brief History of Neoliberalism*, Oxford: Oxford University Press.

—— (2005b), *Spaces of Neoliberalization: Towards a Theory of Uneven Geographical Development*, Stuttgart: Franz Steiner Verlag.

Hick, Steven (1997), 'Participatory research: An approach for structural social workers,' *Journal of Progressive Human Services*, 8(29): 63–78.

Higashide, Seiichi (1993), *Adios to Tears: The Memoirs of a Japanese-Peruvian Internee in US Concentration Camps*, Seattle: University of Washington Press.

—— (1995), (Koyama Yukinori, ed.), *Namida no adiosu*, Tokyo: Sairyūsha.

Hill, Michael (2000), *Conversion and Subversion: Religion and the Management of Moral Panics in Singapore*, Victoria, NZ: Asian Studies Institute.

Hiroshima City (2006), 'Hiroshima digital migration space,' Retrieved on August 11, 2007 from http://dms-hiroshima.eg.jomm.jp/.

Hiroshima-City and Nagasaki-City (1979), *Hiroshima Nagasaki no genbaku saigai* (Atomic bomb effects in Hiroshima and Nagasaki), Tokyo: Iwanami Shoten.

Hiroshima International Council for Health Care of the Radiation Exposed (2006), Premier figures of the Ministry of Health, Labor and Welfare, March 2006. Retrieved on 24 June 2007 from http://www.hiroshima-cdas.or.jp/HICARE/11/index.html.

Hiroshima Peace Site (2001), 'Lucky Dragon No. 5,' Retrieved on 15 October 2007 from http://www.pcf.city.hiroshima.jp/virtual/VirtualMuseum_e/exhibit_e/exh0503_e/exh05031_e.html.

Hiroshima Prefecture (1938), *Tokō-saki betsu shukkoku no jōkyō* (Current situations of departures from Japan to various countries). Retrieved on 24 June 2007 from http://db1.pref.hiroshima.jp/Folder01/Frame01.htm.

Hiroshima Prefecture (1972), *Hiroshima Ken-shi: Genbaku shiryō-hen* [Hiroshima prefectural history: The atomic bomb], Hiroshima, Japan: Hiroshima Ken Kyōkasyo Tosyo Hanbai Kabushikigaisha.

Hiroshima Prefecture (1988), *Hiroshima-ken sensaishi* (War damages in Hiroshima Prefecture), Tokyo: Daiichi Hōki Shuppan.
Hobsbawm, Eric (1994), *The Age of Extremes: The Short Twentieth Century 1914–1991*, London: Michael Joseph.
Hondagneu-Sotelo, Pierrette (1994), 'Reconstructing Gender through Immigration and Settlement,' in Pierrette Hondagneu-Sotelo (ed.), *Gendered Transitions*, Berkeley: University of California Press, pp. 98–147.
Hondagneu-Sotelo, Pierrette and Ernestine Avila, (2003), '"I'm here, but I'm there": The meanings of transnational Latina motherhood,' in Pierrette Hondagneu-Sotelo (ed.), *Gender and US Immigration*, Berkeley: University of California Press, pp. 317–40.
Ichii, Saburō (1971), *Rekishi no Shinpo towa Nani ka* (What is historical progress?), Tokyo: Iwanami Shoten.
*International Herald Tribune* (2005), 'Loosen up or lose out, Singaporeans are told,' 23 August.
Ishida, Atsushi, Kenji Kosaka and Hiroshi Hamada (2006), 'A Boolean analysis of subjective well-being,' *ABSTRACTS*. International Conference on Comparative Social Sciences. Tokyo: Sophia University, p. 13.
Kamei, Nobutaka (2007), 'Drawing sketches in the field: Sketch literacy for social research,' in Akira Furukawa (ed.), *Frontiers of Social Research: Japan and Beyond*, Melbourne: Trans Pacific Press, pp. 72–99.
Kamishima, Jirō (1961), *Kindai Nihon no seishin kōzō* (Mental structure of modern Japan), Tokyo: Iwanami Shoten.
Kamiya, Chikara (1976), *Ie to mura no hōshi kenkyū—nihon kindai hō no seiritsu katei* (A study on the history of ie and mura—the process of creation of the modern Japanese law), Tokyo: Ochanomizu Shobō.
Kant, Immanuel (1969), *Groundwork of a Metaphysics of Morals*, translated from the German original [1785].
Kaplan, Abraham (1964), *The Conduct of Inquiry: Methodology for Behavioral Science*, Scranton: Chandler Publishing Company.
Kasser, Tim (2000), 'Two versions of the American dream: Which goals and values make for a higher quality of life,' in Ed Diener and Don R. Rahtz (eds), *Advances in Quality of Life Theory and Research*. Dordrecht: Kluwer, pp. 3–12.
Kavalski, Emilian and Magdalena Zolkos (2006), 'The hawks of war: Comparative analysis of the foreign policy discourses of Poland and Bulgaria on Iraq (2003–2005),' *ABSTRACTS*. International Conference on Comparative Social Sciences (July 15–16, 2006), Tokyo: Sophia University pp. 29–30.
Kieselbach, T. (2000), *Youth Unemployment and Social Exclusion: A Comparison of Six European Countries*, Opladen: Leske und Budrich.
Kodama, Masaaki (1992), *Nihon imin-shi kenkyū josetsu* (An introduction to the research into the history of Japanese emigrants), Hiroshima: Keisuisha.
Kosaka, Kenji (2000), 'Realistic foundations of "Being a system"—Systems Theory Revisited,' *Shakai Keizai Systems*, 19, pp. 2–7.
—— (2006a), 'Killing Many Innocent People: An Introduction to the Sociology of Well-being and Ill-being,' in Kenji Kosaka (ed.), *A Sociology of Happiness: Japanese Perspectives*, Melbourne: Trans Pacific Press, pp. 1–39.

―――― (ed.) (2006b), *A Sociology of Happiness: Japanese Perspectives*, Melbourne: Trans Pacific Press.

―――― (2007), 'A sociology for happiness: Beyond Western versus Non-Western perspectives,' SOCIOLOGICAL BULLETIN (*Journal of the Indian Sociological Society*), September–December 56 (3): 369–82.

Kuramoto, Kanji (1999), *Zaibei goju-nen: Watashi to America no hibakusha* (Fifty years in the United States: Me and survivor victims of atomic bombs in America), Tokyo: Kindai Bungeisha.

Kurosaka, Sakiko (2005), 'Research notes of a case study on happiness and unhappiness among the Newar: Challenges and possibilities of the research,' presented at The Joint Seminar on Human Well-being: Comparative Asian Perspectives, Hanoi, 26 February 2005.

Lazarsfeld, Paul, William Sewell and H. L. Wilensky (1967), 'Introduction,' in Paul Lazarsfeld (ed.), *The Uses of Sociology*, New York: Basic Books.

Lee, Hsien Loong (2005), 'Proposal to develop integrated resorts,' Ministerial Statement, *MediaCorp News* website, http://www.channelnewsasia.com/casino/text_pmlee.htm, 18 April.

Lee, Theresa (1991), 'Service directions for the voluntary welfare organisations serving youths,' in Yap Mui Teng (ed.), *Social Services: the Next Lap*, Singapore: Times Academic Press [for the] Institute of Policy Studies, pp. 100–16.

Leong, Wai Teng (1989), 'Culture and the state: Manufacturing traditions for tourism,' *Critical Studies in Mass Communications*, 6(4): 355–75.

Lian, K. F. (2007), 'Is there social policy in Singapore?' in K. F. Lian and C. K. Tong (eds), *Social Policy and Social Development in Singapore*, Leiden and New York: Brill Academic Publishers, pp. 37–58.

Lifton, Robert J. (1968), *Death in Life: Survivors of Hiroshima*, New York: Random House.

Lipovestky, Gilles (2006), *Le Bonheur paradoxal. Essai sur la société d'hyperconsommation*, Paris: Gallimard.

Lyon, David (2001), *Surveillance Society: Monitoring Everyday Life*, Buckingham: Open University Press.

―――― (2003), *Surveillance after September 11*, Cambridge: Polity Press.

Macner-Licht, Berul (1991), 'Service directions for voluntary welfare organisations in the mental health field,' in Yap Mui Teng (ed.), *Social Services: The Next Lap*, Singapore: Times Academic Press [for the] Institute of Policy Studies, pp. 173–87.

Maslow, Abraham H. (1954), *Motivation and Personality*. New York: Harper and Row.

Matsuura, Akira (2005), 'Hyogo-ken ni okeru Chiiki-ryoku to Shuccho-ritsu (Community power and birth rate in Hyogo Prefecture),' *Kenkyu Nenpō* (Research Annual Report), 11: 27–37.

Mauss, Marcel (1978), 'Essai sur le don', in Marcel Mauss, *Sociologie et Anthropologie*, Paris: PUF, pp. 142–279.

McNamara, Robert et al. (1999), *Argument without End: In Search of Answers to the Vietnam Tragedy*, New York: Pacific Affairs.

Menon, Parvathi (2002), 'Against the organ trade,' *Frontline* 19(10), 11–24 May 2002, http://www.hinduonnet.com/fline/fl1910/19100840.htm, as viewed on 6 June 2007.

Miles, Matthew B., and A. Michael Huberman (1994), *Qualitative Data Analysis* (2nd ed.), Thousand Oaks: Sage.
Ministry of Justice, Judicial System Department, Minister's Secretariat (2005–7), *Annual Report of Statistics on Legal Migrants 2004–6*.
Miura, Kōkichirō (2007), 'Lessons on human rights derived from an epistolary style: The sociography of structural discrimination,' in Akira Furukawa (ed.), *Frontiers of Social Research: Japan and Beyond*, Melbourne: Trans Pacific Press, pp. 253–71.
Miyauchi, Taisuke (2007), 'Rethinking case studies: Research as a power to construct lives,' in Akira Furukawa (ed.), *Frontiers of Social Research: Japan and Beyond*, Melbourne: Trans Pacific Press, pp. 39–52.
Mizuno, Takeya (2005), *Nikkei Amerikajin: Kyōsei shūyō to jānarizumu* (Japanese Americans: Incarceration and journalism), Tokyo: Shumpūsha.
Moore, Michael (2002), *Bowling for Columbine*, MGM Distribution Co.
Morin, Edgar (1962), *L'Esprit du temps*, Paris: Grasset Ed.
—— (2001), Seven complex lessons in education for the future, Paris: UNESCO, translated from French, *Les Sept Savoirs nécessaires à l'éducation du future*, Paris: Seuil.
Morris, David B. (1997), 'About Suffering: Voice, Genre, and Moral Community,' in Arthur Kleinman, Veena Das, and Margaret Lock (eds), *Social Suffering*, Oxford University Press, pp. 25–45.
Narayan, Uma (1997), *Dislocating Cultures: Identies, Traditions and Third-World Feminism*, New York: Routledge.
Netting, F. Ellen, Peter M. Kettner and Steven L. McMurtry (1998), *Social work macro practice* (2nd ed.), New York: Addison Wesley Longman, Inc.
Neuhaus, Richard J. (1988), 'Renting women, buying babies and class struggles,' *Society*, 25(3): 8–10.
Ngai, Mae M. (2004), *Impossible Subjects: Illegal Aliens and the Making of Modern America*, Princeton: Princeton University Press.
Nishitani, Osamu (ed.) (2006), *Gurōbaru-ka to naraku no yume* (Globalization and dreams of the abyss), Tokyo: Serica Shobō.
Nussbaum, Martha (1993), 'Non-relative virtues: An Aristotelian approach,' in Martha Nussbaum and Amartya Sen (eds), *The Quality of Life*, Oxford: Clarendon, pp. 242–69.
—— (2000), *Woman and Human Development: The Capabilities Approach*, Cambridge: Cambridge University Press.
Ochi, Noboru (1974), 'Nihon kindaika to chiiki shihai (Japan's modernization and regional control),' in Jirō Kamishima (ed.), *Kindaika no seishin kōzō* (The mental structure of modern Japan), Tokyo: Iwanami Shoten.
Ochiai, Emiko (1997), *The Japanese Family System in Transition: A Sociological Analysis of Family Change in Postwar Japan*, Tokyo: LTCB International Library Foundation.
Ogino, Masahiro and Mayumi Yukimura (2006), 'Katari e nu mono wo tou— shakai chōsa ni okeru animēsyon riyō no kanōsei (Eliciting the implicit: Feasibility of animation films in social research),' *Sentan shakai kenkyū* (Advanced Social Research Series), 4: 205–31, Nishinomiya: Kwansei Gakuin University Press.
Otani, Yasuo (1997), *Amerika zaijū Nikkeijin kyōsei shūyō no higeki* (The

tragedy of the forced detention of the Japanese residents in the US), Tokyo: Akashi Shoten.
Parrenas, Rhacel (2001), *Servants of Globalization: Women, Migration and Domestic Work*, Stanford: Stanford University Press.
Pascal, Blaise (2004 [1670]), *Pansée (Thoughts)*, Neeland Media LLC.
Payne, Geoff and Judy Payne (2004), *Key Concepts in Social Research*, London: Sage.
Phuyal, Kamal (2003), 'A Brief Introduction to Participatory Learning and Action (PLA),' Unpublished report on participatory reproductive health programming workshop held 23–30 March 2003 in Katmandu.
Piersma, Hinke (2005), *De drie van Breda: Duitse oorlogsmisdadigers in Nederlandse gevangenschap 1945–1989* (The Breda Three: German War Criminals in Dutch Imprisonment 1945–1989), Amsterdam: Balans.
Popper, Karl R. (1984), *Auf der Suche nach einer besseren Welt* (In search of a better world), München: R. Piper GmbH & Co.
Powers, William (1973), *Behavior: The Control of Perception*, Chicago: Aldine.
Prime Minister's National Day Rally Speech (1999), 'First World Economy, World Class Home,' National Archives of Singapore Speech-Text Archival and Retrieval System, http://stars.nhb.gov.sg/stars/public.
—— (2001), 'New Singapore,' National Archives of Singapore Speech-Text Archival and Retrieval System, http://stars.nhb.gov.sg/stars/public.
—— (2002), 'Remaking Singapore—Changing Mindsets,' National Archives of Singapore Speech-Text Archival and Retrieval System, http://stars.nhb.gov.sg/stars/public.
—— (2003), 'From the Valley to the Highlands,' National Archives of Singapore Speech-Text Archival and Retrieval System, http://stars.nhb.gov.sg/stars/public.
Ragone, Helena (1994), *Surrogate Motherhood: Conception in the Heart*, Boulder: Westview Press.
Rasmussen, David (ed.) (1995), *Universalism vs. Communitarianism: Contemporary Debates in Ethics*, Cambridge, MA: MIT Press.
Raymond, Janice (1993), *Women as Wombs: Reproductive Technologies and the Battle Over Women's Freedom*, Melbourne: Spinifex Press.
Reason, James (1997), *Managing the Risks of Organizational Accidents*, Hampshire, UK: Ashgate Publishing Limited.
Ristock, Janice and Joan Pennell (1996), *Community Research as Empowerment: Feminist Links, Postmodern Interruptions*, Don Mills, Ontario: Oxford University Press.
Roberts, Dorothy (1997), *Killing the Black Body: Race, Reproduction, and the Meaning of Liberty*, New York: Pantheon Books.
Roemer, John E. (1996), *Theories of Distributive Justice*, Cambridge: Cambridge University Press.
Rosenberg, Morris (1968), *The Logic of Survey Analysis*, New York: Basic Books.
Rothman, Barbara (1988), 'Reproductive technology and the commodification of life,' in Elaine H. Baruch, D'Adamo F. Amadeo and Joni Seager (eds), *Embryos, Ethics and Women's Rights*, Hawthorn Press: New York, pp. 95–100.

Rothwell, C. and P. Cohen (2003), 'P + 5E + 3H is how happy you are,' *The New Paper*, 8 January.
Saito, Natsu Taylor (1998), 'Justice Held Hostage: US Disregard for International Law in the World War II Internment of Japanese Peruvians—A Case Study,' *Boston College Law Review*, 15:1 (December 1998), and *B.C. Third World Law Journal*, 19:1 (fall 1998): 303–15.
Saito, Takao (2004), *Anshin no fashizumu* (Fascism for security), Tokyo: Iwanami Shoten.
Sarri, Rosemary and Catherine Sarri (1992), 'Participatory action research in two communities in Bolivia and the United States,' *International Social Work*, 35: 267–80.
Sassen, Saskia (2002), *Globalization and Its Discontents: Essays on the New Mobility of People and Money*, New York: Free Press.
Satz, Debra (1992), 'Markets in women's reproductive labor,' *Philosophy and Public Affairs*, 21(2): 107–31.
Savage, Victor (2004), 'Singapore's environmental ideology,' in Kah Choon Ban, Anne Pakir and Chee Kiong Tong (eds), *Imagining Singapore*, Singapore: Marshall Cavendish, pp. 210–39.
Scheper-Hughes, Nancy (1999), "One previous owner", *New Scientist*, 164: 48–9.
——— (2003), "Keeping an Eye on the Global Traffic in Human Organs," *Lancet* 361: 1645–8.
Schutz, Alfred (1996), *Collected Papers IV*, Dordrecht: Kluwer Academic Publishers.
Seah, C. N. (2006), 'One grade too serious,' *Star Newspaper*, Malaysia, 23 July.
Seiyama, Kazuo (2007), 'Explanation and narrative: What should social research aim for?,' in Akira Furukawa (ed.) (2007), *Frontiers of Social Research: Japan and Beyond*, Melbourne: Trans Pacific Press, pp. 19–38.
Sekizawa, Mayumi (1988), '"Mura no nenrei" wo sazukeru mono—Ōmi ni okeru chōrō to "zajin chō" (The man who grants "village-years"—village seniors and "list of meeting members" in Ōmi),' *Nihon Minzoku Gaku* (Bulletin of the Folklore Society of Japan), 174.
Sen, Amartya (1981), *Poverty and Famines: An Essay on Entitlements and Deprivation*, Oxford: Oxford University Press.
——— (1987), 'The Standard of Living: Lecture I and Lecture II,' in A. Sen (ed.), *The Standard of Living*, Cambridge: Cambridge University Press, pp. 1–38.
——— (1992), *Inequality Reexamined*, Cambridge: Harvard University Press.
——— (1999), *Development as Freedom*, New York: Alfred A. Knopf.
——— (2003), *Development, Rights and Human Security: Commission on Human Security/Final Report*, New York: United Nations Publications.
Shimamoto, Yasuko (2006), *Sensō de shinu to iukoto* (Dying in War), Tokyo: Iwanami Shoten.
Shino, Cedric (2006), 'Share your research or experience,' Lecture at the Japanese American National Museum, 7 September 2003.
Singer, Peter W. (2003), *Corporate Warriors: The Rise of the Privatized Military Industry*, Ithaca: Cornell University.
Singh, Bilveer (2004), 'A small state's quest for security: Operationalizing deterrence in Singapore's strategic thinking,' in Kah Choon Ban, Anne Pakir

and Chee Kiong Tong (eds), *Imagining Singapore*, Singapore: Marshall Cavendish, pp. 106–37.
Smith, Adam (1976 [1776]), *An Inquiry into the Nature and Causes of the Wealth of Nations*, R.H. Campbell and A.S. Skinner (eds), Oxford: Clarendon Press.
Sodei, Rinjirō (1978), *Watashitachi wa teki datta noka* (Were we the enemy?), Tokyo: Ushio Shuppansha.
―――― (1998), *Were We the Enemy? American Survivors of Hiroshima*, Boulder: Westview Press.
Spar, Debora L. (2006), *The Baby Business: How Money, Science, and Politics Drive the Commerce of Conception*, Cambridge, MA: Harvard Business School Publishing Corporations.
Spivak, Gayatri C. (1988), 'Can the subaltern speak?' in C. Nelson and L. Grossberg (eds), *Marxism and the Interpretation of Culture*, Chicago: University of Illinois Press.
Suzuki, Eitarō (1968 [1940]), *Nihon nōson shakai genri* (The principles of Japanese rural communities), Tokyo: Miraisha.
Takeda, Joe (2005), 'PLA (Participatory Learning and Action) ni yoru mainoritī kenkyū no kanousei (Using PLA as a means of empowering minority communities),' *Advance Social Research*, 3: 163–207.
―――― (ed.) (2005), *Firipin Josei Entateinā no Raifu Sutōrī* (Life stories of Filipina entertainers), Nishinomiya: Kwansei Gakuin University Press.
Takeda, Jun'ichi (1929), *Zaibei Hiroshima kenjin-shi* (A history of emigrants from Hiroshima Prefecture in the United States), Los Angeles: Zaibei Hiroshima Kenjin-shi Hakkō-sho.
Tamney, Joseph B. (1996), *The Struggle over Singapore's Soul: Western Modernization and Asian Culture,* Berlin: Walter de Gruyter.
Tas, J. (1946), 'Psychische stoornissen in concentratiekampen en bij teruggekeerden (Psychological disorders in concentration camps and among the returned),' *Maandblad Geestelijke gezondheid* (MGv) (Monthly on Public Mental Health), vol.1: 143–50.
Thatcher, Margaret (1993), *The Downing Street Years*, London: HarperCollins.
The Atomic Heritage Foundation (2007), 'Chronology for the origin of atomic weapons,' Retrieved on 28 August 2007 from http://www.mphpa.org/index.php?option=com_content&task=view&id=287&Itemid=201.
*The Economist* (2007), "Medical tourism to India", 10 September 2004 as viewed on 6 May.
*The Rafu Shimpo* (1946), '*Nisei* in Japan may get permit to return to US' (4 March), p. 1.
*The Straits Times* (1992), 'BG Lee quashes "worse off" claims,' 16 January.
*The Straits Times* (1992), 'Buying power test of whether we are better off,' 17 January.
*The Straits Times* (1998), 'Police-I'll be watching you—Take off shirt? OK,' 5 October.
*The Straits Times* (2007), 'Bye bye, bar top babes', 27 April.
The United States Strategic Bombing Survey (1946), 'The Effects of Atomic Bomb on Hiroshima and Nagasaki,' Washington, DC: United States Government Printing Office.
*Times International* Asia Ed. (2007), 'Singapore soars,' 4 June.

Toppan (2006), 'Sekyuritī chōsa shirīzu dai-san-dan, "Seikatsu kankyō no anshin/anzen ni kansuru chōsa" kekka hōkoku: ōku no hito ga ikikisuru kōkyō no ba ni, yaku hachiwari no hito ga sekkyokuteki ni kanshi kamera o setchi subeki to kaitō (Report on results of the security survey series, part 3, "Survey on the security and safety of the living environment:" approximately eighty percent of respondents say that surveillance cameras should be installed proactively in public places where large numbers of people come and go)', http://www.toppan.co.jp/news/newsrelease455.html#top, 20 October.

Torigoe, Hiroyuki (1982), *Ie to mura no shakai gaku* (Sociology of ie and mura), Kyoto: Sekai Shisōsha.

Tule Lake Committee (2004), 'Tule Lake Pilgrimage 2004: Citizens betrayed July 2–5, 2004,' Retrieved on 21 August 2007 from http://www.tulelake.org/2004-pilgrimage/.

Uchiyama, Takashi (2006), *Sensō to iu shigoto* (The job of war), Nagano: Shinano Mainichi Shimbunsha.

UNRRA Inter-Allied Psychological Study group (1945), 'Psychological problems of displaced persons,' London, June.

Veenhoven, Ruut (1989), *How Harmful is Happiness? Consequences of Enjoying Life or Not.* Rotterdam: Universitaire Press.

—— (1991), 'Questions on happiness: Classical topics, modern answers, blind spots,' in Fritz Strack, Michael Argyle and Norbert Schwarz (eds), *Subjective Well-Being: An Interdisciplinary Perspective*, Oxford: Pergamon Press, pp. 7–26.

—— (1996), 'Happy life expectancy: A comprehensive measure of quality of life in nations,' *Social Indicators Research*, 39: 1–57.

—— (2000), 'The four qualities of life,' *Journal of Happiness Studies*, 1: 1–39.

Wajcman, Judy (1994), 'Delivered into men's hands? The social construction of reproductive technology,' in Gita Sen (ed), *Power and Decision: the Social Control of Reproduction*, Cambridge: Harvard School of Public Health, pp. 153–75.

Warnock, Mary (1985), *A Question of Life: The Warnock Report on Human Fertilization and Embryology*, Cambridge: Blackwell Publishers.

Watsuji, Tetsurō (1979), *Fūdo*, Tokyo: Iwanami Shoten.

Watts, Michael J. (2002), 'Hour of darkness: vulnerability, security and globalization,' *Geographica Helvetica*, 57(1): 5–18.

Woods, Gordon G. (1969), *The Creation of the American Republic, 1776–1787*, New York: W.W. Norton and Co.

Wright, Eric Olin (2006), 'Compass points: Towards a socialist alternative,' *New Left Review*, 41: 93–124.

Yamaguchi, Keiko (2006), 'Toshi kūkan no hen'yō to nojukusha—kyūjūnendai ni okeru Shinjuku-eki nishiguchi chika no jirei yori (The transformation of urban space and the homeless: From cases [concerning] the Shinjuku station west entrance underground in the [nineteen-]nineties),' in Ayumi Kariya (ed.), *Furachi na kibō—hōmuresu: yoseba o meguru shakaigaku* (Nefarious hopes: Homeless—the sociology around the day-labour market), Kyoto: Shōraisha, pp. 56–98.

Yamakura, Akihiro (1996), 'Nikkei Perū jin Beikoku kyōsei renkō: Senshōkoku no sensō sekinin (Forced removal of the Japanese Peruvians to the US: The victor's war responsibility),' *Amerikasu Kenkyū* (The Journal of the Americas Studies), 1: 69–84.

―――― (1997), 'Zai Peru Nikkeijin Beikoku kyōsei renkō no jittai: Dai 5 ji tsuihō no jirei (Forced removal of Peruvian Japanese to the US: The Case of the 10 January 1943 removal),' *Amerikasu Kenkyū* (The Journal of the Americas Studies), 2: 79–98.

―――― (2000), 'Nikkeijin senji yokuryū no ronri: Sensō kengen to riberarizumu no genkai (Logic of Japanese incarceration: War powers and the limitation of liberalism),' *Amerikasu Kenkyu* (The Journal of the Americas Studies), 5: 89–107.

―――― (2001), 'Senji ni hō wa chinmoku suruka: Nikkeijin yokuryū shohanketsu wo chūshin to shite (*Inter arma silent leges?*: The Japanese American internment decisions),' *Amerikasu Kenkyū* (The Journal of the Americas Studies), 6: 45–63.

Yamamoto, Eric K., Margaret Chon, Carol L. Izumi, Jerry Kang, and Frank H. Wu (2001), *Race, Rights and Reparation: Law and the Japanese American Internment*, Gaithersburg, NY: Aspen Law & Business.

Yamamoto, Takeo (1997), *Esunishiti to toshi komyuniti* (Ethnicity and urban communities), Tokyo: Minerva Shobō.

Yeich, Susan (1996), 'Grassroots organizing with homeless people: A participatory research approach,' *Journal of Social Issues*, 52(1): 111–21.

Yeo, Anthony (1985), *Living with Stress*, Singapore: Times Books International.

Yergin, Daniel, and Joseph Stanislaw (1998), *The Commanding Heights: The Battle for the World Economy*, New York: Touchstone Books.

Yin, Robert K. (1994), *Case Study Research: Design and Methods* (2nd ed.), Thousand Oaks: Sage.

Young, Jock (1999), *The Exclusive Society: Social Exclusion, Crime and Difference in Late Modernity*, London: Sage.

Young, Robert J. C. (2001), *Postcolonialism: An Historical Introduction*, Oxford, UK: Blackwell.

Žižek, Slavoj (2002), *Welcome to the Desert of the Real: Five Essays on September 11 and Related Dates*, London: Verso.

# Index

9/11, 34–5, 40

abnormal society, 21–2, 28
a-bomb, *see* atomic bomb
a-bomb survivors, *see* atomic bomb survivors
absolute poverty, 148
abstract space, 10
academic absence, 231–2
achievement, 29, 64, 90–3, 192–5, 214
Africa, 22
African Americans, 27
agricultural, 13, 25, 146–7, 150, 166–9, 181, 204–5, 210, 213–14, 234, 245, 247
agriculture, 25, 145–6, 150, 152, 156, 211
air raids, 13, 180
alien, 22–3, 25–6, 110
alternative society, 220, 226, 229, 237–8
alternative sociology, 90, 219–21, 223, 225, 227, 229, 231–3, 235–40
ambivalent, 3, 140, 186
American, 12, 17–18, 20–7, 29–30, 73, 78, 105–6, 108–116, 119–21, 138, 199, 241–2
Asian Americans, 27
Asian financial crisis, 192

asylum seekers, 92
atomic bomb, 3, 105–9, 110–21, 153
atomic bomb certificate, 105
atomic bomb survivors, 3, 105, 108–9, 111–13
authoritarian, 33, 159

*banlieu*, 89
baseline vulnerability, 97
BATIS aware, 55–6, 60–7, 70
BATIS center for women, 53, 56, 60
Belarus, 142–6, 153–4, 157, 159, 243–5
Bikini atoll, 111, 114
birthrate, 7, 224–5
Bourdieu, Pierre, 89, 93–5
Buddhism, 204–5, 212
Buddhist, 7, 15, 211–12, 241
bullying, 4–9, 12, 222–3, 225

camp, 25, 28, 30, 38–9, 105, 110, 116, 122–4, 126–30, 132–9, 242
capabilities, 58–9, 92–100
capability, 56, 88, 92, 95–9, 101, 224
categorical imperative, 35
Central and South America, 18, 21, 28

Chernobyl, 141–5, 148–51, 154–9, 243–4, 246
Chinai village, 169–71, 173–4, 176–7, 179–81, 247
Christian charity, 42
civil liberties, 24, 28
civil rights, 20, 190, 241, *see also* human rights
  movement, 27, *see also* human rights movement
cold war, 122, 129, 135–9
Committee of Atomic Bomb Survivors in the United States (CABSUS), 113
commodities, 6, 78, 91
commodity market, 6
communal, 47–8, 191–2, 224
communism, 135–6, 155, 157, 191–2
communist, 135–40, 157, 159, 193, 244
communitarian, 32–3, 228, 242
communitarianism, 34, 40, 189–90
community, 5–16, 18, 24–6, 28–9, 32–4, 39–40, 47–9, 56–60, 68–70, 83, 91–2, 100, 105, 107–8, 116, 150, 165–6, 168–9, 174–81, 189, 191, 200, 219, 225, 242, 244, 247
community development, 13
concentration camp, 25, 28, 116, 122–4, 126–7, 130, 133–5, 137–9
contamination, 142, 144–50, 152–3, 156, 245
conversational analysis, 221
coping, 55, 63, 96, 98, 114, 116
cultural capital, 94–5
cultural diversity, 224
culture of fear, 35

culture of suspicion, 35

Daigo Fukuryū Maru, *see* Lucky Dragon No. 5
Dahrendorf, Ralf, 91
death, 3–5, 7, 9, 11, 13–16, 93, 113, 115–16, 126–7, 129, 141–2, 153, 156, 168, 170, 173–4, 180, 230, 233, 241, 243
Declaration of Independence, 17, 22, 191
decontamination, 146–7, 156
demilitarize, 12
Derrida, Jacques, 42–8
Department of War, 18, 28
Do Thien Kinh, 201, 204–5, 212–13
drug abuse, 98
due process of law, 17–18, 26
Dutch Jews, 122, 126
Dutch resistance, 122, 131
dying, 15, 127

Emperor, 165, 171, 173, 181, 227
empowerment, 54–60, 64–7, 237
entitlement, 92–5, 98, 133
environmental issues, 10
ethical, 45–6, 72, 74, 230, 235
ethics, 45–7, 71–4, 86
ethnicity, 24, 48, 72, 86, 108, 204–5, 211
ethnomethodology, 221
Etzioni, Amitai, 33–4, 40, 242
Europe, 10, 23, 82, 89–90, 92, 144, 154, 184, 214–16, 244, 246
European Commission, 89
exclusion situation, 99
extermination camps, 127
Expogé, 135–6

family, 4, 7, 16, 18, 33, 55, 73, 76, 78, 80–3, 86–7, 91, 94, 100, 108, 110, 116–17, 128–9, 131, 144, 147–8, 156–7, 174–5, 178–9, 181, 185, 189, 194, 201–16, 242–3, 245
feminist, 57–8, 73, 78–9, 86
Filipino entertainers, 53–5, 57, 59, 61, 63, 65, 67, 69
forced labor, 19
free market, 23, 32
freedom of the individual, 23
friendship, 6, 56, 111, 113, 185

Geneva Convention, 19
German occupation, 122, 131
gestational services, 79
Glenn, Evelyn Nakano, 79
globalization, 31, 34, 42, 49, 71–3, 79, 87, 89, 169, 229, 232, 242
Green and Happiness Index, 239
Gross National Happiness Index, 228

happiness, 17, 32, 91, 96, 124, 128–9, 141–2, 144, 150–1, 154–6, 158, 160, 183, 185–91, 193, 195, 197, 199–209, 215–16, 223, 227–8, 230–3, 238–9, 247–8
Happiness Index, 183–4, 190, 228, 239, 248
happy, 31–2, 66, 82, 85, 155, 157–8, 181, 185–7, 191, 202–3, 211–12, 227, 229, 247–8
happy family, 201–3, 205, 207, 209–16
Hawaii, 18, 109–10, 121
health sociology, 91, 96

*hibakusha*, 105–7, 111–12
hierarchy of suffering, 140
Hirabayashi, Gordon, 18
Hiroshima, 3, 105–6, 109–13, 115, 117–19, 121
Holocaust, 45
housework, 83–4, 86, 207–8, 213–16
Human Development Index (HDI), 228
human rights, 24, 27, 30, *see also* civil rights movement, 27, *see also* civil rights movement
humanitarian, 123
hybrid landscape, 3, 8, 10–12, 15–16, 241
hydrogen bomb, 111, 114

ideological, 21, 188
ideology, 22–3, 32–3, 136, 159, 188–9, 194
*ijime*, 4–6, 11–12, 14, 225, 241
ill-being, 88–9, 91, 93, 95–101, 227–30, 233–6, 238–9
immigrant, 21–3, 79–80, 83, 86, 109–10, 184, 195
immigration, 23, 25, 105, 109–10, 116, 184
imperial, 25, 110, 163–7, 169, 171–5, 177, 179–81
in vitro fertilization (IVF), 75
incarceration, 17–29, 36, 38, 241
India, 71–2, 74–9, 81–2, 99, 184, 232, 243, 247
Indian Council for Medical Research (ICMR), 81
indigenous knowledge, 58, 68
individual freedom, 24
international law, 18–19, 28

# Index

International Organization for Migration, 64
internment, 18–21, 26–8, 30, 242
internment camps, 105
*Issei*, 21, 109

Japanese American National Museum, 29–30, 242
Japanese Americans, 17–18, 20–2, 24–7, 29–30, 105, 110–13, 241–2
Japanese Civil Code, 179
Japanese-Filipino children, 55
*Japayukis*, 54

Kasumigaura Air Base, 12
Kasumigaura Naval Aviation Base, 13
*Kibei*, 106, 111
Kieselbach, Thomas, 89–90
Kirov, 145, 150, 152, 157
*kolkhoze*, 147–8, 152
Korematsu, 18, 20, 30, 241
Kosaka, Kenji, 96, 98–9, 101, 219, 227, 233, 235–6, 238–9
Kwak Kwi Hun, 112, 115

labor market, 78, 98–9
language, 11, 42–4, 55, 97, 107, 116, 142, 223–4
lawsuits, 106, 112, 114–16, 241
Lee Hsien Loong, 195–6, 199
Lee Kuan Yew, 191, 199
Lefebvre, Henri, 10
liberal theory, 24
liberalism, 23–4, 32–4, 47–8, 242
libertarianism, 34
life situation concept, 90–92
life-course perspective, 107, 116

logic of hospitality, 42
logic of surveillance, 31, 34–43, 47–8
Loukachenko, Alexander, 150, 154, 159, 244
Lucky Dragon No.5, 111, 114

Marx, Karl, 233
Manchurian Incident, 170, 173, 179, 180
marginalized, 58, 60–2, 66–9, 121, 148
market, 6, 8, 16, 23, 32, 38, 47, 73–5, 78, 94, 98–9, 146, 148–9, 152, 196
market capitalism, 73
market principles, 6, 16, 23
Maslow, Abraham, 200
materialism, 183, 187–8
Mauss, Marcel, 15
medical science, 125
medical tourism, 75–6
Meiji period, 21, 163–4, 169, 174, 181
Mexican, 23
military facilities, 12–13, 15
military reservations, 12–14
minorities, 212, 229, 232
minority, 18, 29, 36, 40, 42–3, 106, 204–5, 232
money, 6, 16, 29, 73, 80–6, 88, 98, 131, 146, 170, 172–3, 179, 202, 208, 211, 246
moral decline, 128–9
morality, 32, 45–7, 71, 73
Moscow, 145, 246

Nagasaki, 111, 113, 121
Narovlia, 142–6, 149–2, 155, 157, 243, 245–6
national defense, 24

national emergency, 18, 22, 24
National Mobilization Law, 165, 171, 179
natural environment, 7–8, 153
natural space, 10–11
naturalization, 22, 25–6
negative experience, 3–4
neo-conservatism, 32–3
neo-conservative, 32
neo-liberalism, 32–4, 47–8, 242, *see also* liberalism
neo-marxism, 226
neo-Nazi, 40, 123
Netherlands, 122, 129, 135, 137, 139–40
*Nisei*, 21, 106, 110–13, 116–17
nuclear power, 234
Nussbaum, Martha, 99–100, 231

O'Connor, Sandra, 20

pain, 55–6, 118, 137, 142, 236
Panama Canal, 19
Pareto optimum, 228
Participatory Appreciative Planning Approach (PAPA), 63
Participatory Learning and Action (PLA), 57–68, 237
participatory research, 54, 56–7, 59, 67–70
Pearl Harbor, 25, 110
Peru, 18–19, 21, 27–8
Peruvian, 18–19, 21, 27–8
Peruvian Japanese, 19, 21, 27–8
Philippines, 53–4, 64, 224
pleasure, 36, 126, 144, 151, 155–8, 186, 215, 236
post traumatic stress disorder (PTSD), 124
postwar development, 12, 15

poverty, 53, 55, 78, 86–95, 97, 100–1, 148, 189, 191, 229, 247
poverty trap, 89
pragmatism, 183, 187–8
prostitution, 54, 73
psychiatry, 125, 128–9
public works, 13, 247
pursuit of happiness, 17, 183

quality of life, 53, 113, 183–7, 195, 197

racial discrimination, 18, 20, 24, 26
radiation exposure, 105
radioactivity, 146–7, 243
reconstruction moralism, 129
relativism, 24
religion, 40, 42, 167, 204, 211
reproductive labor, 71–4, 78–9, 86–7, 243
resource concept, 90–1
risk, 20, 33, 37, 44, 56, 82, 89–91, 95, 106, 135, 142, 144, 148–9, 153, 155
Roosevelt, Franklin D., 23

*Sansei*, 21, 112
SARS epidemic, 192
Second World War, 7, 12
security, 32–6, 38–9, 41–2, 115, 181, 190, 200, 238, 242
self-actualization, 189, 200
self-esteem, 84–5, 185, 189, 194, 200
shell-shock, 129
Sen, Amartya, 92–5, 100, 238
Singapore, 183–5, 187–200, 247–8
Sino-Japanese War, 163–4, 170

## Index

Smith, Adam, 91
social capital, 94–5, 98, 100–1, 195
social chaos, 128–9, 132
social democratic, 34
social development unit, 189
social exclusion, 90
social order, 33, 36, 226, 231
social reform, 56
social research, 53, 121, 219–21, 223–4, 226, 231–2, 237–8
social sciences, 121, 228, 235, 237
social stigma, 53–4
social systems theory, 229
social welfare, 88–9, 97, 99, 121
sociology of education, 91
sociology of missed opportunities, 233, 238
Son Gin Doo, 111, 114
South Korea, 75, 78, 115
Soviet Union, 147, *see also* USSR
spatial codes, 10
spatial symbols, 7–8, 10–11
standard of living, 183–5, 190, 192, 204–6, 213–14, 216, 245
stranger, 35, 47, 53, 129
suicide, 4–6, 9, 11–12, 14, 16, 18, 123, 225, 241
surrogacy, 71–87
surrogate mother, 71–3, 75–7, 79, 81–2, 86, 232
surveillance, 9, 18, 25, 31, 34–43, 47–8, 146, 242–3
Survivors Special Medical Care Law, 114
sustainability, 228
sustainable development, 239
Switzerland, 90, 92, 100

Taisho period, 170, 216
terrorism, 34, 191
terrorist, 35
Thatcher, Margaret, 31–2
tolerance, 23, 41–4, 48
totalitarianism, 136, 139
tyranny of reproduction, 73

unconditional hospitality, 44–5
United Nations Development Program (UNDP), 228
universities, 14, 154, 245
university, 108, 121, 154, 219, 223, 245
urban poor, 97, 99
USSR, 145, 149, 159, 243, 245, *see also* Soviet Union
utilitarian state, 188

victim, 3–9, 15–16, 19, 26–7, 29, 72, 83, 86, 117, 120, 122–4, 126, 128–30, 131, 133–41, 147–8, 157, 200, 245
Vietnam, 99, 201, 203–4, 211–16, 224, 233–4
violence, 4, 31, 38–40, 45–6, 48–9, 55–6, 136, 193, 242

war trauma, 122, 124–6, 129, 136–8, 140
wartime measure, 20
Watsuji, Tetsurō, 9–10
Weber, Max, 15, 235
well-being, 67, 69–70, 94–7, 108, 115–16, 120–1, 123, 127–8, 159, 163, 173, 181–2, 186–7, 189–90, 208, 210, 212, 219, 226–9, 231, 233–4, 236, 239, 248
women's movement, 73
woods, 17

World Bank, 90
World Index on Happiness, 183
worship, 7, 170–1

Yamamoto, Eric, 20